The Identity in Question

The Identity in Question

edited by

John Rajchman

Routledge

New York and London

Published in 1995 by
Routledge
29 West 35th Street
New York, NY 10001

Published in Great Britain by
Routledge
11 New Fetter Lane
London EC4P 4EE

The following essays originally appeared in *October* (vol. 61, Summer 1992), published by MIT Press: Joan W. Scott, "Multiculturalism and the Politics of Identity"; Cornel West, "Matter of Life and Death"; Chantal Mouffe, "Democratic Politics and the Question of Identity"; Homi Bhabha, "Freedom's Basis in the Indeterminate"; Jacques Rancière, "Politics, Identification, and Subjectivization"; Andreas Huyssen, "The Inevitability of Nation: German Intellectuals after Unification"; Ernesto Laclau, "Universalism, Particularlism, and the Question of Identity"; and Stanley Aronowitz, "Reflections on Identity." Cornel West, "The New Cultural Politics of Difference," was originally published in *Out There* (MIT Press, 1990). "Wounded Attachments," by Wendy Brown, from Political Theory, vol. 21, No. 3, pp. 390–410, copyright © 1993 by Sage Publications. Fredric Jameson, "On *Cultural Studies*," originally appeared in *Social Text* (vol. 34, 1993).

Library of Congress Cataloging-in-Publication Data

The identity in question / edited and with an introduction by John Rajchman.
   p.   cm.
"This volume grew out of a symposium held in New York in 1991"—Introd.
ISBN 0-415-90617-2 (cl.) — ISBN 0-415-90618-0 (pbk.)
   1. Identity. 2. Political science—Philosophy. 3. Culture-
-Philosophy. 4. Critical theory. 5. Nationalism. 6. Philosophy,
Modern—20th century. I. Rajchman, John.
BD236.I42   1995
306—dc20   94-24832
                                     CIP

Contents

PART II ELABORATIONS

Introduction

This volume grew out of a symposium held in New York in 1991, at the height of a wave of debate in America over two phenomena, which then seemed inseparable from one another: "multiculturalism" and "political correctness." The aftermath of this debate is still very much with us. Two of the writers highlighted by Homi Bhabha in his contribution, Derek Walcott and Toni Morrison, have gone on to receive Nobel Prizes. Terms of the day, such as "diversity" and "sensitivity to difference," have now entered the language, together with their familiar legal and political purports. Yet many questions or difficulties, conceptual and political, raised by this debate remain unsettled. And it was precisely the experiment of this symposium to bring these sorts of questions out into open public exchange, and so to initiate a critical examination of how the problems and objectives had been framed, the meanings determined, the categories fixed.

For at this time "the public" already enjoyed an important role in the controversy—a very American sort of role. The debate had become a mass-mediated pastime, the new topic of talk shows and T-shirts, bringing unaccustomed notoriety and fortune to certain academic authors. Multiculturalism had become a fad and a style, and everyone knew what to think about it. Indeed it seemed that we were living in a new, monolithic *culture* of multiculturalism. And yet all this "publicity" had tended to obscure the more difficult questions, to cover over an unspoken diversity in approach, concern and analysis, to discourage singular creative efforts—in short to reduce or smooth over complications and differences. Even the key word, "multiculturalism," came to cover quite different ideas and practices, which a critical reflection or a creative practice might want to separate, or reassemble in other ways. The symposium was an attempt to make public such diversity and such possibility behind the mediatized homogenization of the terms in which the debate was being carried on, so as to better diagnose what was really at stake, to better define the nature of the *politics* at issue. It was an attempt to introduce some *movement* into the concepts at work—concepts like "culture," "identity" and "plurality," which themselves had had a particularly resonant history in America. To this end, the symposium assembled a small group of people engaged in the debate in different fields and countries to take part in a public encounter. The edited outcome of this experiment comprises Part I of this volume. Part II includes longer and more elaborate discussions from those who were invited to participate but who, for one reason or another, did not.

A number of lines of questioning emerged in the free-flowing debate of Part I. Joan Scott tackled the conservative and neoconservative campaign against the whole multicultural phenomenon, and tried to distinguish its politics from liberalism. But in the discussion that followed, there arose a clash in viewpoints that further complicated matters. Chantal Mouffe raised the problem of the heritage of liberal pluralism in a different light; and in a fine, conceptual analysis, Ernesto Laclau tried to show how universality and particularity figured in the new vantage point. Cornel West introduced his distinctive brand of "tragic" pragmatism, in which suffering bodies compete for the resources to weave hopeful webs of meaning. His pragmatism found one prolongation in Stanley Aronowitz's attempt to bring back George Herbert Mead. In Aronowitz's view, the identities which are formed in social movements (or which require social movements to be formed) are not only many-sided, but are also politically "heteronomous." Minority identity is thus not only tragic and hopeful; it also becomes problematizing when it mobilizes something "other"—something which cannot be assimilated within visible, established, public categories, and which causes them to be rethought.

This theme of the heteronomous character of identity in social movements was elaborated in another way by Jacques Rancière. It had emerged in the course of his study of how the very name "worker" functioned in the French workers' movement, how it became the name of something "other," inseparable from the political process of "subjectivization" which the movement itself sought to introduce into society. In this way, Rancière raised the problem of such problematic identities in *history*—the problem of the *kind* of history which can be transformed by the "movement" of heteronomous subjectivizations. In this case, history is more than context or tradition. Rather, context and tradition are something like the negative conditions for the attempt to set into motion something as yet unconceived or unnamed, which opens society to a transformation whose outcome is unforeseen—conditions for a sort of experiment. The potential for such movement and critical experimentation within society shows that history is not linear or progressive, any more than it is circular or cyclical. It shows that if history is a "web," it is one with many gaps and holes which allow it to be constantly rewoven in other ways, and that it thus always carries with it the sort of "in-between" times and spaces to which Homi Bhabha draws attention in postcolonial writing. Thus one can see minority not as a given, monolithic, traditional identity, but rather as a multiple, unpredictable force which comes out from the *intervals* of official memory to problematize and recompose traditions. And while traditional liberalism has the honor of defending the rights of minorities, it has been much less able to understand the violence of this sort of alterity, this sort of movement.

Together with Rancière, Andreas Huyssen introduced a European perspective into the discussion. He raised the question of German nationalism, and so of nationalism itself, and the negative attitudes to it traditionally on the Left. He thus indirectly raised the question of the "complex" of amnesia and mourning that the debacle of such nationalism left in Europe, and particularly in Germany. It was a useful reminder. For there is a sense in which our current notions of "multiculturalism" are as peculiarly American as were our earlier ideas of pluralism. In response to some insistent questioning from the floor, some participants started to worry that there were too many Europeans in this American symposium, furthering a "hegemony on the level of knowledge." But questions of "cultural identity" and nationalism have since exploded with tragic fatality and unspeakable brutality in Europe, and "multicultural" America has remained rather indifferent to this fact. And, as Chantal Mouffe remarked in the discussion, it is often those with this type of "European experience" who today are the most sympathetic to American pluralism, the most puzzled by its blanket rejection by some on the American Left. Yet no one, European or American (or other), was unreservedly satisfied with such pluralism, even if there was no consensus on the alternatives to it, or on the manner in which contemporary questions of identity serve to complicate or rethink it. Thus Rancière captured a common concern when he declared that we must *reinvent* politics today. For there is something in the nature of power and of "the political" which traditional pluralism fails to understand, and which current multiculturalism seems to bring to the fore: what would a democracy be which allows for the unpredictable movement of those unnamed "others" within, without, or "in-between" that would serve to transform the very idea of who comprises it, and therefore, of what it is and can do?

A central feature of multiculturalist talk in America that enjoyed much less currency in this symposium is to be found in the ubiquitous, but often unanalyzed, term of *culture*. The more elaborate essays in Part II help explain why. It is remarkable that the current American discussion of "difference" is couched in the terms of a widespread culturalism, such that to untangle what is being said about identity is to understand to what sort of "culture" appeal is being made. Thus, when Cornel West uses the term in introducing "the new cultural politics of difference," he is content to leave it somewhat unexplained in a pragmatic way. A more detailed and more critical view is offered by Fredric Jameson, in his elaborate look at "the desire called 'cultural studies' " in America. Jameson finds that the new emphasis on culture has come at the expense of the larger sense of history and politics one finds in the Marxist tradition.

In a lecture first presented at UNESCO, Etienne Balibar goes further; he tries to critically dissect the very idea of "cultural identity," arguing that what is discussed under this heading might be better formulated in terms of the relation between subjects and historical institutions. In the analysis of such relations, he contends, psychoanalysis has an important role to play, since there is no racism that does not include some form of sexism. Thus Balibar distinguishes different kinds of identification. He refers to Jean-Claude Milner's reading of Lacan's categories in terms of the logical problem of the assemblage of elements into groups; thus one may talk of "symbolic" identities, "imaginary" ones and, finally, "paradoxical" ones, which Milner thinks always emerge in the course of a psychoanalysis. It is the last category, associated with what Lacan called "the real," which perhaps offers the psychoanalyst's most original contribution to the question of identity. In referring to it, Balibar thus touches on a problem pursued by Wendy Brown and Judith Butler in their essays. They are concerned with two seemingly opposed theoretical perspectives that have been influential when questions of sex and sexuality have been raised in the "new cultural politics of difference" in America—one coming from Nietzsche and Foucault, the other from Freud and Lacan. And perhaps the "paradoxical" kind of identity linked to what Lacan called "the real" is just the kind which Foucault urged that we make the object of the critical historical experimentation which problematizes and opens our "cultures" to new possibilities, new subjectivies.

In its two parts, this volume is thus an attempt to introduce a certain critical "diversity" into the very concept of multiculturalism and the uniform mediatized way in which it has come to be served up to us in America. The aim is not to represent all viewpoints, and no doubt there are many other ways to take up this endeavor. For the point of the experiment was not to be all-inclusive, or to propound an overarching viewpoint; it was to initiate a critical activity to be taken up by others elsewhere, in different ways. It was to this end that I prepared a series of questions that were sent to all the participants in 1990; I have reproduced them here.

The Identity in Question: The central aim of this symposium is to problematize and to complicate the very terms of the debate over multiculturalism and political correctness: "culture," "identity," "representation," "power," "experience," and so forth, formulating thereby new questions or raising old ones in new ways. What is at stake is the nature of political community and what it can be for us today. A (nonexhaustive) list of issues to be addressed includes:

1. Universality   Do there exist values, principles or objectives that transcend all particular identifications, and to which all particular oppressed or disadvantaged groups can, or must, appeal? Need such appeals postulate fixed rules or formal procedures derived from a foundational philosophy of humanity or reason, and what relation would they have to the particularities of the "identity" or "culture" of the various groups? Does or can there exist such a thing as a universal "culture," or only the particular ones that secure the identities of groups? What is universality, what is particularity, and what is the relation between the two?

2. Agency Does the erosion of, or skepticism about, the great progressivist or teleological, social-historical models and Utopias of the last century allow for any form of political organization other than that of the "empowerment" of particular groups? What would be the nature of a collective "agency" which did not require those models or Utopias, or which would rethink them along new lines? After the model of the self-consciousness of progress in a party, what is political "agency"?

3. Liberalism What role should "liberal" values of the rule of law, the claims to rights, and equal opportunities play in the politics of minority "empowerment"? Does the old liberal consensus, or its revivals, entail a "depoliticization"? What relation does, or should, it have to the struggle for "power" on the part of minorities? What is power; what is "the political"?

4. Plurality Is society, or political community, irreducibly plural, or "dispersed" in nature? Or does there, rather, exist some systemic organization, the analysis of which might unify the community and its struggles? Is such "plurality" or "diversity" to be understood as a group of tribes each with its own "cultural identity," or is there a more radical type of "plurality" or "multiplicity" prior to existing classifications, that would involve the political temporality of those "in-between" such groups, those with "hybrid" identifications, or simply those identifying with no one group? What is "diversity"?

5. Nationality In the wake of the end of the settlement of the great European War of Nations, does there exist, outside the Marxist treatment of the nationality question and the Leninist doctrine of imperialism, a conception of citizenship which is not *de facto* defined in terms of nation-states? Does there exist another political solution to the question of minority than that of the egalitarian or republican law of particular nations, or the Romantic notion that each people must have its state? After the Cold War, what are nationality and nationalism?

6. Avant-garde Does the mainstream absorption of the great movements of cultural modernism entail that there can, or should, no longer exist a dissident art other than an art of subcultural empowerment, with its concomitant embrace of mass and artisanal cultural forms? What is the "politics" of art, and of its forms?

7. Alterity   Does it make sense to speak of an "Other" whose logic would not be one of contrast or opposition (as in the idea of the "non-Western")—something "other to" identity, rather than an "other identity"; something which, therefore, no group (not even a "non-Western" one) may be said to "represent"? What or who is "the Other"?

8. Subjectivity   Does the question of the subject (as distinct from that of the individual) raised by psychoanalysis and by Lacan introduce a "politics of identity" that is distinct from and even opposed to a "politics of identification" with a culture, tribe, nation, way of life, community (and notably the type of identification Freud analyzed in the church and the army)? What is the relation of identity to "sexuality"? Is it a matter of the "culture" of sexual minorities, their "self-esteem" and their "empowerment"? Or is the assertion of "proper" or unproblematic identity itself the symptom of a fundamental anxiety, a fundamental "discontent" in civilization, that is unleashed in "modernity"? What is the relation of the "subjectivity" or "spirituality" of desire to the political?

9. Methodology   Do minority studies require methods appropriate to each group, and irreducible to those of more traditional disciplines such as history, social science and literary or art criticism? Is each group methodologically obliged to have its own historians, its own critics, its own intellectuals? Are "women's studies" or "African-American studies," beyond the study of women or African-Americans, particular *kinds* of study, characterized by their own particular procedures or styles of analysis, inference and explanation? In particular, what relation do minority studies have to those methods or types of analysis credited with being the achievements of "Western Civilization"? Is there, and should there be, such a thing as "methodological separatism"?

10. Theory   Is all theory, if not all knowledge, necessarily "ethnocentric"? Is truth or objectivity something more or different from solidarity with one's tribe? Is the historical contextualization of knowledge or theory of this tribal sort? Are claims or appeals to universality really only a matter of Western, European tribalism? Can one speak from any other position than one's own "subject position" or one's own "site"? What is "critical theory," what sort of truth claims does it make, and to whom is it addressed?

The Identity in Question

DEBATE

Joan W. Scott

Multiculturalism and the Politics of Identity

If there were any doubt that the production of knowledge is a political enterprise that involves a contest among conflicting interests, the raging debates of the last few years should have dispelled them. What counts as knowledge? Who gets to define what counts as knowledge? These are difficult problems, never easy to resolve, but it is the function of teachers and scholars to grapple with them.

Those who deny the existence of these problems and who would suppress discussion of them are not without their politics; they simply promote their orthodoxy in the name of an unquestioned and unquestionable tradition, universality or history. They attack challenges to their ideas as dangerous and subversive, antithetical to the academic enterprise. They offer themselves as apostles of timeless truths, when in fact they are enemies of change. The cry that politics has recently invaded the university, imported by sixties radicals, is an example of the defense of orthodoxy; it is itself a political attempt to distract attention from the fact that there are serious issues at stake and more than one valid side to the story in the current debates about knowledge.

What we are witnessing these days is not simply a set of internal debates about what schools and universities should teach and what students should learn. Journalists and politicians have joined the fray and added a new dimension to it. There is much more at stake in their campaign against "political correctness" than a concern with excessive moralism, affirmative action and freedom of speech in the academy. Rather, the entire enterprise of the university has come under attack, and with it the aspect that intellectuals most value and that the humanities most typically represent: a critical, skeptical approach to all that a society takes most for granted.

The far-ranging investigations of university practices—curricular change, admissions standards, financial aid, fellowship awards, disciplinary codes, hiring and tenure procedures, teaching loads, time spent on research, accreditation standards, even, I would argue, the investigation of the misuse of overhead funds—are all attempts to delegitimize the philosophical and institutional bases from which social and cultural criticism have traditionally come. We are experiencing another phase of the ongoing Reagan-Bush revolution which, having packed the courts and privatized the economy, now seeks to neutralize the space of ideological and cultural nonconformity by discrediting it. This is the context within which debates about political correctness and multiculturalism have taken shape.

"Political correctness" is the label that has been attached to any program or position that attacks or calls into question the status quo. Coined by the Left as an internal criticism of moralizing dogmatisms, the term has been seized by the Right and used to disqualify all critical efforts. It seems to be working so well as a form of intimidation that it became a theme in the Bush presidential campaign for 1992. Demands for change in the name of tolerance, fairness and justice are, under the "P.C." label, described as dangerous orthodoxies, attempts to impose thought control on otherwise benign individuals. In the name of defending the individual's right to think and act as he pleases, the conservative ideologists protect existing structures and practices from all critical scrutiny and even moderate attempts at reform.

If "political correctness" is the label attached to critical attitudes and behavior, "multiculturalism" is the program it is said to be attempting to enact. This project of somehow recognizing the demographic diversity that has become characteristic of many colleges, universities and urban schools has been reviled by conservatives as a dangerous orthodoxy. One writer refers to the "cult of multiculturalism," distinguishing a few reasonable proponents among a preponderance of fanatics. Another suggests that multiculturalism's "Europhobia" will undermine the unity and the com-

Joan W.
4   *Scott*

mon culture of the American nation. Proponents insist, on the other hand, that multiculturalism will increase both fairness (by representing the range and richness of America's different ethnicities) and tolerance (by exposing students to multiple perspectives on the meaning of history). In this view, multiculturalism pluralizes the notion of an American identity by insisting on attention to African-Americans, Native Americans and the like, but it leaves in place a unified concept of identity.

It is this unified concept of identity that informs the debate on multiculturalism. And it is the extreme polarization of sides—for and against multiculturalism, liberal pluralism or conservative individualism—that makes critical reflection on the terms of the debate so difficult. Despite its difficulty, and fully cognizant of the political risks involved, it is such a critical reflection that I want to undertake.

Within the pluralist framework that seeks to contain and resolve the debate, identity is taken as the referential sign of a fixed set of customs, practices and meanings, an enduring heritage, a readily identifiable sociological category, a set of shared traits and/or experiences. "Diversity" refers to a plurality of identities, and it is seen as a condition of human existence rather than as the effect of an enunciation of difference that constitutes hierarchies and asymmetries of power.[1] When diversity is seen as a condition of existence, the questions become whether and how much of it is useful to recognize; but the stakes people have in the answers to those questions are obscured, as are the history and politics of difference and identity itself. Without a way to theorize the history and politics of identity outside the pluralist framework, it is difficult to respond to the conservative onslaught.

Something of this can be seen in the report of the New York State Social Studies Review and Development Committee, issued last June and called "One Nation, Many Peoples: A Declaration of Cultural Interdependence." The report is an impressive document from many perspectives, and it makes a persuasive case for a multicultural curriculum, arguing, among other things, that democratic participation is enhanced when students understand that change occurs because groups pursue their interests through collective action. Pride in one's heritage is, the report suggests, an important ingredient in citizenship, particularly for those whose identities and viewpoints have been excluded or marginalized in accounts of American history. What the report does not do is conceive of difference as in any way constitutive, and so it leaves itself open to a charge delivered by Nathan Glazer (one of the dissenting members of the committee) that ethnicities should not be treated as monolithic and unchanging because that ignores the very real history of their assimilation to "American culture." Glazer's argument, that the report's "hypostatization" of identities creates a dangerously divided reality, is eminently political; by asserting the essential unity of the identity of "American," it underplays the extent to which processes of difference and discrimination have structured (and continue to structure) American life.

By looking only at the effects of the enunciation of difference, and not at the contested process itself, both Glazer and the authors of the report naturalize identity, making it a matter of biology or history or culture, an inescapable trait that can matter more or less, but is inherently a part of one's being. The report assumes that people are discriminated against *because* they are already different, when, in fact, I would argue, it is the other way around: difference and the salience of different identities are produced by discrimination, a process that establishes the superiority or the typicality or the universality of some in terms of the inferiority or atypicality or particularity of others.

Two citations seem to me to illustrate this point. One is from Stuart Hall, whose theoretical explorations prepare us for his insight:

> The fact is "black" has never been just there either. It has always been an unstable identity, psychically, culturally, and politically. It, too, is a narrative, a story, a history. Something constructed, told, spoken, not simply found. People now speak of the society I come from in totally unrecognizable ways. Of course Jamaica is a black society, they say. In reality it is a society of black and brown people who lived for three or four hundred years without ever being able to speak of themselves as "black." Black is an identity which had to be learned and could only be learned in a certain moment. In Jamaica that moment is the 1970s.[2]

The second quote is from someone whose insight we might attribute to "experience" (as long as we understood experience to be discursively mediated). A white, middle-class student, living in a Latino dormitory at Stanford, told a *New York Times* reporter what she had come to understand about her identity:

Joan W. Scott

"Sometimes I'd get confused," she said because she never knew when a simple comment she made would offend someone else. She finally appreciated the difference between herself and the Hispanic students when one of them asked her what it felt like to be an Anglo. "I'd never heard anyone use the word Anglo for me before. ... Where I came from no one was Anglo; everyone was just Irish Catholic. But after being [here] a while I realized that an Anglo can be an Anglo only if there's someone who's not."[3]

cf, orthodox Jew, etc

Most discussions of multiculturalism avoid this kind of insight about the production of knowledge of identity, and therefore undercut their most radical potential. It may be precisely because they wanted to avoid appearing too radical that the authors of the New York State report assumed that identity groups preexisted rather than followed from discrimination; it may also be that to have historicized the question of identity would have antagonized a significant and vociferous minority constituency, one invested in establishing its autonomous and unified historical existence. (Support for this argument might come from the curious absence of attention to gender in the report and from the committee's contorted apology about it at the end:

> We were repeatedly cautioned to avoid letting issues related to sex-role differences come to dominate the work of this Committee. We were reminded that, too often, when matters of cultural, ethnic, and language biases are addressed and attention is called to the importance of sex-role differences and sexism, the sexism question dominates discussion and action. Thus we treated sex-role group-ings as contexts for the development of culture-like consistencies. (draft version, p. 68)

The paragraph goes on to acknowledge the "double and even triple" bur-den carried by women in "low status" cultural groups (as if such an acknowledgment in the report could compensate for the exclusion of atten-tion to gender and sexuality in the proposed curriculum). Whatever the explanation—and I suspect many factors were at work—the result leaves the discussion safely within a liberal pluralist framework, and makes emi-nently plausible the objection of another of the dissenters on the committee,

Arthur Schlesinger, Jr., that in the proposed curriculum there was too much emphasis on the *"pluribus"* and not enough on the *"unum."*

The alternative strategy—to historicize the question of identity—is to introduce an analysis of its production, and thus an analysis of constructions of and conflicts about power; it is also, of course, to call into question the autonomy and stability of any particular identity as it claims to define and interpret a subject's existence. Oddly enough, given the charges of incoherence and anarchy made against multicultural approaches, historicizing the question of identity also offers the possibility of a more unified view than that of the liberal pluralists. Here is S. P. Mohanty, taking up an argument made by Cornel West against a notion of separate canons, of new canons entirely replacing old:

> How do we negotiate between my history and yours? How would it be possible for us to recover our commonality, not the ambiguous imperial-humanist myth of our shared human attributes, which are supposed to distinguish us from animals, but, more significantly, the imbrication of our various pasts and presents, the ineluctable relationships of shared and contested meanings, values, and material resources? It is necessary to assert our dense particularities, our lived and imagined differences; but could we afford to leave untheorized the question of how our differences are intertwined and, indeed, hierarchically organized? Could we, in other words, afford to have *entirely* different histories, to see ourselves as living—and having lived—in entirely heterogeneous and discrete spaces?[4]

His answer is obviously no. Instead he calls for an alternative to pluralism that would make difference and conflict the center of a history "we" all share.

If Mohanty's solution seems obvious to many of us, we are in a clear minority, as the struggle over multiculturalism unfolds in the context of a prevailing ideology of individualism. Individualism is the language of the conservatives' critique of multiculturalism, of the liberal universities' accommodation to its newly diverse populations, and of the identity politics of minority groups. In the 1960s and 1970s, proponents of affirmative action and identity politics took economic, political and social structures for granted in their analyses (one could invoke "experience," for example,

Joan W. Scott

and mean something historically, culturally and discursively produced, as feminists did in consciousness-raising sessions to great political effect); but in the 1980s and 1990s, the ideological pendulum has swung back to individualism (and "experience" now signifies a prediscursive, direct and unmediated apprehension of social truth). The courts are reversing affirmative action decisions; the President vetoes civil rights legislation; and the history of discrimination as evident in statistics is being denied. All this is being done in the name of justice for individuals, who are conceived to be entirely equal units, living in a cultural and historical vacuum.

The logic of individualism has structured the approach to multiculturalism in many ways. The call for tolerance of difference is framed in terms of respect for individual characteristics and attitudes; group differences are conceived categorically and not relationally, as distinct entities rather than interconnected structures or systems created through repeated processes of the enunciation of difference. Administrators have hired psychological consulting firms to hold diversity workshops which teach that conflict resolution is a negotiation between dissatisfied individuals. Disciplinary codes that punish "hate-speech" justify prohibitions in terms of the protection of individuals from abuse by other individuals, not in terms of the protection of members of historically mistreated groups from discrimination, nor in terms of the ways language is used to construct and reproduce asymmetries of power. The language of protection, moreover, is conceptualized in terms of victimization; the way to make a claim or to justify one's protest against perceived mistreatment these days is to take on the mantle of the victim. (The so-called Men's Movement is the latest comer to this scene.) Everyone—whether an insulted minority or the perpetrator of the insult who feels he is being unjustly accused—now claims to be an equal victim before the law. Here we have not only an extreme form of individualizing, but a conception of individuals without agency.

There is nothing wrong, on the face of it, with teaching individuals about how to behave decently in relation to others, and about how to empathize with each other's pain. The problem is that difficult analyses of how history and social standing, privilege and subordination are involved in personal behavior entirely drop out. Chandra Mohanty puts it this way:

> There has been an erosion of the politics of collectivity through the reformulation of race and difference in individualistic terms. The

1960s and '70s slogan "the personal is political" has been recrafted in the 1980s as "the political is personal." In other words, all politics is collapsed into the personal, and questions of individual behaviors, attitudes, and life-styles stand in for political analysis of the social. Individual political struggles are seen as the only relevant and legitimate form of political struggle.[5]

Paradoxically, individuals then generalize their perceptions and claim to speak for a whole group, but the groups are also conceived as unitary and autonomous. This individualizing, personalizing conception has also been behind some of the recent identity politics of minorities; indeed it gave rise to the intolerant, doctrinaire behavior that was dubbed, initially by its internal critics, "political correctness."

It is particularly in the notion of "experience" that one sees this operating. In much current usage of "experience," references to structure and history are implied but not made explicit; instead, personal testimony of oppression replaces analysis, and this testimony comes to stand for the experience of the whole group. The fact of belonging to an identity group is taken as authority enough for one's speech; the direct experience of a group or culture—that is, membership in it—becomes the only test of true knowledge.

The exclusionary implications of this are twofold: all those not of the group are denied even intellectual access to it, and those within the group whose experiences or interpretations do not conform to the established terms of identity must either suppress their views or drop out. An appeal to "experience" of this kind forecloses discussion and criticism, and turns politics into a policing operation: the borders of identity are patrolled for signs of nonconformity; the test of membership in a group becomes less one's willingness to endorse certain principles and engage in specific political actions, less one's positioning in specific relationships of power, than one's ability to use the prescribed languages that are taken as signs that one is inherently "of" the group. That all of this is not recognized as a highly political process that produces identities is troubling indeed, especially because it so closely mimics the politics of the powerful, naturalizing and deeming as discernably objective facts the prerequisites for inclusion in any group.

Indeed, I would argue more generally that separatism, with its strong insistence on an exclusive relationship between group identity and access

Joan W. Scott

to specialized knowledge (the argument that only women can teach women's literature or only African-Americans can teach African-American history, for example), is a simultaneous refusal and imitation of the powerful in the present ideological context. At least in universities, the relationship between identity-group membership and access to specialized knowledge has been framed as an objection to the control by the disciplines of the terms that establish what counts as (important, mainstream, useful, collective) knowledge and what does not. This has had an enormously important critical impact, exposing the exclusions that have structured claims to universal or comprehensive knowledge. When one asks not only where the women or African-Americans are in the history curriculum (for example), but why they have been left out and what are the effects of their exclusion, one exposes the process by which difference is enunciated. But one of the complicated and contradictory effects of the implementation of programs in women's studies, African-American studies, Chicano studies, and now gay and lesbian studies is to totalize the identity that is the object of study, reiterating its binary opposition as minority (or subaltern) in relation to whatever is taken as majority or dominant.

The alternative, to treat identity as the unstable, never-secured effect of a process of enunciation of cultural difference, is often dismissed as impractical for pedagogy and political mobilization. But, as Denise Riley has persuasively argued, except for the "catastrophic loss of grace in the wording," it makes far more sense for feminist politics to have Sojourner Truth ask "Ain't I a fluctuating identity?" and thereby recognize both the dangers and benefits of the collective consolidation implied in the category "women."[6] In a similar way, it makes more sense to teach our students and tell ourselves that identities are historically conferred, that this conferral is ambiguous (though it works precisely and necessarily by imposing a false clarity), that subjects are produced through multiple identifications, some of which become politically salient for a time in certain contexts, and that the project of history is not to reify identity but to understand its production as an ongoing process of differentiation, relentless in its repetition, but also— and this seems to me the important political point—subject to redefinition, resistance and change. Such an outlook might also call for a more complicated strategy than organizing political campaigns around identity groups (conceived in pluralist terms), and that, in the current context in this country at least, might be all to the good.

NOTES

Other longer and somewhat different versions of this essay have appeared in *Change,* November/December 1991, and in the *Boston Review,* March 1992.

1. On difference as a process of enunciation, see Homi Bhabha, "The Commitment to Theory," in *Third Cinema Reader,* ed. J. Pines and P. Willemen (London: British Film Institute, 1989), pp. 111–132, especially p. 125.
2. Stuart Hall, "Miminal Selves," in *Identity: The Real Me,* (London: ICA, 1987), p. 45.
3. Anthony de Palma, "Campus Ethnic Diversity Brings Separate Worlds," *New York Times,* (May 18, 1991), p. 7.
4. S. P. Mohanty, "Us and Them: On the Philosophical Bases of Political Criticism," *Yale Journal of Criticism* 2 (Spring 1989), p. 13.
5. Chandra Talpade Mohanty, "On Race and Voice: Challenges for Liberal Education in the 1990s," *Cultural Critique* 14 (Winter 1989–90), p. 204.
6. Denise Riley, *"Am I That Name?" Feminism and the Category of "Women" in History* (Minneapolis: University of Minnesota Press, 1988), p. 1. An example of the literalness of the worst kind of political correctness can be found in Tania Modleski, *Feminism Without Women: Culture and Criticism in a "Postfeminist" Age* (New York: Routledge, 1991). Modleski deliberately misreads Riley's reference to Sojourner Truth as ahistorical, antiwoman, and certainly racist, thereby completely missing Riley's accomplishment for feminism, which is to *historicize,* not repudiate, the category "women."

Joan W. Scott

DEBATE

Cornel West

A Matter of Life
and Death

I would first like to congratulate those who had the vision and determination to bring us together, for one can see that this is quite a relevant and pertinent issue. And I am sure that the organizers did not know that the
conference would be held the same day that David Duke was up for election
in the state where my mother and father were born—old Jim and Jane Crow,
Louisiana. Nor did they know that it would be the day after Michael Jackson
decided to make his statement about identity—Black or White—in a video.
But I think this matter raises three fundamental questions that I want to
zoom in on very quickly. The first is "What do we mean by *'identity'?*" Since
this term itself can be a rather elusive, amorphous and even vaporous one,
we need to have heuristic markings for it. The second is "What is the moral
content of one's identities?"—because we all have multiple positions in
terms of constructing our identities; there's no such thing as having one
identity or of there being one essential identity that fundamentally defines
who we actually are. And third, "What are the political consequences of our
various identities?"—which is what Joan Scott was talking about with such
insight.

So let us begin with a heuristic definition. For me, identity is fundamentally about desire and death. How you construct your identity is predicated on how you construct desire, and how you conceive of death: desire

for recognition; quest for visibility (Baldwin—no name in the street; nobody knows my name); the sense of being acknowledged; a deep desire for association—what Edward Said would call affiliation. It's the longing to belong, a deep, visceral need that most linguistically conscious animals who transact with an environment (that's us) participate in. And then there is a profound desire for protection, for security, for safety, for surety. And so, in talking about identity, we have to begin to look at the various ways in which human beings have constructed their desire for recognition, association and protection over time and in space, and always under circumstances not of their own choosing.

But identity also has to do with death. We cannot talk about identity without talking about death. That's what a brother named Julio Rivera had to come to terms with: the fact that his identity had been constructed in such a way that xenophobes would put him to death. Or brother Youssef Hawkins in Benson Hurst. Or brother Yankel Rosenbaum in Crown Heights. Persons who construct their identities and desires often do it in such a way that they are willing to die for it—soldiers in the Middle East, for example—or, under a national identity, that they're willing to kill others. And the rampant sexual violence in the lives of thousands of women who are attacked by men caught up in vicious patriarchal identities—this speaks to what we are talking about. But if, in fact, identity has something to do with these various kinds of desires, these various conceptions of death (we are beings-toward-death), it is because we have, given our inevitable extinction, to come up with a way of endowing ourselves with significance.

So we will weave webs of existential meaning. We will say something about the terrors of nature, the cruelties of fate, the unjustifiability of suffering. It sounds very much like religion. But let us understand: religion not in the theological sense, but in the etymological sense of *ligare*, which means to bind. Identity is about binding, and it means, on the one hand, that you can be bound—parochialist, narrow, xenophobic. But it also means that you can be held together in the face of the terrors of nature, the cruelties of fate and the need for some compensation for unjustified suffering: what theologians used to call the problem of evil. And believe me, identity cuts at that deep existential level where religion resides. That is what is frightening, especially for the Left that, like Habermas, has linked itself to an Enlightenment bandwagon. For it is a shaking of the rationalist foundation.

Cornel
West

But keep in mind, here, the crucial interplay between desire and death, the quest for existential meaning and material resources. For identity is about bodies, land, labor and instruments of production. It is about the distribution of resources. That is, in part, what David Duke is all about. He is addressing a background condition of the maldistribution of resources, in which downward mobility is forcing a working class, squeezed by taxes and exploited by a ruling group, to race-bait and scapegoat Black folk, Jewish people and women. So we must always keep in mind the role of material resources and the various systems that generate their distribution and consumption. There has to be a dialectical interplay in talking about these things; and of course, that is one of the problems of narrow and xenophobic identity politics or political positions. Such positions cause us to lose sight of the fact that we linguistically conscious animals have, up to this moment, had to labor under a radically inegalitarian distribution of resources.

And we thus come to our second question: "What is the moral content of your identity?" It is another way of raising the question of how radically democratic you are when you talk about defining your identity, especially in relation to this maldistribution of resources. If this is important, it is because one of the most disturbing things about identity talk—especially in America, but my hunch is, it is true around the world—is that when people speak about identity, they always begin by talking about the victims. Having a conference on race? Bring on the Black folk. We do not want to invite some White racists so they can lay bare the internal dynamics of what it is to be a White racist. No. Having a conference on gender? Bring on women. As if Whiteness is not as fundamentally constructed within the discourse of race as Blackness is. As if maleness is not as fundamentally structured in the discourse of gender as is femaleness, or woman. As if straightness were inscribed into the nature of things, and those who are not straight have to provide some account of their identity. No, let us talk about identity-from-above as well as identity-from-below. That is something rarely stressed, rarely examined, rarely specified. We need to get a handle on how this Whiteness, maleness, and straightness functions over time and space in relation to Blackness or Brownness or Yellowness or womanness or gayness or lesbianness and so on.

I would hope that, in our studies as well as in our discussions, we recognize the very different status—the different political status—between identity from above and from below. I think this has much to do with the degree to which, when we talk about identities, we rarely speak of some of the larger identities that shape us. For example, national identity—which is very different from having a nation-state—is one of the most powerful means of constructing desire and death in our present moment. It functions on a different axis from that of race or gender, but with dialectic affinities. Why? Because there are racialized subjects who are deeply linked to national identity. That is one of the fascinating things about Black neoconservatives: they are against identity (they are thinking about Black identity), but they are also the most rampant American nationalists in the country. The same thing would be true on other axes as well.

Thus addressing the moral content of one's identity forces us to raise the question of what and where the radical democratic project is. To what degree is that project called into question by certain narrow forms of identity politics? And what social basis could there be for a radical democratic project? I am not going to answer that, but I am raising the question. I think this is something that we have to grapple and come to terms with.

But I want to end by saying something about the last question, the one about the political consequences of one's identities. Since this has to do with strategies and tactics, it is something the Left rarely talks about. Intellectuals usually have little to say about this. How do you go about binding people? What is the political version of the *ligare* activity, which is to say, mobilizing and organizing? Although at this present moment, one cannot, must not, give up on the radical democratic project, yet we find ourselves up against a wall in trying to put forward effective ways of mobilizing and organizing.

Yes, the Left is Balkanized; yes, the Left is fragmented. The older universalist projects of the Left have been shattered—shattered in part because they did not speak effectively to desire and death: they are an Enlightenment project whose critical acumen we must preserve, but whose glib pseudouniversalisms we must radically call into question. As long as we simply hide various particularisms, but without that critical acumen, there cannot be a radical democratic project. So there must be strategies and tactics that cut across identity politics, cut across region, and gender, race and class. Class is still around, even though it has been unable to constitute an identity that has the saliency and potency of the other identities. And we must attempt to think about how we create and sustain organizations that acknowledge this. Because we are in the bind we are in partly because we have been unable to generate the transgendered, transracial, transsexual orientation of social motion, social momentum, social movement. And if we cannot do that, then there will be many, many more David Dukes by the end of the twentieth century, even while we engage in our chatter about identity.

So we have a crucial organizational, strategic and tactical imperative. It is not that we have to have an organizational meeting, but we have to engage the question of mobilization as an object of reflection, because, as Joan Scott said, politics and thinking go hand and hand. And while our politics are understood in a multidimensional and multilayered way, it is also true that, on the ground, without the kind of social motion, momentum and movement that I am talking about, we will feel ourselves more and more pushed against the wall as the xenophobes—be it the Lombard League in Italy, or the skinheads in Germany, or Le Pen in France—more and more speak their right-wing constructs of desire and death to mobilize and organize *their* populace.

And that is serious business. When you get working-class folk, lower-middle-class folk in Louisiana saying that what they see reminds them of Germany in 1930, that is not a plaything. And of course, Black folk know that by experience. That is a serious challenge.

DEBATE

Discussion

AUDIENCE (ANDERS STEPHANSON): I was pleased, Cornel, to see that you introduced the question of resources, labor and land into the conversation.

CORNEL WEST: And bodies, too.

AUDIENCE: And bodies. What I'd like you to elaborate on is how that actually relates to identity, because you said very little about that. And in particular, I'd like for you to relate it to the third section of your talk, where you spoke of the political effects of identities. You gave an account that was normative. You said we should bind together. But you gave no real historical or political account of why it is that the American Left has not been able to do so. Here I apologize for bringing up the Swedish example. But the fact of the matter is that, if you look at the land, resources, labor and so forth of the particular identity of the Swedish Left and the class upon which it has based itself, you'll not find an essence, but instead something extremely stable, almost an absolute identity over a whole century, which is a long time. And now that identity, of course, is falling apart as a result of what you might call the postmodern or postindustrial traversing of the national territory by a whole series of new things. That is what I thought was missing in your account.

CORNEL WEST: I alluded just very briefly to the complex, mediated relation between weaving webs of meaning and these material resources—how they're produced, distributed and consumed. When I spoke of the social base of David Duke, I talked about how the maldistribution of resources was such that when in fact human beings find themselves engaged in downward mobility or social slippage, identities are appropriated from above in order to scapegoat those below. We know that downward mobility is not the only factor and variable, although in this instance it's a significant one. When we look at the United States, we can see relatively stable, continuous, White-supremacist identities among large numbers of the population, even among those who didn't know they were White until they got here. That's primarily because they looked around and saw resources available to them—White skin privilege—so that Sicilian and Irish peasants, who themselves had been subordinated and degraded within their own Old World conditions, made their bid for resources over and against people of color, especially Black folk. So material interest creates fundamental linkages between the quest for resources and the quest for identities-from-above. White-supremacist identities are identities-from-above, and they're powerful ones, as we see in Louisiana. And this is also true of the patriarchal identities or anti-Semitic identities in mid-twentieth-century Europe that continue until this day, unfortunately. That's not an answer, but it's the beginning of an answer. I think the Swedish case is an interesting one because you've got a certain homogeneity there. There are cleavages and conflicts, but still a certain homogeneity.

AUDIENCE: I'm talking less about identity than I am about the working class. And what I'd like to know is how, according to you, is the process in the United States supposed to take place that would provide resources for those from below to weave their own existential webs of meaning?

CORNEL WEST: One of the problems in the United States is that we don't have strong infrastructures and institutions on the Left to transmit identities that go across race, gender, region, class. Our trade unions are weak, for example. So we don't have what Sweden has, strong trade unions that can constitute subcultures—which the Communist Party tried to do here in the 1930s. It represented a great effort to constitute an alternative subculture based on institutions. But that has not taken place, which is precisely why I say that the best we can do is social motion, momentum and movements. Because when you don't have institutions and infrastructures that can sustain the transmitting of values, or the constitution of subcultures over time and space, the best you can do is to try to initiate momentum and possible movement. And we do that first by stressing a moral discourse that cuts across divisions, an analytical discourse that makes linkages and connections, and then places values on qualities like courage and sacrifice and risk, qualities which go hand in hand with any serious sense of struggle. That's how I would begin to answer your question.

STANLEY ARONOWITZ: I'd like to address my question to both Chantal and Cornel. The Duke phenomenon in Louisiana, and similar kinds of right-wing working-class developments in the United States, may indicate that there are some very deep radical impulses at the base of working-class life in the United States. How come the Left is so conservative? Although Chantal talks about radical democracy and citizenship, I would like to know if she has any insight into why the Left is so conservative. Is it possible that in some way, caught up in one of our multiple identities, we are middle class? Because obviously if we're talking about radical democracy, in the United States the radicalism clearly seems to be coming from the Right.

CORNEL WEST: Stanley, just a quick clarification before we answer. Could you say more clearly what the radical impulse is that underlies what's going on in Louisiana?

STANLEY ARONOWITZ: I think this is revealed when Duke supporters make statements about feeling excluded by the political discourse in the United States and the terms of democratic, or for that matter liberal, discussion; and that their "needs," demands and situation are by and large completely ignored. It can easily be argued, that insofar as the intellectual Left is part of that mainstream discourse in this country, it too ignores right-wing populism. Last night I heard a man saying on television, "The White working class is completely ignored in America. I support Duke because he hears us." That's pretty radical. It doesn't mean that it's radical in the way we like it; but it's radical in the sense that it says, "This liberal democracy isn't working for me, and it continually marginalizes and excludes my needs." Look at the struggles that took place around the issue of this pitiful unemployment compensation legislation that went on in Congress in the last couple of weeks. I'm just wondering whether, in the discourse of identity politics, you could render an account of how that exclusion has taken place in the United States.

CORNEL WEST: But Stanley, there have certainly been Left intellectuals who recognize that we've been in a solid depression for eighteen years. There's been a 19.1 percent decline in real, inflation-adjusted wages. Louisiana has been especially hit—150,000 jobs owing to an oil crash. That kind of downward mobility that the White, male working class feels, that Nixon began addressing in 1972 and that Reagan spoke to in 1980, has a long history. If you're going to use the term radical—which is a kind of loose usage, I think—to say, "Look, I'm talking about being excluded," yes, we both give an account of that exclusion. But at the same time, as we know, the response to that is culturally filtered and colored by Duke and others. So if the question is, how does the Left speak to White men who, when they feel excluded, begin to call for the necks of Black folk and the bodies of women . . . what do you do? I think we need some progressive White males to speak to these brothers. We need leadership in the White, progressive, male community especially. That's the beginnings of it.

JOAN SCOTT: I think, Cornel, that posing the question in the kind of class terms you used doesn't help either. I think we need a different analysis of their sense of exclusion and of the ways in which difference is constructed politically. That's not the same as the traditional kind of class analysis that you're implying we need to deal with in this question.

STANLEY ARONOWITZ: I didn't imply this at all. The old Left linked class exclusively to questions of ownership and control of the means of production. Moreover, the various Marxisms that grew up in the United States believed the "working class" to be capitalism's gravedigger because of "its" exploitation and structural location. When workers support candidates such as Duke—or Bush, for that matter—the Old Left ascribes this to "false consciousness." My comments have nothing to do with these elements of Marxism as a master discourse on the inevitability of class struggle and socialist outcomes. It has to do with the character of contemporary US politics. For example, it can be safely argued that the key field of combat in the 1992 Democratic presidential primaries will not only be the question of the economy, but specifically, the fate of the working class, with all of the candidates "rediscovering" the discourse of class as the key signifier to economic alternatives to those of the Bush Administration. In contrast to the past three presidential elections, which were still mired in Cold War debates, the ruling arguments of this one will revolve around who can deal most effectively with the issues affecting workers. All I am asking is how radical democratic discourse addresses the subject-position of workers who have, as Cornel has shown, taken a serious beating in the past two decades. I have not identified "exclusion" with "radical"; but when a group recognizes its own exclusion, it tends to signify the formation of an identity that has political consequences.

Among both ideological and popular Lefts, the move—over this period—to address gender, race and sexuality is nothing but admirable. But unfortunately, our haste to distance ourselves from the Old Left has resulted, for many of us, in a *de facto* abandoning of *any* coherent discourse on class. I suppose I wanted to say that this rush away from formulaic Marxism has permitted the right to present itself as the authentic representative of working-class interests, and to constitute class discourse as racist, sexist and antidemocratic. The simple fact that the Right has noticed that many White workers are in deep shit has considerable resonance among many who occupy what, in the wake of the disarticulation of traditional industrial structures, is a new, "abject" subject-position.

CHANTAL MOUFFE: I'm not quite sure I like the terms *radical* and *conservative* for the Left. Of course, you can always speak in that way, but I think the basic problem with the Left is not that it is conservative, but that there is a complete lack of any idea of what politics is about. This is something that is true in the case of Duke, as it is for the followers of Le Pen in France. Because in fact people have been saying, "Look, there is a democratic impulse behind those movements." I wouldn't go so far as to say that. But clearly those people are saying that democracy doesn't work, that "Nobody has asked us to participate." So this is a phenomenon which is not particular to America, but is a basic crisis of liberal democratic societies. And one of the reasons that the Left is not able to understand this, and doesn't know how to provide an alternative to it, is that for a long time the Left has identified liberal or pluralist democracy with capitalism. The result is that here in America, particularly, you can't defend liberalism or pluralism. The issue, however, is that we must distinguish *between* a pluralist democracy as a political form of society *and* capitalism. And by the way, we are now seeing how this distinction works, because of the effect it has in Eastern Europe, where they say, "We want pluralist democracy even if we have to buy capitalism with it."

Because we've been insisting that those things go together, we wanted to get rid of the whole package. But in this moment it is important to say that we are fighting for the principles of liberal, pluralist democracy, because I don't think there is anything more radical than liberty and equality for all. The problem is that those ideas are not put into practice in those societies which call themselves "liberal democratic." It's for that reason that the Left has said liberalism is a sham, is pure ideology, and we must construct a society that will really be democratic. But the way in which radical democracy is understood in our work is to *radicalize* the ideas of liberty and equality, to extend them to more and more areas of social life.

AUDIENCE: I am troubled by a few things. One is the reification of Duke. I'm concerned that you're making him seem like an aberration, when fundamentally he represents the way this society constructs race. The professors in the academy, whom Joan Scott referred to earlier, in their critique of multiculturalism pretty much echo his language. So we have to be clear that this is in fact a fundamental aspect of American culture, one which is being reinscribed in order to maintain a sense of hegemony and control over all the forces that have been asking for change. I'm also concerned about the credibility of Black women as speakers, and I think you need to deal with that. The Anita Hill hearing brought that to my attention, as, I'm sure, to everyone else's. There's a sense in which we are not credible speakers in just any context. Third, the point that Joan Scott made about Sojourner Truth: it seems to me that the question of power has been elided in your discussion. The fact is that Sojourner Truth, in making that statement, "Ain't I a woman," was not dealing with fluctuating identities but was actually inserting herself into a discourse that was excluding her. So I think this whole question of identities needs to look at power and where one speaks from, and at how one becomes a credible speaker. And I wish you would clarify the point you made about the various studies being separate, because that is also problematic as I see it.

JOAN SCOTT: I certainly think you're right about the context of power in which people are saying things, and I think that although the quote from Denise Riley about Sojourner Truth does not mention specific context, it makes an important point about identity and power—one you are making. It says—as Sojourner Truth does—that identity is not fixed, nor is it self-evident, and it becomes meaningful differently in different contexts. Sojourner Truth is calling into question the self-evident claim of a group of White women about what it means to be a woman, about what rights mean, and how difference and power matter. On your point about separatism, I'm not at all opposed to separate programs of women's studies, African-American studies, and so on. I organized a program I want to see continue at Brown, and I've argued for Women's Studies at other places I've taught as well. I was simply suggesting that part of the contradiction we're caught in whenever we claim an identity—an unavoidable political strategy at some moments—is that we reaffirm the differences we are seeking to challenge. In liberal, pluralist universities there tends to be an essentializing of identities—that was the point of my paper. Instead of difference being understood as part of the process by which power is constituted, it is taken as a separate sociological fact, as the reflection of some enduring or preexisting "culture." Then we have women here and African-Americans there and Latinas and Jews and the list goes on, and they're studied as discrete entities. Sociological categories and all questions of power and difference, of the inter-relationships that produced difference, are gone. That's a kind of happy pluralism I want to avoid, and this is where I get nervous with some of the things Chantal was saying, because they seem to leave out analysis of the process by which difference is enunciated. How can our politics expose this process instead of simply appealing to preexisting identity groups?

Discussion 27

AUDIENCE: I understand what you're saying; I'm familiar with that analysis. I'm just saying that something is missing in terms of not historicizing why these programs exist and how they came to be separatist, and how the university itself maintains that separatism by keeping them without resources so that they have continually to be fighting to maintain a presence and a right to speak.

CORNEL WEST: Doesn't that have something to do with the kind of fighting over crumbs that is the consequence of the maldistribution of resources I was talking about? What you said about David Duke was important, and I hope none of us gets the impression that Duke is an anomaly. He's quite continuous with the kind of campaign that has been run by the Republican party since 1972—having learned from Wallace's '68 race—but is also part of the legacy of the White folk democracy, which the United States had been up until 1960. The White folk democracy is one in which large numbers of White males gain access to resources by excluding Black folk and women. That's part of American history; that's constitutive American civilization. And that legacy is still there, you see. So when they get hot under the collar, after drinking beer and so forth, they're upset at Negroes and women and gays and lesbians.

JOAN SCOTT: And Jews, too.

CORNEL WEST: And Jews as well. And Catholics for a while. This is not to demonize the White, male, working class. It is to situate dominant tendencies within that group historically. But getting back to Stanley's point, we have to deal with that dominant tendency and hit it head on. It's that slice of the group that is responsible for the Republican presidential crossover. And yet we get a Wofford who can play both the populist card and the social conservative card. This is why liberal politics finds itself between a rock and a hard place. The Democratic conservatives can push the populist line, and downplay race, gender, sexual orientation and so forth. And if it's a weak position, those of us on the Left are even weaker, because we don't even have a significant social base, although we've had the better arguments and the deeper vision.

CHANTAL MOUFFE: I want to say something with regard to that, and also in response to Joan. Because we must not forget the old question of hegemony in this discussion. It is central, because you say, "Well, Bush speaks about radical democracy; therefore we cannot." And of course Bush does not speak about radical democracy in our sense of the term; obviously he could not. For too long the Left has ceded all of the important concerns to the Right because it thought there was something *essentially* wrong about certain ideas if they were used by its opponents. But the strategy against their hegemony is to occupy the terrain, to redefine the terms, to redefine the question of democracy, redefine the question of pluralism, redefine the question of liberalism. That's what I'm advocating. The Left has not come to terms with the fact that liberal pluralist democracy is something worth fighting for—but only in the context of reformulating pluralism in a way that *of course* is different. We've got to impose our conception; that is absolutely central in the struggle for democratic politics.

AUDIENCE (GEORGE YUDICE): My comment might seem a little facetious at first, but some of the remarks that have been made presuppose the importance of the media: Cornel's references to Michael Jackson; Stanley's to David Duke on television. In a perverse way, it seems to me that the project of radical democracy has been achieved by television, MTV, the media. During the Gulf War there was no better depiction of a multicultural democracy than the army. MTV also has its panoply of different groups, not only the antiracist ones, but Guns N' Roses, the whole gamut. The reason I'm referring to this is that it seems to me that a project for radical democracy has to go through what Cornel was speaking about as desire. And the instruments of mobilizing and convincingly engaging people's desires are very much in the hands of the media. Thus we can talk ourselves to death about radical democracy, but unless we engage the relationship of the media to the constitution of identities with regard to desire, we're going to end up in the same place as the Old Left.

CORNEL WEST: I think you're right. But it's important to keep in mind that, when we're talking about the media, we're still talking about corporate means of production and communication, and therefore we need to democratize that—not in the sense of making the figures in the glass menagerie more colorful for an audience or constituency of passive consumption, but in the sense of power positions. Democracy is about ordinary people participating in decision-making and in institutions that guide and regulate their lives, so that those people have power and wield power. And that's precisely what we don't have in Hollywood, even though there are now more Black folk, more women, although usually appearing in degraded images. You're absolutely right that the media is a crucial terrain. Part of the Black film renaissance, even in its very narrow and often misogynist forms, is an attempt to engage in acts of cultural resistance. And that kind of upping the ante for contestation and struggle within the media is crucial.

AUDIENCE: Chantal, I was struck by the way that—in the second part of your talk—you repeated two-thirds of the revolutionary motto: equality, liberty and fraternity; but left out the fraternity part. And it raised Carole Pateman's argument about social contract theory for me: her argument that when you talk about the common good's being ultimately not representable, this is because the common good has been represented as a fraternity, a male common good. While I'm intellectually uncomfortable about the common good's being a discursive horizon—and thus being ultimately unrecognizable—it bothers me a little bit too, and I wonder how far you would be willing to go in representing a feminine, or a woman's, subject-position within that common good, specifically in terms of certain public policies or issues of legislation, either in your own context in France or in the United States?

CHANTAL MOUFFE: Yes, I did leave out the fraternity part, not only because it's a sexist way to put it, but also because I think it is not really necessary, since if we speak of equality and liberty for all, we are talking about a kind of solidarity, one of the meanings of fraternity. For me, the question is how to have liberty, equality and solidarity. To come to the question of Carole Pateman, she's right in her analysis when she shows how the idea of the citizen was defined by the modern project, such that the citizen was a man, and that women were excluded. Where I don't follow is her proposal that the solution is to add to the male idea of the citizen a *female* idea of the citizen—the role that woman as woman can bring to society. Which means her quality as mother, her motherhood. I think this is essentialist and I'm against all forms of essentialism. It's important to criticize the way in which citizenship has been constructed on the basis of women's exclusion, but much more radically than by just having a Janus-faced citizen, with a woman's and a man's face. The issue is to create a new conception of citizenship in which the distinction of gender becomes nonpertinent.

AUDIENCE: But yet, if, as you suggest in your paper, we all inhabit an ensemble of positions, wouldn't you agree that one part of that ensemble is being a woman or being a man, or, as your paper suggests, being gay or being lesbian? Your paper seems to suggest that possibility, but I'm wondering how you can represent that.

CHANTAL MOUFFE: We are always multiple subjects. We are woman, but also many other things, belonging to many other communities. What I'm against is a certain type of identity politics that says what politics is about is the representation of all those identities as they already exist. For me this is basically the bad liberal framework, the one I want to get rid of, the individualistic liberal framework. It's important to believe that our identity, when we act politically, should not be defined exclusively by the fact that we belong to one particular constituency. I think we should inscribe our demands in a much wider chain of equivalences, and if one is going to act politically as a radical democratic citizen, it can't just be on the basis of pushing for the demands of women, or blacks or other identities. I'm not saying that they're not important, but they can't exclusively determine our actions in the field of the political.

DEBATE

Chantal Mouffe

Democratic Politics and the Question of Identity

In the current debate about identity there is one issue that I consider to be crucial for democratic politics: *political* identity. In this paper I intend to address that question from a specific angle, and ask: What type of political identity should a project of "radical and plural democracy" aim at constructing? I am going to argue that such a project requires the creation of radical democratic *citizens* and that it implies a new understanding of pluralism, one that acknowledges the constitutive role of power and antagonism.

Since a specific theoretical perspective is going to play a key role in my argument, it might be useful to indicate briefly a few points of reference to help grasp the nature of my approach. Let me then make clear at the outset that my reflections will be inscribed within an antiessentialist theoretical framework according to which the social agent is constituted by an ensemble of "subject positions" that can never be totally fixed in a closed system of differences. It is constructed by a diversity of discourses, among which there is no necessary relation but a constant movement of overdetermination and displacement. The "identity" of such a multiple and contradictory subject is therefore always contingent and precarious, temporarily fixed at the intersection of those subject positions and dependent on specific forms of identification. This plurality, however, does not involve the "coexistence," one by one, of a plurality of subject positions but the constant subversion and overdetermination of one by the others, which makes possible the generation of "totalizing effects" within a field characterized by open and determinate frontiers.

There is therefore a double movement: on the one hand, a movement of decentering which prevents the fixation of a set of positions around a preconstituted point; on the other hand, and as a result of this essential nonfixity, the opposite movement: the institution of nodal points, partial fixations which limit the flux of the signified under the signifier. But this dialectics of nonfixity/fixation is posssible only because fixity is not given beforehand, because no center of subjectivity precedes the subject's identifications. For that reason we have to conceive the history of the subject as the history of his/her identifications, and there is no concealed identity to be rescued beyond the latter.

CITIZENSHIP IN THE MODERN POLITICAL COMMUNITY

After those brief remarks, the importance of which will become clear later, I want to move straight to what I see as the main difficulty that we are facing when we intend to scrutinize democratic politics from the point of view of political identity. It can be formulated in this way: How to conceive the political community under modern democratic conditions? Or also: How to conceptualize our identities as individuals and as citizens in a way that does not sacrifice one to the other? The question at stake is to make our belonging to different communities of values, language, culture and others compatible with our common belonging to a political community whose rules we have to accept. As against conceptions that stress commonality at the expense of plurality and respect of differences, or that deny any form of commonality in the name of plurality and difference, what we need is to envisage a form of commonality that respects diversity and makes room for different forms of individuality.

When we scrutinize the current discussion about citizenship from such a perspective, we realize that the terms of the debate have been far too restricted, and such a situation is, I believe, at the origin of many false dilemmas and political misunderstandings. On one side we have those who defend a "communitarian" view of politics and citizenship that privileges a type of community constituted by shared moral values and organized around the idea of "the common good." On the other side is the liberal view,

Chantal Mouffe

which affirms that there is no common good and that each individual should be able to define her own good and realize it in her own way. The communitarians want to revive the civic republican conception of citizenship as the key identity that overrides all others, and their approach runs the risk of sacrificing the rights of the individual. For the liberals, on the contrary, our identity as citizens—which is only envisaged as a legal status and as the possession of a set of rights that we hold against the state—is only one among many others, and does not play any privileged role. Politics, for them, is merely the terrain where different groups compete for the promotion of their specific private interests, and no space is left for the idea of the political community. In this case it is the citizen who is sacrificed to the individual. Many communitarian critiques have rightly pointed to the disintegration of social bonds and the growing phenomenon of anomie which has accompanied the dominance of the liberal view. It is indeed true that this view has had many negative effects for modern democratic politics, and that the current disaffection with political life in Western democracies is one of its products.

But we cannot accept the solution put forward by the communitarians, because their attempt to recreate a type of *Gemeinschaft* community cemented by a substantive idea of the common good is clearly premodern and incompatible with the pluralism that is constitutive of modern democracy. If it is necessary to criticize the shortcomings of liberalism, one should also recognize its crucial contribution to the emergence of a modern conception of democracy. It is, therefore, important to grasp the specificity of modern democracy and the central role played in it by pluralism. By this I mean the recognition of individual freedom, that freedom which John Stuart Mill defends in his essay "On Liberty," and which he defines as the possibility for every individual to pursue happiness as he sees fit, to set his own goals, and to attempt to achieve them in his own way. There are, of course, problems with Mill's formulations, which are still too dependent on a utilitarian and individualistic problematic, and we certainly need to reformulate his conception of pluralism in a different philosophical framework. But this should not lead us to reject it. Pluralism is linked to the abandonment of a substantive and unique vision of the common good and of the *eudaimonia* which is constitutive of modernity. It is at the center of the vision of the world that might be termed "political liberalism," and it is therefore important to understand that what characterizes modern democracy as a new political form of society is the articulation between political liberalism and democracy.

Once this is recognized, we can understand why the core of the problem lies in the way we conceptualize the political community and our belonging to the political community, that is, citizenship, in a way that makes room for pluralism. Let's examine each of these three notions in turn.

1. Political Community.

The reference to the political community is crucial, but it should be conceived as a discursive surface and not as an empirical referent. Politics is about the constitution of the political community, not something that takes place inside the political community. The political community, as a surface of inscription of a multiplicity of demands where a "we" is constituted, requires the correlative idea of the common good, but a common good conceived as a "vanishing point," a "horizon of meaning," something to which we must constantly refer but which can never be reached. In such a view the common good functions, on the one hand, as a "social imaginary": that is, as that for which the very impossibility of achieving full representation gives to it the role of a horizon which is the condition of possibility of any representation within the space that it delimits. On the other hand, it specifies what we can call, following Wittgenstein, a "grammar of conduct" that coincides with the allegiance to the constitutive ethicopolitical principles of modern democracy: liberty and equality for all. Yet, since those principles are open to many competing interpretations, one has to acknowledge that a fully inclusive political community can never be realized. There will always be a "constitutive outside," an exterior to the community that is the very condition of its existence. It is vital to recognize that, since to construct a "we" it is necessary to distinguish it from a "them," and that all forms of consensus are based on acts of exclusion, the condition of possibility of the political community is at the same time the condition of impossibility of its full realization.

But this does not mean that we should abandon any attempt at constructing a political community, because that would imply renouncing democratic politics. It is important to enter that terrain, to engage into that kind of struggle, but with the awareness that a perfect solution will never be available.

Chantal Mouffe

2. Citizenship.

The previous considerations have important implications for the understanding of our identity as citizens. The perspective that I am proposing envisages citizenship as a form of political identity that is created through identification with the political principles of modern pluralist democracy, that is, the assertion of liberty and equality for all. By that I understand the allegiance to a set of rules and practices that construe a specific language game, the language of modern democratic citizenship. A citizen is not in this perspective—as in liberalism—someone who is the passive recipient of rights and who enjoys the protection of the law. It is a common political identity of persons who might be engaged in many different communities and who have differing conceptions of the good, but who accept submission to certain authoritative rules of conduct. Those rules are not instruments for achieving a common purpose—since the idea of a substantive common good has been discarded—but conditions that individuals must observe in choosing and pursuing purposes of their own.

The reflections on civil association developed by Michael Oakeshott in *On Human Conduct* are pertinent here, since they can help us formulate the kind of bond that should exist among citizens in a way that reconciles freedom with authority.[1]

For Oakeshott, the participants in a civil association or *societas* are linked by the authority of the conditions specifying their common or "public" concern. These consist of a manifold of rules or rulelike prescriptions that he calls *respublica* and that specify not performances but conditions to be subscribed to in choosing performances. According to such a view, what is required to belong to a political community is to accept a specific language of civil intercourse, the *respublica*. The identification with those rules creates a common political identity among persons otherwise engaged in many different enterprises and communities. This modern form of political community is held together not by a substantive idea of the common good but by a common bond, a public concern. It is therefore a community without a definite shape and in continuous reenactment.

If we try to connect Oakeshott's views with what I said earlier concerning the principles of modern democracy as a new regime, we can say that in a modern democracy, the *respublica* is constituted by the political principles of such a regime: equality and liberty for all. By putting such a content in

Oakeshott's notion of the *respublica*, we are able to affirm that the conditions to be subscribed to and taken into account by acting as citizens are to be understood as the exigency of treating others as free and equal persons.

It is evident, however, that this can be interpreted in many different ways, and can lead to competing forms of identifications. For instance, a radical democratic interpretation will emphasize the numerous social relations where relations of domination exist and must be challenged if the principles of liberty and equality are to apply. For that reason, citizenship as a form of political identity cannot be neutral, but will have a variety of modes according to the competing interpretations of the *respublica* which construe that identity and the type of articulation that is established among different subject positions of the agent. The creation of political identities as radical democratic citizens, for instance, depends on a collective form of identification among the democratic demands found in a variety of movements: women, workers, black, gay, ecological; as well as against other forms of subordination. This is a conception of citizenship that through a common identification with a radical democratic interpretation of the principles of liberty and equality aims at constructing a "we," a chain of equivalence among their demands so as to articulate them through the principle of democratic *equivalence*. It must be stressed that such a relation of *equivalence* does not eliminate *difference*—that would be simple identity. It is only insofar as democratic differences are opposed to forces or discourses which negate all of them that these differences are substitutable for each other. That is, the "we" of the radical democratic forces is created by the delimitation of a frontier, the designation of the "them"; it is not a homogeneous "we," predicated on the identity of its components. Through the principle of equivalence a type of commonality is created that does not erase plurality and differences and that allows diverse forms of individuality.

Such a view of citizenship is clearly different from both the liberal and the communitarian ones. It is not one identity among others, as it is in liberalism, nor is it the dominant identity that overrides all others, as it is in civic republicanism. It is an articulating principle that affects the different subject positions of the social agent while allowing for a plurality of specific allegiances and for the respect of individual liberty. In the case of a radical democratic citizen, such an approach allows us to visualize how a concern with equality and liberty should inform her actions in all areas of social life. No sphere is immune from those concerns, and relations of domination can be challenged everywhere.

3. Pluralism.

As I have stressed repeatedly, the respect of pluralism and differences must be at the core of a radical democratic conception of citizenship. Nevertheless, it is also necessary to indicate that such a view cannot allow for a total pluralism, and that it needs to acknowledge the limits of pluralism which are required by a democratic politics that aims at challenging a wide range of relations of subordination. This is why I want to distinguish my position from the type of extreme pluralism that is found in certain forms of postmodern politics that emphasize heterogeneity and incommensurability and refuse any attempt at constructing a "we," and at creating a common political identity. According to those views, pluralism—understood as valorization of all differences—should have no limits, and we are left with a multiplicity of identities with no common denominator. The very idea that we should try to construct a common identity through citizenship is considered repressive.

I consider that, despite its claims to be more democratic, such a perspective impedes us from seeing how certain differences are constructed as relations of subordination, and it should therefore be challenged by a radical democratic politics. It makes it impossible to distinguish between differences that exist but should not exist and differences that do not exist but should exist. More generally, what such a pluralism misses is the dimension of the political. Relations of power and antagonisms are erased, and we are left with the typical liberal illusion of a pluralism without antagonism. Indeed, although it tends to be critical of liberalism, that type of postmodern pluralism, precisely because of its refusal of any attempt to construct a "we" and to articulate the demands found in the different movements against subordination, partakes of the liberal negation of the political.

Politics concerns collective, public action, and deals with collective identities; it aims at the construction of a "we" in a context of diversity and conflict. But, as I indicated earlier, to construct a "we," it must be distinguished from a "them," and in the context of politics, that means establishing a frontier, defining an "enemy." Carl Schmitt was right, then, to declare that the friend/enemy distinction was central to politics. The avoidance of such a criterion by both the liberal and the postmodern forms of pluralism has serious consequences for radical politics, because no struggle is possible against relations of subordination without the establishment of a frontier and the definition of the forms of domination to be destroyed.

It is clear, however, that this implies a double movement: on the one hand the consolidation of the "we"—the friend side—by establishing a certain type of relationship among its different components; on the other hand, the designation of the "them"—the "enemy"—whose exclusion from the range of differences that are considered as legitimate inside the circle of the "we" will determine what are the limits imposed to pluralism.

To deny the need for the construction of such collective identities, and to conceive of politics exclusively in terms of a struggle by a multiplicity of minorities to have their rights recognized and represented, is to remain blind to relations of power, and to ignore the limits imposed on the extension of the sphere of rights by the fact that some existing rights have been constructed on the very exclusion or subordination of rights of others.

As against that extreme postmodern pluralism that values differences, but in a way that forecloses the issue of power, the approach that I am defending shows how social relations and identities are always constructed through asymmetrical forms of power. Since some social agents have more power than others, this will force the latter to establish some form of alliances against them, and, in order to do so, they will have to construct their demands by articulating the demands of others. Hence the crucial role of categories such as "hegemony" and "articulation."[2]

There is also another sense in which it is necessary to stress the limits of pluralism. We must be aware that the very possibility of recognizing differences and defending pluralism depends on the existence of modern democracy, understood as a specific regime the political principles of which are the assertion of liberty and equality for all. Far from being based on a relativist conception of the world, modern democracy is defined by a set of ethicopolitical values. It establishes a specific form of coexistence that requires, for instance, the distinction between the realm of the public and the realm of the private, the separation of church and state, the distinction between civil law and religious law. Those institutions are coextensive with pluralism, and cannot be put into question "in the name of pluralism." Those who conceive the pluralism of modern democracy as having, as the only restriction, an agreement on *procedures*

Chantal Mouffe

do not realize that there can never be pure procedural rules without references to normative concerns.

This reveals the profound misunderstanding involved in the liberal tenet of the *neutrality* of the state. To be sure, in order to respect individual liberty and pluralism, a liberal democratic state must be agnostic in matters of religion and morality; but it cannot be agnostic concerning political values, since, by definition, it postulates certain ethicopolitical values that constitute its principles of legitimacy: liberty and equality for all.

An important consequence follows from that point: antagonistic principles of legitimacy cannot coexist inside a political association, because to accept pluralism at that level would automatically entail the disappearance of the state as a political reality. And this, contrary to some views, would mean not more democracy but the very negation of its possibility.

Therefore, our belonging to the political association cannot be conceived as one more identity at the same level as the others. This is why I believe that we need a conception of citizenship as political identity that consists of the identification with the political principles of modern democracy and commitment to defend its key institutions. Citizenship understood as allegiance to the ethicopolitical values constitutive of modern democracy could provide the consensus which is required to make pluralism possible. Such a consensus on the principles does not imply negation of conflict and division and the creation of an homogeneous collective will. Conflicting interpretations of those principles will always exist and provide for different conceptions of citizenship. The radical democratic mode of identification is only one among many others possible, and it cannot claim any privilege in terms of being the "true" interpretation. If it has any chance of becoming the principal one, to become sedimented into what is considered as "common sense," it would be because the radical democratic forces have been able to establish their hegemony. But nothing can guarantee the issue of the struggle, and a neoconservative conception of citizenship might well be the one able to create a new hegemony.

It is necessary to stress here that, as there is no common ground between those conflicting articulations, there is no way of subsuming them under a deeper objectivity which would reveal its true and deeper essence. This is the basis for the assertion of the constitutive and irreducible character of antagonism, and such an idea plays a central role in the new approach to pluralism that I am proposing.

PLURALISM, POWER AND ANTAGONISM

These reflections indicate that what is really at stake in the question of pluralism is power and antagonism and their ineradicable character. The democratic society can no longer be conceived as a society that would have realized the dream of a perfect harmony in social relations. Its democratic character can only be given by the fact that no limited social actor can attribute to herself the representation of the totality and claim in that way to have the "mastery of the foundation." The main question of democratic politics becomes, therefore, not how to eliminate power, but how to constitute forms of power which are compatible with democratic values. To acknowledge the existence of relations of power and the need to transform them, while renouncing the illusion that we could free ourselves completely from power, is what is specific in the project of radical and plural democracy.

Such an approach requires that we do not conceptualize power as an *external* relation taking place between two preconstituted identities, but rather as constituting the identities themselves. It is because the constitutive outside is present within the inside *as an always real possibility* that every identity is purely contingent and that hegemonic arrangements cannot claim any other source of validity than the power basis on which they are grounded. If this is the case we can now understand why, for democracy to exist, no social agent should be able to claim any mastery of the *foundation* of society. This means that the relation between social agents will become more democratic *only* as far as they accept the particularity and the limitation of their claims; that is, only insofar as they recognize their mutual relation as one from which power is ineradicable. It then becomes clear, not only why pluralism must be conceived as being constitutive of modern democracy, but also why it cannot be separated from power and antagonism.

When we examine democratic politics with the help of such a theoretical framework, we can formulate questions that were impossible before, and give a solution to problems that appeared as insoluble. For instance, the question of the relation between democracy and liberalism has long been a disputed issue. For Carl Schmitt, pluralist liberal democracy is a contradictory combination of irreconcilable principles: whereas democracy is a logic of identity and equivalence, its complete realization is rendered impossible by the logic of pluralism which constitutes an obstacle to a total system of

*Chantal
Mouffe*

identification. Franz Neumann, for his part, pointed to the fact that, while both sovereignty and the Rule of Law were constitutive elements of the modern state, they were irreconcilable with each other, for highest might and highest right could not be at one and the same time realized in a common sphere. So far as the sovereignty of the state extends, there is no place for the Rule of Law, and he sees all attempts at reconciliation as coming up against insoluble contradictions.

It cannot be denied that, through the articulation of liberalism and democracy, two logics which are ultimately incompatible have been linked together, but I do not consider that we should therefore accept Schmitt's conclusion concerning the nonviable character of liberal democracy. We can, it seems to me, envisage this question in a different way. It is evident that the complete realization of the logics of democracy, which are a logic of identity and a logic of equivalence, is made impossible by the liberal logic of pluralism and difference, which impedes the establishment of a total system of identifications. But I consider that it is precisely the existence of such a tension between the logic of identity and the logic of difference that makes pluralist democracy a regime particularly suited to the indecidability and indeterminacy which constitute the specific character of modern politics. To be sure, the liberal logic that aims at constructing every identity as positivity and difference necessarily subverts the project of totalization that is inscribed in the democratic logic of equivalence, but, far from complaining about it, it is something that we should see as very positive. Indeed, it is the existence of such a tension, which also manifests itself between the principles of equality and liberty and between our identities as "citizens" and our identities as "individuals," that constitutes the best guarantee against the dangers of final closure or of total dissemination that would be the consequence of the exclusive dominance of one of the two logics. Far from aiming at its suppression—that would lead to the elimination of the political and the end of democracy—we must preserve and enhance it. Between the project of a complete equivalence and the opposite one of pure difference, the experience of modern democracy consists in acknowledging the existence of those contradictory logics as well as the necessity of their articulation: articulation that constantly needs to be recreated and renegotiated, since there is no final point of equilibrium where a final harmony could be reached. It is only in that precarious space "in-between" that pluralist democracy can exist. Therefore such a democracy will always be a democracy "to come," to use the expression of Derrida, insisting not only on the potentialities still to be realized but also on the radical impossibility of a final achievement.

To believe that a final resolution of conflicts is eventually possible—even if it is seen as an asymptotic approaching to the regulative ideal of free, unconstrained communication as in Habermas—is something that, far from providing the necessary horizon of the democratic project, in fact puts it at risk. We must be aware of the fact that pluralit democracy is a self-refuting ideal, because the very moment of its realization will see its disintegration.

This is why the project of radical and plural democracy must be distinguished from other forms of radical or participatory democracy informed by a universalistic and rationalistic theoretical framework. I indicated earlier that it was necessary to come to terms with the fact that pluralism implies the permanence of conflict and antagonism. I hope that, by now, it is clear that conflict and antagonism are not to be seen as disturbances that unfortunately cannot be completely eliminated, or as empirical impediments that render impossible the full realization of a good constituted by a harmony that we cannot reach because we will never be completely able to coincide with our rational universal self.

Pluralism is not merely a *fact* that we have to accept grudgingly, as John Rawls often presents it, but an axiological principle, a valorization of diversity. Instead of trying to reduce the existing plurality through devices like the veil of ignorance or the ideal speech situation, we need to develop a positive attitude towards differences, even if they lead to conflict and impede the realization of harmony. Any understanding of pluralism whose objective is to reach harmony is ultimately a negation of the positive value of diversity and difference.

Nevertheless, the kind of pluralism I am advocating requires the establishment of a common bond, so that the multiplicity of democratic identities and differences do not explode into a separatism that would lead to the negation of the political community; for without any reference to the political community, democratic politics cannot exist. Therefore, those of us who are committed to a radicalization and extension of the principles of liberty and equality should envisage a type of political community that is created through a chain of equivalence among democratic struggles and identities.

A radical democratic conception of citizenship could, I believe, provide that bond created through equivalence, that form of commonality that does not erase differences. It can play such a role because, as I have tried to show, it draws on an antiessentialist framework according to which the commonality that is made possible by equivalence is not the expression of something positive, of a common essence, but something purely negative. Besides, it is linked with an idea of the political community that mobilizes a conception of pluralism according to which conflict and antagonism are recognized as the condition of possibility of pluralist democracy as well as the condition of impossibility of its full realization. Indeed, they name the precondition of such a democracy, a precondition that represents the limit of such a possibility.

NOTES

1. I am drawing here on a more developed version of that argument in my article, "Democratic Citizenship and the Political Community" in Chantal Mouffe, ed., *Dimensions of Radical Democracy, Pluralism, Citizenship, Community*, (London: Verso, 1992).
2. For a full elaboration of those categories, as well as the approach presented here, see Ernesto Laclau and Chantal Mouffe, *Hegemony and Socialist Strategy: Towards a Radical Democratic Politics* (London: Verso, 1985).

DEBATE

Homi Bhabha

Freedom's Basis in the Indeterminate

Postcolonial criticism bears witness to the unequal and uneven forces of cultural representation involved in the contest for political and social authority within the modern world order. Postcolonial perspectives emerge from the colonial or anticolonialist testimonies of Third World countries and from the testimony of minorities within the geopolitical division of East/West, North/South. These perspectives intervene in the ideological discourses of modernity that have attempted to give a hegemonic "normality" to the uneven development and the differential, often disadvantaged, histories of nations, races, communities and peoples. Their critical revisions are formulated around issues of cultural difference, social authority and political discrimination, in order to reveal the antagonistic and ambivalent moments within the "rationalizations" of modernity. To assimilate Habermas to our purposes, we could also argue that the postcolonial project, at its most general theoretical level, seeks to explore those social pathologies—"loss of meaning, conditions of anomie"—that no longer simply "cluster around class antagonism, [but] break up into widely scattered historical contingencies."[1]

These contingencies often provide the grounds of historical necessity for the elaboration of strategies of emancipation, for the staging of other social antagonisms. Reconstituting the discourse of cultural difference demands more than a simple change of cultural contents and symbols, for a replacement within the same representational time frame is never adequate. This reconstitution requires a radical revision of the social *temporality* in which emergent histories may be written: the rearticulation of the "sign" in which cultural identities may be inscribed. And contingency as the *signifying time* of counterhegemonic strategies is not a celebration of "lack" or "excess," or a self-perpetuating series of negative ontologies. Such "indeterminism" is the mark of the conflictual yet productive space in which the arbitrariness of the sign of cultural signification emerges within the regulated boundaries of social discourse.

It is in this salutary sense that various contemporary critical theories suggest that we learn our most enduring lessons for living and thinking from those who have suffered the sentence of history—subjugation, domination, diaspora, displacement. There is even a growing conviction that the affective experience of social marginality—as it emerges in noncanonical cultural forms—transforms our critical strategies. It forces us to confront the concept of culture outside *objets d'art* or beyond the canonization of the "Idea" of aesthetics, and thus to engage with culture as an uneven, incomplete production of meaning and value, often composed of incommensurable demands and practices, and produced in the act of social survival. Culture reaches out to create a symbolic textuality, to give the alienating everyday an "aura" of selfhood, a promise of pleasure. The transmission of "cultures of survival" does not occur in the ordered *musée ordinaire* of national cultures—with their claims to the continuity of an authentic past and a living present—regardless of whether this scale of value is preserved in the organicist national traditions of romanticism or within the more universal proportions of classicism.

Culture as a strategy of survival is both *transnational* and *translational*. It is transnational because contemporary postcolonial discourses are rooted in specific histories of cultural displacement: in the "middle passage" of slavery and indenture; in the "voyage out" of the colonialist civilizing mission; in the fraught accommodation of postwar Third World migration to the West; or in the traffic of economic and political refugees within and outside the Third World. It is translational because such spatial histories of displacement—now accompanied by the territorial ambitions of global media technologies—make the question of *how* culture signifies, or what is signified by *culture*, rather complex issues. It becomes crucial to distinguish between the semblance and similitude of the *symbols* across diverse cultural

Homi Bhabha

experiences—literature, art, music, ritual, life, death—and the social specificity of each of these productions of meaning as it circulates *as a sign* within
specific contextual locations and social systems of value. The transnational
dimension of cultural transformation—migration, diaspora, displacement,
relocations—turns the specifying or localizing process of cultural translation into a complex process of signification. For the natural(ized), unifying
discourse of "nation," "peoples," "folk" tradition—these embedded myths
of culture's particularity—cannot be readily referenced. The great, though
unsettling, advantage of this position is that it makes one increasingly
aware of the construction of culture, the invention of tradition, the retroac-
tive nature of social affiliation and psychic identification.

The postcolonial perspective departs from the traditions of the sociology
of underdevelopment or the "dependency" theory. As a mode of analysis, it
attempts to revise those nationalist or "nativist" pedagogies that set up the
relation of Third and First Worlds in a binary structure of opposition. The
postcolonial perspective resists attempts to provide a holistic social explanation, forcing a recognition of the more complex cultural and political
boundaries that exist on the cusp of these often opposed political spheres.

It is from this hybrid location of cultural value—the transnational *as* the
translational—that the postcolonial intellectual attempts to elaborate a historical and literary project. It has been my growing conviction that the
encounters and negotiations of differential meanings and values within the
governmental discourses and cultural practices that make up "colonial" textuality have enacted, *avant la lettre*, many of the problematics of signification and judgment that have become current in contemporary theory:
aporia, ambivalence, indeterminacy, the question of discursive closure, the
threat to agency, the status of intentionality, the challenge to "totalizing"
concepts, to name but a few.

To put it in general terms, there is a "colonial" countermodernity at work
in the eighteenth- and nineteenth-century matrices of Western modernity
that, if acknowledged, would question the historicism that, in a linear narrative, analogically links late capitalism to the fragmentary, simulacral, pas-
tiche-like symptoms of postmodernity. This is done without taking into
account the historical traditions of cultural contingency and textual indeterminacy that were generated in the attempt to produce an "enlightened"
colonial subject—in both the foreign and native varieties—and that transformed, in the process, both antagonistic sites of cultural agency.

Postcolonial critical discourses require forms of dialectical thinking that do not disavow or sublate the otherness (alterity) that constitutes the symbolic domain of psychic and social identifications. The incommensurability of cultural values and priorities that the postcolonial critic represents cannot be accommodated within a relativism that assumes a public and symmetrical world. And the cultural potential of such differential histories has led Fredric Jameson to recognize the "internationalization of the national situations" in the postcolonial criticism of Roberto Retamar. Far from functioning as an absorption of the particular by the general, the very act of articulating cultural differences "calls us into question fully as much as it acknowledges the Other . . . neither reduc[ing] the Third World to some homogeneous Other of the West, nor . . . vacuously celebrat[ing] the astonishing pluralism of human cultures."[2]

The historical grounds of such an intellectual tradition are to be found in the revisionary impulse that informs many postcolonial thinkers. C.L.R. James once remarked that the postcolonial prerogative consisted in reinterpreting and rewriting the forms and effects of an "older" colonial consciousness from the later experience of the cultural displacement that marks the more recent, postwar histories of the Western metropolis. A similar process of cultural translation, and transvaluation, is evident in Edward Said's assessment of the response from disparate postcolonial regions as a "tremendously energetic attempt to engage with the metropolitan world in a common effort at reinscribing, reinterpreting, and expanding the sites of intensity and the terrain contested with Europe."[3]

How does the deconstruction of the sign, the emphasis on indeterminism in cultural and political judgment, transform our sense of the subject of culture and the historical agent of change? If we contest the grand, continuist narratives, then what alternative temporalities do we create to articulate the contrapuntal (Said) or interruptive (Spivak) formations of race, gender, class and nation within a transnational world culture?

Such problematic questions are activated within the terms and traditions of postcolonial critique as it reinscribes the cultural relations between spheres of social antagonism. Current debates in postmodernism question the cunning of modernity—its historical ironies, its disjunctive temporalities, the paradoxical nature of progress. It would profoundly affect the values and judgments of such interrogations if they were open to the argument that metropolitan histories of *civitas* cannot be conceived without evoking

Homi Bhabha

the colonial antecedents of the ideals of civility. The postcolonial translation of modernity does not simply revalue the contents of a cultural tradition or transpose values across cultures through the transcendent spirit of a "common humanity."

Cultural translation transforms the value of culture-as-sign: as the time-signature of the historical "present" that is struggling to find its mode of narration. The sign of cultural difference does not celebrate the great continuities of a past tradition, the seamless narratives of progress, the vanity of humanist wishes. Culture-as-sign articulates that in-between moment when the rule of language as semiotic system—linguistic difference, the arbitrariness of the sign—turns into a struggle for the historical and ethical *right to signify*. The rule of language as signifying system—the possibility of speaking at all—becomes the misrule of discourse: the right for only some to speak diachronically and differentially, and for "others"—women, migrants, Third World peoples, Jews, Palestinians, for instance—to speak only symptomatically or marginally. How do we transform the formal value of linguistic difference into an analytic of cultural difference? How do we turn the "arbitrariness" of the sign into the critical practices of social authority? In what sense is this an interruption within the discourses of modernity?

This is not simply a demand for a postcolonial semiology. From the postcolonial perspective, it is an intervention in the way discourses of modernity structure their objects of knowledge. The right to signify—to make a name for oneself—emerges from the moment of undecidability—a claim made by Jacques Derrida in "Des Tours de Babel," his essay on "figurative translation." Let us not forget that he sees translation as the trope for the process of displacement through which language names its object. But even more suggestive, for our postcolonial purposes, is the Babel metaphor that Derrida uses to describe the cultural, communal process of "making a name for oneself": "The Semites want to bring the world to reason and this reason can signify simultaneously a colonial violence . . . and a peaceful transparency of the human condition."[4]

This is emphatically not, as Terry Eagleton has recently described it, "the trace or aporia or ineffable flicker of difference which eludes all formalization, that giddy moment of failure, slippage, or jouissance."[5] The undecidability of discourse is not to be read as the "excess" of the signifier, as an aestheticization of the formal arbitrariness of the sign. Rather, it represents, as Habermas suggests, the central ambivalence of the knowledge structure of modernity; "unconditionality" is the Janus-faced process at work in the modern moment of cultural judgment, where validity claims seek justification for their propositions in terms of the specificity of the "everyday." Undecidability or unconditionality "is built into the factual processes of mutual understanding. . . . Validity claimed for propositions and norms transcends spaces and times, but the claim must always be raised here and now, in specific contexts."[6]

Pace Eagleton, this is no giddy moment of failure; it is instead precisely the act of representation as a mode of regulating the limits or liminality of cultural knowledges. Habermas illuminates the undecidable or "unconditional" as the epistemological basis of cultural specificity, and thus, in the discourse of modernity, the claim to knowledge shifts from the "universal" to the domain of context-bound, everyday practice. However, Habermas's notion of communicative reason presumes intersubjective understanding and reciprocal recognition. This renders his sense of cultural particularity essentially consensual and essentialist. What of those colonial cultures caught in the drama of the dialectic of the master and the enslaved or indentured?

This concept of the right to signify is, in the context of contemporary postcolonial poetry, nowhere more profoundly evoked than in Derek Walcott's poem on the colonization of the Caribbean through the possession of a space by means of the power of naming. In Walcott's "Names," ordinary language develops an auratic authority, an imperial persona; but in a specifically postcolonial performance of repetition, the focus shifts from the nominalism of linguistic imperialism to the emergence of another history of the sign. It is another destiny of culture as a site—one based not simply on subversion and transgression, but on the prefiguration of a kind of solidarity between ethnicities that meet in the tryst of colonial history. Walcott explores that space of cultural translation between the double meanings of culture: culture as the noun for naming the social imaginary, and culture as the act for grafting the voices of the indentured, the displaced, the nameless, onto an agency of utterance.

My race began as the sea began,
with no nouns, and with no horizon,
with pebbles under my tongue,
with a different fix on the stars. . . .

Have we melted into a mirror,
leaving our souls behind?
The goldsmith from Benares,
the stonecutter from Canton,
the bronzesmith from Benin.

A sea-eagle screams from the rock,
and my race began like the osprey
with that cry,
that terrible vowel,
that I!

. . . this stick
to trace our names on the sand
which the sea erased again, to our indifference.

And when they named these bays
bays,
was it nostalgia or irony? . . .

Where were the courts of Castile?
Versailles' colonnades
supplanted by cabbage palms
with Corinthian crests,
belittling diminutives,
then, little Versailles
meant plans for the pigsty,
names for the sour apples
and green grapes
of their exile. . . .

Being men, they could not live
except they first presumed
the right of everything to be a noun.
The African acquiesced,
repeated, and changed them.

Listen, my children, say:
moubain: the hogplum,
cerise: the wild cherry,
baie-la: the bay,

with the fresh green voices
they were once themselves
in the way the wind bends
our natural inflections.

These palms are greater than Versailles,
for no man made them,
their fallen columns greater than Castile,
no man unmade them
except the worm, who has no helmet,
but was always the emperor,

and children, look at these stars
over Valencia's forest!

Not Orion,
Not Betelgeuse,
tell me, what do they look like?
Answer you damned little Arabs!
Sir, fireflies caught in molasses.[7]

In this poem, there are two myths of history, each related to opposing versions of the place of language in the process of cultural knowledge. There is the pedagogical process of imperialist naming:

Being men, they could not live
except they first presumed
the right of everything to be a noun.

Opposed to this is the African acquiescence, which, in repeating the lessons of the masters, changes their inflections:

moubain: the hogplum
cerise: the wild cherry
baie-la: the bay
with the fresh green voices
they were once themselves. . . .

Walcott's purpose is not to oppose the pedagogy of the imperialist noun to the inflectional appropriation of the native voice; he proposes instead to go beyond such binaries of power in order to reorganize our sense of the process of language in the negotiations of cultural politics. He stages the slaves' right to signify not simply by denying the imperialist "right for everything to be a noun," but by questioning the masculinist, authoritative subjectivity produced in the colonizing process. What is "man" as an effect of, as subjected to, the sign—the noun—of a colonizing discourse? To this end, Walcott poses the problem of beginning outside the question of origins, beyond that perspectival field of vision which constitutes human consciousness in the "mirror of nature" (as Richard Rorty has famously described the project of positivism). According to this ideology, language is always a form of visual epistemology, the miming of a pregiven reality; knowing is implicated in the confrontational polarity of subject and object, Self and Other.

Within this mode of representation, naming (or nouning) the world is a mimetic act. It is founded on an idealism of the iconic sign, which assumes that repetition in language is the symptom of an inauthentic act, of nostalgia or mockery. In the context of imperialist naming, this can only lead to ethnocentric disdain or cultural despair:

Where were the courts of Castile?
Versailles' colonnades
supplanted by cabbage palms
with Corinthian crests,
belittling diminutives. . . .

Thus Walcott's history begins elsewhere: in that temporality of the negation of essences to which Fanon led us; in that moment of undecidability or unconditionality that constitutes the ambivalence of modernity as it executes its critical judgments or seeks justification for its social facts. Against the possessive, coercive "right" of the Western noun, Walcott places a different mode of speech, a different historical time envisaged in the discourse of the enslaved or the indentured—the goldsmith from Benares, the stonecutter from Canton, the bronzesmith from Benin.

My race began as the sea began,
with no nouns, and with no horizon. . . .

I began with no memory,
I began with no future. . . .

I have never found that moment
When the mind was halved by a horizon. . . .

And my race began like the osprey
with that cry,
that terrible vowel,
that I!

Is there a historical timelessness at the heart of slavery? By erasing the sovereign subject of the Western mind, of the mind "halved by the horizon," Walcott erases the mode of historicism that predicates the colonial civilizing mission on the question of the origin of races. "My race began . . . with no nouns." With this Walcott destroys the Eurocentric narrative of nouns, the attempt to objectify the New World, to enclose it in the teleology of the noun, in the fetish of naming. In destroying the teleology of the subject of naming, Walcott refuses to totalize differences, to make of culture a holistic, organic system. What is more, he emphatically stills that future-drive of the (imperialist) discourse of modernization or progress that conceals the disjunctive, fragmented moment of the colonial "present" by overlaying it with grand narratives and grandiose names or nouns: Castile, Versailles. Walcott reveals the space and time in which the struggle for the proper name of the postcolonial poet ensues.

Walcott's timeless moment, that undecidability from which he builds his narrative, opens up his poem to the historical present that Walter Benjamin, in his description of the historian, characterizes as a "present which is not a transition, but in which time stands still and has come to a stop. For this notion defines the present in which he himself is writing history."[8] Yet what is the history that is being rewritten in this present? Where does the postcolonial subject lie?

With "that terrible vowel, that I," Walcott opens up the disjunctive present of the poem's writing of its history. The "I" as vowel, as the arbitrariness of the signifier, is the sign of iteration or repetition; it is nothing in itself, only ever its difference. The "I" as pronominal, as the avowal of the enslaved colonial subject-position, is contested by the repetition of the "I" as vocal or vowel "sign," as the agency of history, tracing its name on the shifting sands, constituting a postcolonial, migrant community-in-difference: Hindu, Chinese, African. With this disjunctive, double "I," Walcott writes a history of cultural difference that envisages the production of difference as the political and social definition of the historical present. Cultural differences must be understood as they constitute identities—contingently, indeterminately—between the repetition of the vowel *i* (which can always be reinscribed, relocated) and the restitution of the subject "I." Read like this, between the I-as-symbol and the I-as-sign, the articulations of difference—race, history, gender—are never singular, binary or totalizable. These cultural differentials are most productively read as existing in-between each other. If they make claims to their radical singularity or separatism, they do so at the peril of their historical destiny to change, transform, solidarize. Claims to identity must never be nominative or normative. They are never nouns when they are productive; like the vowel, they must be capable of turning up in and as an other's difference and of turning the "right" to signify into an act of cultural translation.

The postcolonial revision of modernity I am arguing for has a political place in the writings of Raymond Williams. Williams makes an important distinction between emergent and residual practices of oppositionality, which require what he describes as a "non-metaphysical and non-subjectivist" historical position. He does not elaborate on this complex idea, but I hope that my description of agency as it emerges in the disjunctive temporality of the "present" in the postcolonial text may be one important instance of it. This concept has a contemporary relevance for those burgeoning forces of the Left who are attempting to formulate a "politics of difference" that avoids both essentialism and cultural "nationalism"; Williams suggests that in certain historical moments—ours certainly among them—the profound deformation of the dominant culture will prevent it from recognizing "political practices and cultural meanings that are not reached for."[9]

Such a notion of the emergence of a cultural "minority" has a vivid realization in the work of many Black American women writers—writers who emphasize, according to Houston Baker, "the processual quality of meaning . . . not material instantiation at any given moment but the efficacy of passage."[10] Such a passage of time-as-meaning emerges with a sudden ferocity in the work of the African-American poet Sonia Sanchez:

life is obscene with crowds
of black on white
death is my pulse.
what might have been
is not for him/or me
but what could have been
floods the womb until i drown.[11]

You can hear it in the ambiguity between "what might have been" and
"what could have been"—again, in that undecidability through which
Sanchez attempts to write her history of the present. You read it in that considerable shift in historical time between an obscene, racist past—the
"might have been"—and the emergence of a new birth that is visible in the
writing itself—the "could have been." You see it suggested in the almost
imperceptible displacement in tense and syntax—might, could—that
makes all the difference between the pulse of death and the flooded womb
of birth. And it is this repetition—the repetition of the could-in-the-
might—that expresses the right to signify.

The postcolonial passage through modernity produces a form of retroac-
tion: the past as projective. It is not a cyclical form of repetition that circulates around a lack. The time *lag* of postcolonial modernity moves *forward*,
erasing that compliant past tethered to the myth of progress, ordered in the
binarisms of its cultural logic: past/present, inside/outside. This forward is
neither teleological, nor is it an endless slippage. It is the function of the
lag to slow down the linear, progressive time of modernity to reveal its gesture, its *tempi*—"the pauses and stresses of the whole performance." This can
only be achieved—as Walter Benjamin remarked of Brecht's epic theater—
by damming the stream of life, by bringing the flow to a standstill in a
reflux of astonishment.

When the dialectic of modernity is brought to a standstill, then the temporal action of modernity—its progressive future drive—is *staged*, revealing "everything that is involved in the act of staging per se."[12] This slowing
down, or lagging, impels the past, projects it, gives its "dead" symbols the
circulatory life of the "sign" of the present, of passage, of the quickening of
the quotidian. Where these temporalities touch contingently, their spatial
boundaries overlap; at that moment their margins are sutured in the articulation of the "disjunctive" present. And this time lag keeps alive the mak-

Homi
Bhabha

ing and remaking of the past. As it negotiates the levels and liminalities of that spatial time that I have tried to unearth in the postcolonial archaeology of modernity, you might think that it "lacks" time or history. But don't be fooled!

It appears "timeless" only in that sense in which, for Toni Morrison, African-American art is "astonished" by the belated figure of the ancestor . . . "the timelessness is there, this person who represented this ancestor."[13] And when the ancestor rises from the dead in the guise of the murdered slave daughter, Beloved, then we see the furious emergence of the projective past. Beloved is not the ancestor, the elder, whom Morrison describes as benevolent, instructive and protective. Her presence, as *revenant*, is profoundly time-lagged, and moves forward while continually encircling the moment of the "not there" that Morrison sees as the stressed, dislocatory absence that is crucial for the reconstruction of the narrative of slavery. Ella, a member of the chorus, standing at that very distance from the "event" from which modernity produces its historical sign, now describes the projective past:

> The future was sunset; the past something to leave behind. And if it didn't stay behind you might have to stomp it out. . . . As long as the ghost showed out from its ghostly place . . . Ella respected it. But if it took flesh and came in her world, well, the shoe was on the other foot. She didn't mind a little communication between the two worlds, but this was an invasion.[14]

The emergence of the "projective past" introduces into the narratives of identity and community a necessary split between the time of utterance and the space of memory. This "lagged" temporality is not some endless slippage; it is a mode of breaking the complicity of past and present in order to open up a space of revision and initiation. It is, in other words, the articulation between the pronominal "I" and verbal/vocal *i* that Walcott stages in the process of creating a postcolonial, Caribbean voice that is heard in the *interstitial* experience of diaspora and migration, somewhere between the "national" origins of the Benin bronzesmith, the Cantonese stonecutter, and the goldsmith from Benares.

The histories of slavery and colonialism that create the discursive conditions for the projective past and its split narratives are tragic and painful in the extreme, but it is their agony that makes them exemplary texts for our moment. They represent an idea of action and agency more complex than either the nihilism of despair or the Utopia of progress. They speak of the reality of survival and negotiation that constitutes the lived moment of resistance, its sorrow and its salvation—the moment that is rarely spoken in the stories of heroism that are enshrined in the histories we choose to remember and recount.

NOTES

Short sections of this talk have been published elsewhere.

1. Jürgen Habermas, *The Philosophical Discourse of Modernity* (Cambridge: MIT Press, 1978), p. 348.
2. Roberto Fernandez, *Caliban and Other Essays*, trans. Edward Baker, foreword Fredric Jameson (Minneapolis: Minnesota University Press, 1989), pp. xi–xii.
3. Edward Said, "Intellectuals and the Post-Colonial World," *Salmagundi* 70/71 (Spring/Summer 1986).
4. Jacques Derrida, "Des Tours de Babel," in *Difference in Translation*, ed. Joseph F. Graham (Ithaca: Cornell University Press, 1985), p. 174.
5. Terry Eagleton, *The Ideology of the Aesthetic* (Oxford: Blackwell, 1990), p. 370.
6. Habermas, *The Philosophical Discourse of Modernity*, p. 323.
7. Derek Walcott, *Collected Poems 1948–1984* (New York: Noonday Press, 1990), pp. 305–308.
8. Walter Benjamin, "Theses on the Philosophy of History," *Illuminations,* trans. Harry Zohn (New York: Schocken, 1969), p. 262.
9. Raymond Williams, *Problems in Materialism and Culture* (London: Verso, 1980), p. 43.
10. Houston Baker, "Our Lady: Sonia Sanchez and the Writing of a Black Renaissance," in *Reading Black, Reading Feminist,* ed. Henry Louis Gates (New York: Meridian, 1990).
11. Sonia Sanchez, quoted in Baker, "Our Lady: Sonia Sanchez," pp. 329–330.
12. Walter Benjamin, *Understanding Brecht*, trans. Stanley Mitchell (London: New Left Books, 1973), pp. 11–13. I have freely adapted some of

Homi Bhabha

Benjamin's phrases and interpolated the problem of modernity into the midst of his argument on Epic theater. I do not think that I have misrepresented his argument.

13. Toni Morrison, "The Ancestor as Foundation," in *Black Women Writers*, ed. Mari Evans (London: Pluto Press, 1985), p. 343.
14. Toni Morrison, *Beloved* (New York: Plume, 1987), pp. 256–257.

DEBATE

Jacques Rancière

Politics, Identification, and Subjectivization

In a sense, the whole matter of my paper is involved in a preliminary question: In what language will it be uttered? Neither my language nor your language, but rather a dialect between French and English, a special one, a dialect that carries no identification with any group. No tribal dialect, no univeral language, only an *in-between* dialect, constructed for the aims of this discussion and guided by the idea that the activity of thinking is primarily an activity of translation, and that anyone is capable of making a translation. Underpinning this capacity for translation is the efficacy of equality, that is to say, the efficacy of humanity.

I will move directly to the question that frames our discussion. I quote from the third point of the list of issues we were asked to address: "What is the political?"

Briefly and roughly speaking, I would answer: the political is the encounter between two heterogeneous processes. The first process is that of governing, and it entails creating community consent, which relies on the distribution of shares and the hierarchy of places and functions. I shall call this process *policy*.

The second process is that of equality. It consists of a set of practices guided by the supposition that everyone is equal and by the attempt to verify this supposition. The proper name for this set of practices remains *eman-*

cipation. In spite of Lyotard's statements, I do not assume a necessary link between the idea of emancipation and the narrative of a universal wrong and a universal victim. It is true that the handling of a wrong remains the universal form for the meeting between the two processes of policy and equality. We can question that encounter. We can argue, for example, that any policy denies equality, and that there is no commensurability between the two processes. In my book, *The Ignorant Schoolmaster*, I advocated the thesis of the French theorist of emancipation, Joseph Jacotot, according to whom emancipation can only be the intellectual emancipation of individuals. This means that there is no political stage, only the law of policy and the law of equality. In order for a political stage to occur, we must change that assumption. Thus, instead of arguing that policy *denies* equality, I shall say that policy *wrongs* equality, and I shall take the political to be the place where the verification of equality is obliged to turn into the handling of a wrong.

So we have three terms: policy, emancipation and the political. If we want to emphasize their interplay, we can give to the process of emancipation the name of *politics*. I shall thus distinguish policy, politics and the political—the political being the field for the encounter between emancipation and policy in the handling of a wrong.

A momentous consequence follows from this: politics is not the enactment of the principle, the law or the self of a community. Put in other words, politics has no *arche*, it is anarchical. The very name *democracy* supports this point. As Plato noted, democracy has no *arche*, no measure. The singularity of the act of the *demos*—a *cratein* instead of an *archein*—is dependent on an originary disorder or miscount: the *demos*, or people, is at the same time the name of a community and the name for its division, for the handling of a wrong. And beyond any particular wrong, the "politics of the people" wrongs policy, because the people is always more or less than itself. It is the power of the *one more*, the power of *anyone*, which confuses the right ordering of policy.

Now, for me, the current dead end of political reflection and action is due to the identification of politics with the *self* of a community. This may occur in the big community or in smaller ones; it may be the identification of the process of governing with the principle of the community under the heading of universality, the reign of the law, liberal democracy and so on. Or it may be, on the contrary, the claim for identity on the part of so-called minorities against the hegemonic law of the ruling culture and identity.

Jacques
Rancière

The big community and the smaller ones may charge one another with "tribalism" or "barbarianism," and both will be right in their charge and wrong in their claim. I don't assume that they are practically equivalent, that the outcomes are the same; I only assume that they stem from the same questionable identification. For the *primum movens* of policy is to purport to act as the self of the community, to turn the techniques of governing into natural laws of the social order. But if *politics* is something different from *policy*, it cannot draw on such an identification. One can object that the idea of emancipation is historically related to the idea of the self in the formula of "self-emancipation of the workers." But the first motto of any self-emancipation movement is always the struggle against "selfishness." This is not only a moral statement (for instance, the dedication of the individual to the militant community); it is also a logical one: the politics of emancipation is the politics of the self as an other, or, in Greek terms, a *heteron*. The logic of emancipation is a heterology.

Let me put this differently: the process of emancipation is the verification of the equality of any speaking being with any other speaking being. It is always enacted in the name of a category denied either the principle or the consequences of that equality: workers, women, people of color or others. But the enactment of equality is not, for all that, the enactment of the self, of the attributes or properties of the community in question. The name of an injured community that invokes its rights is always the name of the anonym, the name of anyone.

Are there universal values transcending particular identifications? If we are to break out of the desperate debate between universality and identity, we must answer that the only universal in politics is equality. But we must add that equality is not a value given in the essence of Humanity or Reason. Equality exists, and makes universal values exist, to the extent that it is enacted. Equality is not a value to which one appeals; it is a universal that must be supposed, verified and demonstrated in each case. Universality is not the *eidos* of the community to which particular situations are opposed; it is, first of all, a logical operator. The mode of effectivity of Truth or Universality in politics is the discursive and practical construction of a polemical verification, a case, a demonstration. The place of truth is not the place of a ground or an ideal; it is always a *topos*, the place of a subjectivization in an argumentative plot. Its language is always idiomatic, which, on the contrary, does not mean tribal. When oppressed groups set out to cope with a wrong, they may appeal to Man or Human Being. But the universality is not in those concepts; it is in the way of demonstrating the consequences that follow from this—from the worker being a citizen, the Black being a human being, and so on. The logical schema of social protest, generally speaking, may be summed up as follows: Do we or do we not belong to the category of men or citizens or human beings, and what follows from this? The universality is not enclosed in *citizen* or *human being*; it is involved in the "what follows," in its discursive and practical enactment.

Such a universality may develop through the mediation of particular categories. For instance, in nineteenth-century France, workers might construct the logic of a strike in the form of a syllogism: Do French workers belong to the category of Frenchmen? If not, the Declaration of Rights has to be changed. If so, they must be treated as equals, and they act to demonstrate it. The question might become more paradoxical. For instance, does a French woman belong to the category of Frenchmen? The question may sound nonsensical or scandalous. However, such nonsensical sentences may prove more productive in the process of equality than the mere assumption that a woman is a woman, or a worker, a worker. For they allow these subjects not only to specify a logical gap, that in turn discloses a social bias, but also to articulate this gap as a relation, the nonplace as a place, the place for a polemical construction. The construction of such cases of equality is not the act of an identity, nor is it the demonstration of the values specific to a group. It is a process of subjectivization.

What is a process of subjectivization? It is the formation of a one that is not a self but is the relation of a self to an other. Let me demonstrate this with respect to an outmoded name, "the proletarian." One of its first uses occurs in nineteenth-century France, when the revolutionary leader Auguste Blanqui was prosecuted for rebellion. The prosecutor asked him: "What is your profession?" He answered: "Proletarian." Then the prosecutor: "It is not a profession." And the response of Blanqui was: "It is the profession of the majority of our people who are deprived of political rights." From the vantage point of policy, the prosecutor was right: it is no profession. And obviously Blanqui was not what is usually called a worker. But, from the vantage point of politics, Blanqui was right: *proletarian* was not the name of any social group that could be sociologically identified. It is the name of an outcast. An outcast is not a poor wretch of humanity; outcast is the name of those who are denied an identity in a given order of policy. In Latin, *pro-*

letarii meant "prolific people"—people who make children, who merely live and reproduce without a name, without being counted as part of the symbolic order of the city. *Proletarians* was thus well suited for the workers as the name of anyone, the name of the outcast: those who do not belong to the order of castes, indeed, those who are involved in undoing this order (the class that dissolves classes, as Marx said). In this way, a process of subjectivization is a process of disidentification or declassification.

Let me rephrase this: a subject is an outsider or, more, an *in-between*. *Proletarians* was the name given to people who are together inasmuch as they are between: between several names, statuses and identities; between humanity and inhumanity, citizenship and its denial; between the status of a man of tools and the status of a speaking and thinking being. Political subjectivization is the enactment of equality—or the handling of a wrong—by people who are together to the extent that they are between. It is a crossing of identities, relying on a crossing of names: names that link the name of a group or class to the name of no group or no class, a being to a nonbeing or a not-yet-being.

This network has a noticeable property: it always involves an impossible identification, an identification that cannot be embodied by he or she who utters it. "We are the wretched of the earth" is the kind of sentence that no wretched of the world would ever utter. Or, to take a personal example, for my generation politics in France relied on an impossible identification—an identification with the bodies of the Algerians beaten to death and thrown into the Seine by the French police, in the name of the French people, in October 1961. We could not identify with those Algerians, but we *could* question our identification with the "French people" in whose name they had been murdered. That is to say, we could act as political subjects in the interval or the gap between two identities, neither of which we could assume. That process of subjectivization had no proper name, but it found its name, its cross name, in the 1968 assumption "We are all German Jews"—a "wrong" identification, an identification in terms of the denial of an absolutely essential wrong. If the movement began with that sentence, its decline might be emblematized by an antithetical statement, which served as the title of an essay published some years after by a former leader of the movement: "We were not all born proletarians." Certainly we were not; we are not. But what follows from this is an inability to draw consequences from a "being" that is a "nonbeing," from an identification with an anybody that has no body. In the demonstration of equality, the syllogistic logic of the *either/or* (are we or are we not citizens or human beings?) is intertwined with the paratactic logic of a "we are *and* are not."

In sum, the logic of political subjectivization, of emancipation, is a heterology, a logic of the other, for three main reasons. First, it is never the simple assertion of an identity; it is always, at the same time, the denial of an identity given by an other, given by the ruling order of policy. Policy is about "right" names, names that pin people down to their place and work. Politics is about "wrong" names—misnomers that articulate a gap and connect with a wrong. Second, it is a demonstration, and a demonstration always supposes an other, even if that other refuses evidence or argument. It is the staging of a commonplace that is not a place for a dialogue or a search for a consensus in Habermasian fashion. There is no consensus, no undamaged communication, no settlement of a wrong. But there is a polemical commonplace for the handling of a wrong and the demonstration of equality. Third, the logic of subjectivization always entails an impossible identification.

Only by dismissing the complexity of this logic can one oppose the past grand narratives and the universal victims to present-day little narratives. The so-called grand narrative of the people and the proletariat was in fact made of a multiplicity of language games and demonstrations. And the concept of narrative itself, like the concept of culture, is highly questionable. It entails the identification of an argumentative plot with a voice, and of a voice with a body. But the life of political subjectivization is made out of the difference between the voice and the body, the interval between identities. So narrative and culture entail the reversion of subjectivization to identification. The process of equality is a process of difference. But difference does not mean the assumption of a different identity or the plain confrontation of two identities. The place for the working out of difference is not the "self" or the culture of a group. It is the *topos* of an argument. And the place for such an argument is an interval. The place of a political subject is an interval or a gap: being *together* to the extent that we are *in-between*—between names, identities, cultures and so on.

This is, to be sure, an uncomfortable position, and the discomfort gives way to the discourse of metapolitics. Metapolitics is the interpretation of politics from the vantage point of policy. Its tendency is to interpret heterology as illusion, and intervals and gaps as signs of untruth. The paradigms of the metapolitical interpretation approach is the Marxist interpretation of the *Declaration of the Rights of Man and of the Citizen* of 1789. It assumed that the very difference between *man* and *citizen* was the hallmark of delusion: lurking behind the celestial identity of the citizen was the mundane identity of a man who was in fact an owner. Today the current style of metapolitics teaches us, on the contrary, that man and citizen are the same liberal individual, enjoying the universal values of human rights embodied in the constitutions of our democracies. But the style of politics as emancipation is a third one: it assumes that the universality of the declaration of 1789 is the universality of the argument to which it gave way, and that is due precisely to the very interval between the two terms, which opened the possibility of appealing from one to the other, of making them the terms of innumerable demonstrations of rights, including the rights of those who are counted neither as men nor as citizens.

My conclusion is twofold: both optimistic and pessimistic. First, we are not trapped within the opposition of universalism and identity. The distinction is rather between a logic of subjectivization and a logic of identification—between two ideas of multiplicity, not between universalism and particularism. The discourse of universalism may be as "tribal" as the discourse of identity. We could experience this during the Gulf War, when many heralds of universal culture turned out to be heralds of clean, universal weapons and undetailed death. The true opposition runs between the tribal and the idiomatic. Idiomatic politics constructs locally the place of the universal, the place for the demonstration of equality. It dismisses the desperate dilemma: either the big community or the smaller ones—either community or nothing at all. It leads to a new politics of the in-between.

My second conclusion is less optimistic. Much of the discussion earlier dealt with new forms of racism and xenophobia, and our failure to formulate effective responses. There is more at issue here, however. In France, for instance, the new racism and xenophobia should not be viewed as consequences of social problems that we cannot confront, for instance, as the effects of objective problems raised by the immigrant population. Rather, they are the effects of a void, of a previous collapse—the collapse of emancipatory politics as a politics of the other. Twenty years ago, we were "all German Jews"; that is to say, we were in the heterological logic of "wrong" names, in the political culture of conflict. Now we have only "right" names. We are Europeans and xenophobes. It is the demotion of the political form, of the political polymorphism of the other, that creates a new kind of *other*, one that is infrapolitical. Objectively, we have no more immigrant people than we had twenty years ago. Subjectively, we have many more. The difference is this: twenty years ago the "immigrant" had an *other* name; they were workers or proletarians. In the meantime, this name has been lost as a *political* name. They retained their "own" name, and an other that has no *other* name becomes the object of fear and rejection.

The "new" racism is the hatred of the other that comes forth when the political procedures of social polemics collapse. The political culture of conflict may have had disappointing outlets. But it was also a way of coming to terms with something that lies before and beneath politics: the question of the other as a figure of identification for the object of fear. Earlier Cornel West told us that identity is about desire and death. I would say that identity is first about fear: the fear of the other, the fear of nothing, which finds on the body of the other its object. And the polemical culture of emancipation, the heterological enactment of the other, was also a way of civilizing that fear. The new outcomes of racism and xenophobia thus reveal the very collapse of politics, the reversion of the political handling of a wrong to a primal hate. If my analysis is correct, the question is not only "How are we to face a political problem?" but "How are we to reinvent politics?"

DEBATE

Andreas Huyssen

The Inevitability of Nation: Germany after Unification

Having come back recently from a one-year stay in Berlin, I am afraid that I will discuss a topic that is very narrowly circumscribed. I will discuss Germany and the problem of nation as one of those identities that has not yet been discussed extensively in this symposium, and that I think has to be addressed.

The German 1980s could be described as a decade obsessed with memory. Wedged between the Berlin Prussian exhibition of 1981 and the recent burial rites for Frederick the Great at Sans Souci, there has been a trail of anniversaries of the key moments in twentieth-century German history, replete with public debate, television documentaries and media commentaries. Most of these fifty-year anniversaries were of a deeply troubling nature, and all of them had to do with the dark side of the German nation: 1983—the fiftieth anniversary of Hitler's rise to power and the book burnings; 1985—defeat of Nazi Germany; 1988—*Kristallnacht*; 1989—the outbreak of Hitler's war; 1991—*Unternehmen Barbarossa*, the German invasion of the Soviet Union. More than any of the earlier postwar decades, the 1980s seemed stuck in the past, and by no means only in Germany: the museum debate, the multiple oral and local history projects, the unprecedented boom in museum architecture have led some observers to claim that musealization was the signature of the decade. Even the attempts to overcome this past by "normalizing" it, or by relying, in Helmut Kohl's words, on the "*Gnade der späten Geburt*" (grace of late birth), were not able to escape the gravity and pull of this past, which continues to circumscribe German nationhood today.

A second point can be made about the 1980s. The more distant the cataclysmic events of twentieth-century German history, the more intense the debate about their adequate representation and their function for German identity today, the identity of the *Nachgeborenen*. Just as, after the mid-1950s, Goodrich and Hackett's dramatization of the diaries of Anne Frank initiated a whole series of dramatic treatments of the Holocaust—from Lenz's *Zeit der Schuldlosen* and Frisch's *Andorra*, via Hochhuth's *Deputy*, to Peter Weiss's *Investigation*—it was again an American product that triggered this latest phase of the negotiation of the present's relationship to the past: the television series *Holocaust*, which found its most significant German response in Edgar Reitz's celebrated *Heimat*. But while the Anne Frank play, in a totally conventional dramaturgy, brought the facts of the Holocaust into public consciousness and was received in that light, the debate over *Holocaust* focused primarily not on historical events, but on how they could be represented.

Questions of representation indeed took the foreground in the 1980s, not only in cultural products and postmodern theory, but in political events as well: think of the staging of Reagan and Kohl at the Bitburg cemetery and the Bergen-Belsen concentration camp, or of the public uproar over the missing quotation marks in Philip Jenninger's controversial speech, in which the politician commemorated the *Kristallnacht* pogrom by adopting, rhetorically, the subject position of an assumed average German of 1938. Here, as elsewhere, the fault lines between present consciousness and past events became ever more a political issue in their own right. How is this past to be represented if the vast majority of the population knows the period of National Socialism from representations only? To what extent can the media even foster the often ritualistically demanded working-through of this past if all we get—as some would argue—is the medium as the message, or, worse, simulation? And what bearing does this observation have on that much-discussed issue of German national identity, which, as Charles Maier pointed out in his book on the German historians' debate, is not reducible to history, or even less, I would add, to its representations?

Andreas
Huyssen

But then the East German crisis of 1989 radically switched the temporal mode of the 1980s from representation to event, and from past to present: from a past that remains visibly inscribed in German nationhood to a present greeted by many as the rebirth of history, and celebrated by conservatives as the hidden *telos* of the whole postwar period. But this rebirth of history out of the ruins of state socialism brought to life another specter from the past that has haunted German postwar intellectuals ever since 1945: the specter of nation. Even the fact that the wall fell on November 9 seemed to suck the present itself ever deeper into the orbit of historical remembrance: 1938, 1923, 1918. And events since the fall of the wall and the demise of one of the most extensive spying and denunciation apparatuses the world has ever known have led to another German conundrum: a second kind of *Vergangenheitsbewältigung* (coming to terms with the past), different from the first, to be sure, and yet serious enough in its implications for the future shape of the unified Germany.

Thus it would be quite deceptive to suggest a dichotomy here between past and present, between a mode of passive remembrance and musealization on the one hand, and one of renewed historical action on the other. Just as the past never relinquished its hold over even the most present of present events, the various anniversaries of the 1980s were never just occasions for disinterested recollection and meditation. They were—all of them—deeply implicated in what one might call the reorganization of cultural and intellectual capital in Germany from the years of the West German *Wende* in the early 1980s and the early stages of the German postmodernism debate, via Bitburg and the *Historikerstreit* (the historian's debate), to the Jenninger affair, and, most recently, the reunification debate, the Christa Wolf debate, and the Gulf War debate. As I have argued elsewhere, these most recent public debates on domestic politics (unification), culture (Christa Wolf), and international politics (the Gulf War) seem to mark a significant breakdown of a long-standing Left and Left-liberal consensus among leading German intellectuals.[1] And the question of nation, I would suggest, is the common, if sometimes hidden, denominator driving the dissolution of this consensus.

Already by the mid-1980s, historians such as Karl-Ernst Jeismann and Wolfgang Mommsen observed a shift in German historiography from writing history with emancipatory intent (especially the critical social history since the 1960s) to the writing of history with the purpose of creating identity. Clearly there is a broader cultural linkage here, though perhaps not yet much explored, between shifting modes of historiography and the literature of the new subjectivity of the 1970s: the focus on experience and memory, the everyday, the *Lebenswelt*. The desire to shore up German identity also energized the neoconservative view that cultural musealization—the enacting of nation through the performance of national culture in the museum—could function as compensation for the ravages of modernization. This at first imperceptible and then quickening shift from a salutary emancipation from traditional conservative notions of German history to a reinscription of questions of identity was, of course, always deeply contested and double-edged. On the one hand, the focus on subjective experience, on the local or regional aspects of historical *Lebenswelten*, was still energized by the democratizing impetus of the late 1960s, a counterposition, as it were, to the revolutionary abstractions of Left sectarianism. On the other hand, it also fed the discourse of normalization as it emerged in the historians' debate, and in the ever more frequently heard claim that Germany has to lay its past to rest in order to become again a "normal" nation. The renewed discourse of national identity on the Right is, I suspect, also much closer to the 1980s' celebration of regionalism than the regionalists would like to admit. Thus Reitz's sixteen-hour television serial *Heimat*, a key text for the reemergent regionalism debate, contains all of the narrative structures of exclusion and inclusion—country versus city; *Weggeher* (emigrants) versus *Dableiber* (those who stay "home")—that typically shaped nationalist discourse; and Reitz himself described his work as a German response to the American *Holocaust* series, which allegedly deprived the Germans of their history. If, as Slavoj Žižek has shown in a recent article,[2] nationalism is based on the conviction that some Other allegedly steals from us that which we never possessed in the first place, then the project of *Heimat* (at least the way it was framed by Reitz), rather than being innocently regionalist, was nationalist to the core.

I will suggest that this whole cultural trajectory of the 1980s, with all its ambiguities and conflicts between leftist and conservative intellectuals over questions of nation and identity, can now be described as "culminating" in the unification of October 3, 1990. Against postmodernist critiques of a notion of historical linearity, and against the leftist taboo on German nationhood, the logic of history and what one might call the cunning of nationhood seem to have asserted themselves yet another time.

Andreas Huyssen

One does not, of course, have to cast this observation in a Hegelian framework, nor would I want to suggest that nation is somehow manifest destiny. But the leftist taboo on nationhood, the antinationalist consensus so central to the self-understanding of the Federal Republic of Germany since the 1960s, had already been fractured before unification, and has become obsolete since. To say this is not to embrace conservative celebrations of reunification as the most natural thing in the world. One may just as well emphasize the haphazardness of a chaotic and multilayered process where only the retrospective glance can construct order, and then only at the price of complexity. But there is no doubt in my mind that historians of the 1980s, far from buying into facile notions of merely specular musealization, *posthistoire*, or history as simulacrum, will be able to show how the totally unexpected event of national unification was subterraneanly structured and steered by the various public discourses of memory and identity that had been so prominent in the 1980s. After all, the parts that were now unified had been torn asunder as a result of precisely those events whose anniversaries contributed to the debates about identity now. Just as the national present is never unto itself on the shifting grounds of the time-space of nation, as Homi Bhabha put it recently, neither is the past—least so in a nation like Germany, whose modern history is characterized by rupture rather than continuity, instability of representation rather than security of self-understanding.

But now the twist in the argument: If indeed one can establish a link between the reemergence of a multilayered discourse of national identity in the West German 1980s and national unification, then this is precisely the point where the logic of history breaks down. October 3 is not fulfillment, but rather the sharpening of the question, the opening up of new fissures and fault lines in the problematic of nation. Once again there is a German nation-state, but the question of national identity remains as elusive as before. It is made even more problematic by the doubling of *Vergangenheitsbewältigung*, and by the East/West split that has now been displaced from outside, as it were, to inside, from an international East/West confrontation that kept the question of German nation diffused and neutralized, to a domestic conflict in which achieved national unity is fissured both by the past forty years of separation *and* by the process of unification itself. If the question of national identity before 1989 seemed to be driven in the Federal Republic by a feeling of lack, of insufficiency regarding the always-provisional nature of the Federal Republic, it was frozen in the German Democratic Republic in the simulacrum of a socialist nation. But there now seem to be emerging, as a result of unification, two national identities, an FRG and a GDR identity, within what is supposed to be *one* nation. Unification on the level of state and currency, as most observers agree, is indeed not accompanied by unification on the level of discourse, culture, experience and everyday life, and will not be for years to come. The consequences are considerable, both for the Habermasian concept of a constitutional patriotism, and for Günter Grass's privileging of *Kulturnation* (nationality as a function of cultural identity) as against the nation-state. If the antinationalist consensus of the Left—one of the few things East and West German intellectuals shared—has been overtaken by the raw fact of unification, then the concept of *Kulturnation*, which Grass, with surprising oblivion to its history, uses as the only permissible substitute for a more political concept of nation, has revealed its inherent weakness and abstractness. For the very real cultural differences between the GDR and the FRG are now clashing directly, rather than being kept apart by that safely dividing wall. And what help, one might ask, is the noble political minimalism of a constitutional patriotism in a situation in which all of the presumably obsolete libidinal investments in nationhood are thrown up again in our faces, as a result of the wrenching pressures of unification?

There is a perverse paradox here. When Germany was divided, there was no national German question, and (at least in the West) the notion that the unified nation had merely been an episode in the long wave of German history had been thoroughly internalized and accepted, except perhaps on the right-wing fringes. The dimly felt need for a national identity, to the extent that it reemerged during the 1980s, operated more on a subjective and regional, perhaps even narcissistic, level than on the level of hard politics. Even the politically motivated proposal put forth in the mid-1980s for two German history museums in Bonn and Berlin seemed a feeble substitute for something that was not to be: a unified German nation. Now that Germany is united again, the German question, even if not (yet?) a question of borders, is back with a vengeance. And while Willy Brandt, counting on a broad consensus, could claim, not too long ago and with admirable motives, that the German question was no longer open, he can now claim, after the events of 1989, with perhaps equal persuasiveness for many, "*daß zusam-*

Andreas
Huyssen

menwächst, was zusammengehört" (that which belongs together is now growing together).

But things are not quite that simple. The question of German nationhood looms as large as it ever did, causing apprehensions abroad and over-
reactions among those German intellectuals who are disturbed by the loss of
what for years seemed to be the stable Left-liberal consensus that there
would now always be two German states, and thus that the "national" was
at an end. Even Bonn often seemed uncomfortable with its own policy of
breakneck national unification, which, in public pronouncements by the
Chancellor and Foreign Minister, was rhetorically retracted by the ritualis-
tic, if no doubt genuine, incantations of good Europeanism. Nobody in
Germany, it seems, knows exactly how to handle the question of nation, and
one may still find that preferable to a potentially dangerous resurgence of
an older type of nationalism, such as we can observe in Yugoslavia or in
parts of the crumbling Soviet empire.

Having grown up in West Germany in the 1950s, and having become a
good antinationalist in the 1960s, I myself have deep apprehensions about
German nationhood in particular, and about nationalism in general. At the
same time, it seems clear that the continuing adherence to an antinationalist Left conformism is an inadequate political response to current realities.
It is out of step with the facts, and has become increasingly abstract. Of
course, the solution cannot be simply to affirm various conservative positions on German nationality and their mutations into a good Europeanism.
Nor would it be adequate to suggest, with paranoid leftist self-righteous-
ness, that the German wolf has swallowed European chalk (the dire warn-
ings of a Fourth Reich). The attempt must be made to get out of the
deadening dichotomies that structure the German discourse on nationhood,
dichotomies in which even someone like Habermas remains caught in his
attempt to define a postconventional identity.

What strikes the outside observer most is that the German debate is
quite insular, almost exclusively oriented toward the past, and mired in the
conviction that nationhood can only be defined in conservative, if not reactionary, terms. Recent attempts to challenge the traditional and long-standing Left bias against nationhood, as they have been articulated in Britain,
France and the United States, have not left much of a mark on the discourse
of German intellectuals. The German Left remains tied to conservative definitions of nationality, in that it simply rejects what the Right wants to cel-

ebrate. Both adversaries and proponents of German nationhood indeed see the nation-state as the ultimate *telos* of nation, and identical with it. Both sides are caught in a definition of nation that is constructed out of nineteenth-century fictions of autonomy. The provincialism of the German debate is not only characteristic of official Bonn discourse, but it also affects the anti- or postnational discourse on the Left, from Peter Glotz to Jürgen Habermas and Günter Grass, as well as Karl Heinz Bohrer's presumedly antiprovincialist but ultimately merely nostalgic call for national elites. The argument can even be driven further: the antinationalist conformism of the Left (and this has become very clear during and after the 1989 events) is itself quite nationalist in an inverted way; West Germany's very vital protest culture lived off the conviction, as Klaus Hartung recently put it in a column in *Die Zeit*, "that we solved all world conflicts in our heads, apportioned guilt (mostly to the U.S.) and identified ourselves without question as victims."[3] Just as the regionalism of the late 1970s and eighties can be seen as a problematic substitute for nationalism, the Left *Sonderweg*, too, may have more in common with conservative German exceptionalism than it would care to admit.

Again, how does one get out of this dilemma of an unconditional for-or-against, in which frozen positions are performed as mere rituals? There certainly are no easy solutions. But what may be desirable as a first modest step might be a broad public debate about an alternative notion of nation, one that emphasizes negotiated heterogeneity rather than homogeneity imposed from above, federalism rather than centralism, regionalism as indeed an important layer of national identity rather than its alleged opposite.

Of course, this is not to suggest that antiforeigner pogroms, such as the one at Hoyerswerda (September 1991) and many other sites in all parts of Germany, can be prevented simply by opening up a public debate on German nationhood on the Left. And yet I do think that such a debate is more pressing in the current conjuncture than a debate about the Constitution, for which some Habermasians were still calling even after events had established that the Basic Law (*Grundgesetz*) of the Federal Republic would serve as a constitution for the united Germany. The left has to ask itself whether its refusal to engage constructively in the discourse of nation might not actually be a factor in the resurgence of militant nationalism and xenophobia, both in the former GDR and in the former FRG. Like the Weimar Left, castigated by Ernst Bloch in *Erbschaft dieser Zeit,* the Left today, though in

Andreas Huyssen

vastly different circumstances, may again be underestimating the libidinal and imaginary powers of national discourse. The decision to opt for a European identity in order to avoid the Germanness in question, so typical of postwar intellectuals, was and remains a delusion. Europe was always the privileged space in which modern nationhood took shape, and it still is in many Western writings that see, for instance, postcolonial nationalism as merely borrowed from Europe. Rather than representing an alternative to nation, Europe was always its very condition of possibility, just as it enabled empire and colonialism. The mechanisms separating the non-European as barbarian, primitive, uncivilized were ultimately not that different from the ways in which European nations perceived each other. The traditional national border conflicts that led to inner-European wars have now, it seems, simply been displaced to the outside: Europe, for all its divergent national identities, cultures and languages, as one metanation *vis-à-vis* the migrations from other continents. Fortress Europe as the contemporary reinscription of the nineteenth-century fictions of national autonomy: this is the danger, and perhaps already a reality. The leaflets put out by the People's Union in the October 1991 Bremen elections appealed to German nationalism by warning that the continuing influx of foreigners would lead to "the destruction of European culture" and that "integrationists are hateful racists who want to destroy all cultures by mixing."

Indeed, the European and national aspects of German xenophobia cannot be separated. But there are important specifics to the German case that make its xenophobia different from outbreaks of xenophobia in France, Italy or England. It seems to me that it would be too simple to claim that what we are seeing is a revival of traditional German chauvinism and racism, and that the lack of nationalist fervor during unification was simply a sham. Such an explanation would remain too tied to unhistorical notions of national character. German nationalism was not simply kept under a lid by Communism, by the division of the country, and by its limited sovereignty from 1945 until 1990. The lid theory might explain the outbreak of racist and chauvinist violence in the GDR, but it does not explain the parallel events in the Federal Republic, where notions of multiculturalism had taken deeper roots than would have even been possible in the GDR, a country that was hermetically sealed from much of the rest of the world. My hypothesis is that the astonishing levels of real and verbal violence directed against foreigners in all of Germany these days results from a complex displacement of an inner-German problematic. It is not just the scapegoating of foreigners by those Germans who now experience themselves as second-class citizens, as colonized by the victorious West—the scapegoating that expresses the unquenchable human thirst for always finding someone still lower down than oneself. It is rather the displacement onto the "non-Germans" of forty years of an inner-German hostility, where another kind of foreign body was identified as the source of most problems: the other Germany. The whole *Ossi/Wessi* (Easty/Westy) split, symptomatically expressed in this infantilized language, is not so much a function of objectively separate developments since the late 1940s, nor is it only the result of the current problems with unification. On the psychosocial level, I see it rather as a function of the fact that the other Germany was always inscribed as the other into one's own sense of being either a West or an East German. If one assumes, as I do, that the desire for some form of national identity as a form of belonging and anchoring oneself must not necessarily be pathological, then a postwar German's inability or difficulty to belong could always be blamed on the other German: the other German as thief of one's own potential identity. And that bad, other German could be found either on the respective other side of the wall or, through a complex web of political identifications, on one's own side. In such ways, the history of East Germany is inescapably intertwined with that of West Germany. It is not only their history, it is ours as well, and we begin to understand that only now. My desperately hopeful hypothesis would be that the discursive space of nation might be a space in which such problems of inner-German hostility and resentment could be debated and worked through, the space in which, paradoxically, if my hypothesis were right, antiforeigner chauvinism could eventually be diffused. For that to happen, however, nation would have to be understood as an ongoing process of negotiating identity and heterogeneity, both *vis-à-vis* the East/West split and *vis-à-vis* the foreigners living in Germany. As long as German intellectuals do not wake up to the fact that the laws governing German citizenship, with their reliance on blood lineage rather than place of birth and length of residence, betray a massive deficit of westernization, the chances for such a discourse to emerge are slim. But who else if not the intellectual Left could take up the question of conventional identity in ways that would make unification workable without forcing foreign residents in Germany to pay the price?

Andreas
82   *Huyssen*

NOTES

This piece started as an attempt to make Homi Bhabha's work in *Nation and Narration*, and Slavoj Žižek's reflections on nationalism, which appeared in *New Left Review* in 1990, bear on the German situation. It gained its political urgency with the fall 1991 pogroms directed against foreigners that were widely reported in the U.S. press.

1. Andreas Huyssen, "After the Wall: The Failure of German Intellectuals," *New German Critique* 52 (Winter 1991), pp. 109–143.
2. Slavoj Žižek, "Republics of Gilead," *New Left Review* 183 (September/October 1990), pp. 50–62.
3. Klaus Hartung, *Die Zeit* (August 16, 1991).

DEBATE

Discussion

AUDIENCE: This is addressed to Andreas Huyssen. Until the very last comments you made, it seemed that your recuperation of nationhood was not about political, electoral expediency, but about trying to be in step with what is happening in terms of national cultural politics in a unified Germany. My concern is that German national culture in the twentieth century is not just any European national culture—just as American national culture understood, racially speaking, in its dominant hegemonic sense, is not just any European-derived national culture. Those of us who belong to peoples that have been trampled over by either one or the other, or both, thus have serious doubts about the option you're posing. I understand that the Left in Germany has historically had serious problems in terms of establishing a social base, but I don't quite see how what you're posing is a real alternative, particularly given the dangers involved.

ANDREAS HUYSSEN: I share those kinds of concerns. At the same time—and I'm not very far at this point in my thinking about the question of nationhood and national identity in Germany—I have tried to critique a certain taboo on the Left and to show the necessity of opening up a debate on the question. No more, no less. I think this is as far as

I would go. I could argue that there should be and that there will be a different kind of German national identity from the one that has been dominant in the past, and I emphasized at the beginning of the paper that if there were a productive discussion of national identity in Germany, then the recent history of Germany (that's why I started by focusing on the various anniversaries) will have to remain strongly inscribed within it. Where such a discussion would lead in terms of electoral politics, I have no way to predict; one may very well argue that it might not lead very far. The issue, however, has to be addressed. Evasion will only strengthen conservative definitions of nation.

I also agree with you when you say that German national culture is not like any other; but one might of course ask whether there is any one that is like any other? I don't mean that as a facile response. It just seems to me that the question of national identity has been put on the table in a new way by the raw facts of the political events since 1989; that it has to be addressed publicly by the Left; and that the discursive terrain should not be left only to the conservatives and, potentially, to a new far Right.

HOMI BHABHA: I just wonder a bit about your discussion of the negotiating of this sign of nationhood now: the process of opening up a discursive terrain. The rest of your talk was so focused on the double nature of nation and its internal boundary; but at the end, in the current Germany you describe, how do you provide a space, even within the Left, from which those different discourses and their genealogies could be represented in a dialogue where negotiating power would be shared? That is the major problem, I think. The Turks, the East Germans—what would the representative bodies be?

ANDREAS HUYSSEN: I admit my paper is very speculative on that level and somewhat distant from what is happening at this point in Germany. But I think that what would have to happen, concretely, is that there would have to be a discussion of a problem that the Left has simply avoided. There would have to be a discussion of what actually constitutes German citizenship. German citizenship is still decided by blood lineage; it's based on a pre-World War I law. Now, if citizenship were to be determined automatically by place of birth—which would solve a major problem for many of the second- and third-generation Turks, for instance, who live in Germany and have lived in Germany for a long time—then the Habermasian claim, the attempt to hook Germany up with Western liberal culture, would perhaps be more persuasive. But instead of discussing this, the Left has focused on political asylum, where Germany, because of its history of forced exile, has very liberal legislation. "Citizenship" would thus be a concrete space for discussion that should be opened up. However, I'm very pessimistic about the current political situation, where these spaces do not seem to be expanding but actually seem to be shrinking.

AUDIENCE: My question is directed toward the first two speakers. You both used a spatial metaphor—one of interval and the other of a space of indeterminacy, a gap, literally, between two words. And I wanted to know how such indeterminacy could be a useful agent in discussing identity.

HOMI BHABHA: In fact the main frame of what I was talking about was atemporality, belatedness, a way of questioning acts of naming carried out according to Enlightenment and modernist notions of progress. I think it's important to think about temporality, instead, as the possibility of reconstructing other kinds of histories, ones that do not require—as I said in my comments—a kind of sovereignty of desire. And so really, as far as I'm concerned, I wish to take to task the growing spatialization operating in postmodern critical metaphors, metaphors which lead to saying unthinkingly, "New York is a new Calcutta. You know, we are now also living in the Third World, we're all migrants, we're all diasporates." My argument in the longer study of which this is a part ("Race, Time, and Countermodernity") operates against that kind of thing. So I think that my specific point is really about how *belatedness* functions to critique certain priorities and myths about culture and modernization.

JACQUES RANCIÈRE: In answer to your question, I would say that it is really just the opposite: the social construction of an identity must be conceived in terms of a logic of the subject, that is, in terms of the logic of an actor who cannot be identified with any sociological category or constituent group, who always bears the name of the other and incorporates an impossible identification. This is not just an abstract idea. For me, it is grounded in my research on French workers' history. There it became obvious that one couldn't simply apply social types and categories to this movement, because, in so doing, one dismissed the inner division that was at the very heart of the assumption of the label *worker* or *proletarian*, both in discourse and in practice. These subjects both assumed and did not assume the label *worker.* Against those who treated them as "workers"—"their" workers—they took on this label. So that they did not identify the name *worker* or *proletarian* with a definite technical and social activity, but with a certain way of being at one and the same time inside and outside the symbolic order of the distribution of social identities. What I wanted to question by means of this example is the deceptive appearance of self-evidence of a "social" movement as the expression of a "social" group. A social movement is not the movement of a sociological group. It is a movement of subjects, of people who try to find or apprehend an identity as fighters through the very dismissal of their sociological identity, the identity given to them by a social order.

AUDIENCE: When Andreas spoke of the libidinal investment in nationhood, he seemed to suggest that we should shy away from those kinds of identifications. But that raises a problem (as I think Cornel said) of how the politics of desire can operate in a world when libidinal politics tends to fragment identities, draw upon racist identifications, years of miscegenation. If we look at the everyday world and the way desire is constructed, it's based on the politics of domination, the politics of oppression. So at the same time as we raise this question, for example, in Germany, how can we think about drawing upon libidinal investment in nationhood in a constructive way? Is there a way to imagine a nonracist, nonrepressive libidinal investment?

ANDREAS HUYSSEN: That is the question I'm posing with the paper: Do we have to identify the politics of desire with racism and oppression? I have not, as I suggested, found an answer for this. But I'm convinced that the question has to be asked in order to create alternatives. If it does not get asked, then that kind of political terrain is left to those who are occupying it so successfully now.

ERNESTO LACLAU: What keeps some room for hope in the question of German nationalism is perhaps that today the ideological changes are taking place in an overdetermined context. That is to say that German national identity is being asserted in a context very different from that of the emerging European nationalism of the nineteenth century. The fact that present-day national identities are being asserted in the context of the construction of the European Community gives progressive forces room to maneuver. I agree with you that negating the reality of a strong German identity is nonsensical. Someone like Habermas was, I think, much happier in the Federal Republic when he was part of a "westernized," European identity. Today he must live with the brute fact of German nationalism, and he is clearly uncomfortable. But I think that the assertion of a German identity can take place in a variety of ways, not all of them producing reactionary effects. The overdetermination of the contexts within which this identity is asserted is what counts, and, as I said earlier, the context of the European Community puts some important limits on the development of a purely xenophobic politics.

ANDREAS HUYSSEN: Ernesto's comment is very pertinent here. European unification contains and alters the ways in which national identities in Europe will be constructed in the future. The relationship between nation and nation-state is already no longer what it used to be. But let us not fool ourselves. Even if the sovereign nation-state disappears, it will only have been displaced by a larger unit—"Europe"—that may very well act like a traditional nation-state toward other parts of the world. And internally, I don't think for one minute that older national identities will simply disappear with European unification. The widely divergent reactions to the Gulf War in England, Germany, France, even Czechoslovakia showed how national histories still determine the thoughts and actions in different parts of Europe.

AUDIENCE: My question is related to postcolonialism and the origins of self, origins of the other—things that Homi Bhabha addressed. In the process of enacting equality, do you have the right, the social right, to imagine, vocalize and author a sense of "I"—whether collectively or individually—that would exist in isolation from your history of racism and colonialization? Because, it seems to me, this issue of postcolonialism doesn't deal with the whole problem of a homogeneous, postcolonial world. I just wanted to know if you could elaborate.

HOMI BHABHA: It would be precisely the response of a once-colonizing world now to see a homogenized postcolonial world. That is why it's very important to mark various different sites of the "I"'s enunciation, as I attempted to do today. You can turn to Derek Walcott or Toni Morrison or Sonia Sanchez, and see how the question of race and history and identification was being negotiated at each one of those sites. So the very idea of a homogeneous, postcolonial response would feed yet again into a kind of polarization. If we think of the Gulf War, we could address the example of what appeared from a certain distance to be a coordinated, homogeneous response on the part of the—I'll use the word—Third World. There was opposition to the Gulf War from India, from Pakistan and from most African countries. Yet, as opposed to this, what was interesting in each one of those responses was the way in which the Gulf War was being used by groups of peace protesters in each country to oppose their own dominant and, in many cases, undemocratic regimes. So the Gulf issue was being used in very differently negotiated ways. Further, I think one of the most interesting nonhomogenizing effects in many Third World countries was the surfacing of a desire actually to identify with loss. The identification was not with Saddam Hussein, with his kind of political regime, but with other sorts of things: with death, with despair, with desires to modernize which would in some senses be to destroy. So there are a number of ways in which that opposition to US policy might be seen to be invariant, but it is not. That's the really important issue. It's too easy to homogenize that response.

DEBATE

Ernesto Laclau

Universalism, Particularism and the Question of Identity

There is today a lot of talk about social, ethnic, national and political identities. The "death of the subject," which was proudly proclaimed *urbi et orbi*
not so long ago, has been succeeded by a new and widespread interest in the
multiple identities that are emerging and proliferating in our contemporary
world. These two movements are not, however, in such a complete and dramatic contrast as we would be tempted to believe at first sight. Perhaps the
death of *the* Subject (with a capital "S") has been the main precondition of
this renewed interest in the question of subjectivity. It is perhaps the very
impossibility of referring any longer the concrete and finite expressions of a
multifarious subjectivity to a transcendental center that makes it possible
to concentrate our attention on the multiplicity itself. The founding gestures of the 1960s are still with us, making possible the political and theoretical explorations in which we are today engaged.

If there was, however, this temporal gap between what had become theoretically thinkable and what was actually achieved, it is because a second
and more subtle temptation haunted the intellectual imaginary of the Left
for a while: that of replacing the transcendental subject by its symmetrical
other, that of reinscribing the multifarious forms of undomesticated subjectivities in an objective totality. From there derived a concept which had a

great deal of currency in our immediate prehistory: that of "subject positions." But this was not, of course, a real transcending of the problematic of a transcendental subjectivity (something which haunts us as an absence is, indeed, very much present). "History is a process without a subject." Perhaps. But how do we know it? Is not the very possibility of such an assertion already requiring what one was trying to avoid? If History as a totality is a possible object of experience and discourse, who could be the subject of such an experience but the subject of an absolute knowledge? Now, if we try to avoid this pitfall, and negate the terrain that would make that assertion a meaningful one, what becomes problematic is the very notion of "subject position."

What could such a position be but a special location within a totality, and what could this totality be but the object of experience of an absolute subject? At the very moment in which the terrain of absolute subjectivity collapses, it collapses also *the very possibility* of an absolute object. There is no real alternative between Spinoza and Hegel. But this locates us in a very different terrain: one in which the very possibility of the subject/object distinction is the simple result of the impossibility of constituting either of its two terms. I am a subject precisely *because* I cannot be an absolute consciousness, because something constitutively alien confronts me; and there can be no pure object as a result of this opaqueness/alienation which shows the traces of the subject in the object. Thus, once objectivism disappeared as an "epistemological obstacle," it became possible to develop the full implications of the "death of the subject." At that point, the latter showed the secret poison that inhabited it, the possibility of its second death: "the death of the death of the subject"; the reemergence of the subject as a result of its own death; the proliferation of concrete finitudes whose limitations are the source of their strength; the realization that there can be "subjects" because the gap that "the Subject" was supposed to bridge is actually unbridgeable.

This is not only abstract speculation; it is instead an intellectual way open by the very terrain in which History has thrown us: the multiplication of new—and not so new—identities as a result of the collapse of the places from which the universal subjects spoke—explosion of ethnic and national identities in Eastern Europe and in the territories of the former USSR, struggles of immigrant groups in Western Europe, new forms of multicultural protest and self-assertion in the USA, to which we have to add the gamut of forms of contestation associated with the new social movements. Now, the question arises: Is this proliferation thinkable just *as* proliferation—that is, simply in terms of its multiplicity? To put the problem in its simplest terms: Is particularism thinkable just *as* particularism, only out of the differential dimension that it asserts? Are the relations between universalism and particularism simple relations of mutual exclusion? Or, if we address the matter from the opposite angle: does the alternative between an essentialist objectivism and a transcendental subjectivism exhaust the range of language games that it is possible to play with the "universal"?

These are the main questions that I am going to address. I will not pretend that the *place* of questioning does not affect the nature of the questions, and that the latter do not predetermine the kind of answer to be expected. Not all roads lead to Rome. But by confessing the tendentious nature of my intervention, I am giving the reader the only freedom that is in my power to grant: that of stepping outside of my discourse and rejecting its validity in terms which are entirely incommensurable with it. So, in offering you some surfaces of inscription for the formulation of *questions* rather than answers, I am engaging in a power struggle for which there is a name: hegemony.

Let us start by considering the historical forms in which the relationship between universality and particularity has been thought. A first approach asserts: (a) that there is an uncontaminated dividing line between the universal and the particular; and (b) that the pole of the universal is entirely graspable by reason. In that case there is no possible mediation between universality and particularity: the particular can only *corrupt* the universal. We are in the terrain of classical ancient philosophy. Either the particular realizes in itself the universal—that is, it eliminates itself as particular and transforms itself in a transparent medium through which universality operates; or it negates the universal by asserting its particularism (but as the latter is purely irrational, it has no entity of its own and can only exist as corruption of being). The obvious question concerns the frontier dividing universality and particularity: is it universal or particular? If the latter, universality can only be a particularity which defines itself in terms of a limitless exclusion; if the former, the particular itself becomes part of the universal, then the dividing line is again blurred. But the very possibility of formulating this last question would require that the *form* of universality as such, then the actual *contents* to which it is associated, are subjected to a clear differentiation. The thought of this difference, however, is not available to ancient philosophy.

The second possibility of thinking of the relation between universality and particularity is related to Christianity. The point of view of the totality exists, but it is God's, not ours, so that it is not accessible to human reason. *Credo quia absurdum*. Thus, the universal is mere event in an eschatological succession, only accessible to us through revelation. This involves an entirely different conception of the relationship between particularity and universality. The dividing line cannot be, as in ancient thought, that between rationality and irrationality, between a deep and a superficial layer *within the thing*, but that between two series of events: those of a finite and contingent succession, on the one hand, and those of the eschatological series, on the other. Because the designs of God are inscrutable, the deep layer cannot be a timeless world of rational forms, but a temporal succession of essential events which are opaque to human reason; and because each of these universal moments has to realise itself in a finite reality which has no common measure with them, the relation between the two orders has to be also an opaque and incomprehensible one. This type of relation was called *incarnation*, its distinctive feature being that between the universal and the body incarnating it there is no rational connection whatsoever. God is the only and absolute mediator. A subtle logic destined to have a profound influence on our intellectual tradition was starting in this way: that of the *privileged agent of History*, the agent whose particular body was the expression of a universality transcending it. The modern idea of a "universal class" and the various forms of Eurocentrism are nothing but the distant historical effects of the logic of incarnation.

Not entirely so, however, because modernity at its highest point was, to a large extent, the attempt to interrupt the logic of incarnation. God, as the absolute source of everything existing, was replaced in its function of universal guarantor by Reason, but a *rational* ground and source has a logic of its own, which is very different from that of a divine intervention—the main difference being that the effects of a rational grounding have to be fully transparent to human reason. Now, this requirement is entirely incompatible with the logic of incarnation; if everything has to be transparent to reason, the connection between the universal and the body incarnating it has also to be so; and in that case the incommensurability between a universal to be incarnated and the incarnating body has to be eliminated. We have to postulate a body which is, in and by itself, the universal.

Ernesto Laclau

The full realization of these implications took several centuries. Descartes postulated a dualism by which the ideal of a full rationality still refused to become a principle of reorganization of the social and political world; but the main currents of the Enlightenment were going to establish a sharp frontier between a past, which was the realm of mistakes and follies of men, and a rational future, which had to be the result of an act of absolute institution. A last stage in the advance of this rationalistic hegemony took place when the gap between the rational and the irrational was closed through the representation of the act of its cancellation as a necessary moment in the self-development of reason: this was the task of Hegel and Marx, who asserted the total transparency, in absolute knowledge, of the real to reason. The body of the proletariat is no longer a particular body in which a universality external to it has to be incarnated: it is instead a body in which the distinction between particularity and universality is cancelled, and as a result the need for any incarnation is definitely eradicated.

This was the point, however, in which social reality refused to abandon its resistance to universalistic rationalism. For an unsolved problem still remained. The universal had found its own body, but this was still the body of a certain particularity—European culture of the nineteenth century. So European culture was a particular one, and at the same time the expression—no longer the incarnation—of universal human essence (as the USSR was going to be considered later the *motherland* of socialism). The crucial issue here is that there were no intellectual means of distinguishing between European particularism and the universal functions that it was supposed to incarnate, given that European universalism had precisely constructed its identity through the cancellation of the logic of incarnation and, as a result, of the universalization of its own particularism. So, European imperialist expansion had to be presented in terms of a universal civilizing function, modernization and so forth. The resistances of other cultures were, as a result, presented not as struggles between particular identities and cultures, but as part of an all-embracing and epochal struggle between universality and particularisms—the notion of peoples without history expressing precisely their incapacity to represent the universal.

This argument could be conceived in very explicit racist terms, as in the various forms of social Darwinism, but it could also be given some more "progressive" versions—as in some sectors of the Second International—by asserting that the civilizing mission of Europe would finish with the establishment of a universally freed society of planetary dimensions. Thus the logic of incarnation was reintroduced—Europe having to represent, for a certain period, universal human interests. In the case of Marxism, a similar reintroduction of the logic of incarnation takes place. Between the universal character of the tasks of the working class and the particularity of its concrete demands, an increasing gap opened which had to be filled by the Party as representative of the historical interests of the proletariat. The gap between class itself and class for itself opened the way to a succession of substitutions: the Party replaced the class, the autocrat the Party, and so on. Now, this well-known migration of the universal through the successive bodies incarnating it differed in one crucial point from Christian incarnation. In the latter a supernatural power was responsible both for the advent of the universal event and for the body which had to incarnate the latter. Human beings were on an equal footing *vis-à-vis* a power that transcended all of them. In the case of a secular eschatology, however, as the source of the universal is not external but internal to the world, the universal can only manifest itself through the establishment of an *essential* inequality between the objective positions of the social agents. Some of them are going to be privileged agents of historical change, not as a result of a contingent relation of forces, but because they are incarnations of the universal. The same type of logic operating in Eurocentrism will establish the ontological privilege of the proletariat.

As this ontological privilege is the result of a process which was conceived as entirely rational, it is doubled into an epistemological privilege: the point of view of the proletariat supersedes the opposition subject/object. In a classless society social relations will finally be fully transparent. It is true that, if the increasing simplification of the social structure under capitalism had taken place in the way predicted by Marx, the consequences of this approach would have not necessarily been authoritarian, because the position of the proletariat as bearer of the viewpoint of social totality and the position of the vast majority of the population would have overlapped. But if the process moved—as it did—in the opposite direction, the successive bodies incarnating the viewpoint of the universal class had to have an increasingly restricted social base. The vanguard party as concrete particularity had to claim to have knowledge of the "objective meaning" of any event, and the viewpoint of the other particular social forces had to be dismissed as false consciousness. From this point on, the authoritarian turn was unavoidable.

Ernesto Laclau

This whole story is apparently leading to an inevitable conclusion: the chasm between the universal and the particular is unbridgeable—which is the same as saying that the universal is no more than a particular that at some moment has become dominant, that there is no way of reaching a reconciled society. And, in actual fact, the spectacle of the social and political struggles in the 1990s seems to confront us, as we said before, with a proliferation of particularisms, while the point of view of universality is increasingly put aside as an old-fashioned totalitarian dream. And, however, I will argue that an appeal to pure particularism is no solution to the problems that we are facing in contemporary societies. In the first place, the assertion of pure particularism, independently of any content and of the appeal to a universality transcending it, is a self-defeating enterprise. For if it is the only accepted normative principle, it confronts us with an unsolvable paradox. I can defend the right of sexual, racial and national minorities in the name of particularism; but if particularism is the only valid principle, I have to accept also the rights to self-determination of all kinds of reactionary groups involved in antisocial practices. Even more: as the demands of various groups will necessarily clash with each other, we have to appeal—short of postulating some kind of preestablished harmony—to some more general principles in order to regulate such clashes. In actual fact, there is no particularism which does not make appeal to such principles in the construction of its own identity. These principles can be progressive in our appreciation—such as the right of peoples to self-determination—or reactionary—such as social Darwinism or the right to *Lebensraum*—but they are always there, and for essential reasons.

There is a second and perhaps more important reason why pure particularism is self-defeating. Let us accept, for the sake of the argument, that the above-mentioned preestablished harmony is possible. In that case, the various particularisms would not be in antagonistic relation with each other, but would coexist one with the other in a coherent whole. This hypothesis shows clearly why the argument for pure particularism is ultimately inconsistent. For if each identity is in a differential, nonantagonistic relation to all other identities, then the identity in question is purely differential and relational; so it presupposes not only the presence of all the other identities but also the total ground which constitutes the differences as differences. Even worse: we know very well that the relations between groups are constituted as relations of power—that is, that each group is not only different from the others but constitutes in many cases such difference on the basis of the exclusion and subordination of other groups. Now, if the particularity asserts itself as mere particularity, in a purely differential relation with other particularities, it is sanctioning the status quo in the relation of power between the groups. This is exactly the notion of "separate developments" as formulated in apartheid: only the differential aspect is stressed, while the relations of power on which the latter is based are systematically ignored.

This last example is important because, coming from a discursive universe—South African apartheid—which is quite opposite to that of the new particularisms that we are discussing, and revealing, however, the same ambiguities in the construction of any difference, it opens the way to an understanding of a dimension of the relationship particularism/universalism which has been generally disregarded. The basic point is this: I cannot assert a differential identity without distinguishing it from a context, and, in the process of making the distinction, I am asserting the context at the same time. And the opposite is also true: I cannot destroy a context without destroying at the same time the identity of the particular subject who carries out the destruction. It is a very well known historical fact that an oppositionist force whose identity is constructed within a certain system of power is ambiguous *vis-à-vis* that system, because the latter is what prevents the constitution of the identity and it is, at the same time, its condition of existence. And any victory against the system destabilizes also the identity of the victorious force.

Now, an important corollary of this argument is that, if a fully achieved difference eliminates the antagonistic dimension as constitutive of any identity, the possibility of maintaining this dimension depends on the very failure in the full constitution of a differential identity. It is here that the "universal" enters into the scene. Let us suppose that we are dealing with the constitution of the identity of an ethnic minority, for instance. As we said earlier, if this differential identity is fully achieved, it can only be so within a context—for instance, a nation-state—and the price to be paid for total victory *within that context* is total integration to it. If, on the contrary, total integration *does not* take place, it is because that identity is not fully achieved—there are, for instance, unsatisfied demands concerning access to education, to employment, to consumption goods and so on. But these demands cannot be made in terms of difference, but of some universal principles that the ethnic minority shares with the rest of the community: the

Ernesto Laclau

right of everybody to have access to good schools, or live a decent life, or participate in the public space of citizenship, and so on.

This means that the universal is part of my identity as far as I am penetrated by a constitutive lack, that is, as far as my differential identity has failed in its process of constitution. The universal emerges out of the particular not as some principle underlying and explaining the particular, but as an incomplete horizon suturing a dislocated particular identity. This points a way of conceiving the relation between the universal and the particular which is different from those that we had explored earlier. In the case of the logic of incarnation, the universal and the particular were fully constituted but totally separated identities, whose connection was the result of a divine intervention, impenetrable to human reason. In the case of secularized eschatologies the particular had to be eliminated entirely: the universal class was conceived as the cancellation of all differences. In the case of extreme particularism there is no universal body—but as the ensemble of nonantagonistic particularities purely and simply reconstructs the notion of social totality, the classical notion of the universal is not put into question in the least. (A universal conceived as a homogeneous space differentiated by its internal articulations and a *system* of differences constituting a unified ensemble are exactly the same.) Now we are pointing to a fourth alternative: the universal is the symbol of a missing fullness and the particular exists only in the contradictory movement of asserting at the same time a differential identity and cancelling it through its subsumption in a nondifferential medium.

I will devote the rest of this paper to discussing three important political conclusions that one can derive from this fourth alternative. The first is that the construction of differential identities on the basis of total closure to what is outside them is not a viable or progressive political alternative. It would be a reactionary policy in Western Europe today, for instance, for immigrants from Northern Africa or Jamaica to abstain from all participation in Western European institutions, with the justification that theirs is a different cultural identity and that European institutions are not their concern. In this way all forms of subordination and exclusion would be consolidated with the excuse of maintaining pure identities. The logic of apartheid is not only a discourse of the dominant groups; as we said before, it can also permeate the identities of the oppressed. At its very limit, understood as *mere* difference, the discourse of the oppressor and the discourse of the oppressed cannot be distinguished. The reason for this we have given earlier: if the oppressed is defined by its difference from the oppressor, such a difference is an essential component of the identity of the oppressed. But in that case, the latter cannot assert its identity without asserting that of the oppressor as well.

Il y a bien des dangers à invoquer des différences pures, libérées de l'identique, devenues independantes du négatif. Le plus grand danger est de tomber dans les représentations de la belle-âme: rien que des différences, conciliables et fédérables, loin des luttes sanglantes. La belle-âme dit: nous sommes différentes, main non pas opposés.[1]

The idea of "negative" implicit in the dialectical notion of contradiction is unable to take us beyond this conservative logic of pure difference. A negative which is part of the determination of a positive content is an integral part of the latter. This is what shows the two faces of Hegel's *Logic*: if, on the one hand, the inversion defining the speculative proposition means that the predicate becomes subject, and that a universality transcending all particular determinations "circulates" through the latter, on the other hand, that circulation has a direction dictated by the movement of the particular determinations themselves, and is strictly reduced to it. Dialectical negativity does not question in the least the logic of identity (= the logic of pure difference).

This shows the ambiguity which is inherent in all forms of radical opposition: the opposition, in order to be radical, has to put in a common ground both what it asserts and what it excludes, so that the exclusion becomes a particular form of assertion. But this means that a particularism really committed to change can only do so by rejecting both what denies its own identity and this identity itself. There is no clear-cut solution to the paradox of radically negating a system of power while remaining in secret dependency on it. It is well known how opposition to certain forms of power requires identification with the very places from which the opposition takes place; as the latter are, however, internal to the opposed system, there is a certain conservatism inherent in *all* opposition. The reason why this is unavoidable is that the ambiguity inherent in *all* antagonistic relation is something we can negotiate with but not actually supersede—we can play with both sides of the ambiguity and produce political results by preventing any of them prevailing in an exclusive way, but the ambiguity as such cannot be properly *resolved*. To surpass an ambiguity involves going beyond *both* its poles, but this means that there can be no simple politics of preservation of an identity. If a racial or cultural minority, for instance, has to assert its identity in new social surroundings, it will have to take into account new situations which will inevitably transform that identity. This means, of course, moving away from the idea of negation as radical reversal.[2] The main consequence that follows is that, if the politics of difference means continuity of difference by being always an *other*, the rejection of the other cannot be radical elimination either, but constant renegotiation of the forms of his presence. Aletta J. Norval asked herself recently about identities in a post-apartheid society:

> The question looming on the horizon is this: what are the implications of recognising that the identity of the other is constitutive of the self, in a situation where apartheid itself will have become something of the past? That is, how do we think of social and political identities as post-apartheid identities?

And after asserting that:

> if the other is merely rejected, externalised *in toto* in the movement in which apartheid receives its signified, we would have effected a reversal of the order, remaining in effect in the terrain in which apartheid has organised and ruled,

she points to a different possibility:

> Through a remembrance of apartheid as other, post-apartheid could become the site from which the final closure and suturing of identities is to be prevented. Paradoxically, a post-apartheid society will then only be radically beyond apartheid in so far as apartheid itself is present in it as its other. Instead of being effaced once and for all, "apartheid" itself would have to play the role of the element keeping open the relation to the other, of serving as watchword against any discourse claiming to be able to create a final unity.[3]

This argument can be generalized. Everything hinges on which of the two equally possible movements leading to the supersession of oppression is initiated. None can avoid maintaining the reference to the "other," but they do so in two completely different ways. If we simply *invert* the relation of oppression, the other (the former oppressor) is maintained as what is now oppressed and repressed, but his inversion of the *contents* leaves the form of oppression unchanged. And as the identity of the newly emancipated groups had been constituted through the rejection of the old dominant ones, the latter continue shaping the identity of the former. The operation of inversion takes place entirely within the old *formal* system of power. But this is not the only possible alternative. As we have seen, all political identity is internally split, because no particularity can be constituted except by maintaining an internal reference to universality as that which is missing. But in that case the identity of the oppressor will equally be split: on the one hand, he will represent a particular system of oppression; on the other, he will symbolise the *form* of oppression as such. This is what makes possible the second move suggested in Norval's text: instead of inverting a particular relation of oppression/closure in what it has of concrete particularity, inverting it in what it has of universality: the *form* of oppression and closure as such. The reference to the other is maintained here also, but as the inversion takes place at the level of the universal reference and not of the concrete contents of an oppressive system, the identities of *both* oppressors and oppressed are radically changed. A similar argument was made by Walter Benjamin with reference to Sorel's distinction between political strike and proletarian strike: while the political strike aims at obtaining concrete reforms that change a system of power and thereby constitute a new power, the proletarian strike aims at the destruction of power as such, of the very form of power, and in this sense it does not have any particular objective.[4]

These remarks allow us to throw some light on the divergent courses of action that current struggles in defence of multiculturalism can follow. One possible way is to affirm, purely and simply, the right of the various cultural and ethnic groups to assert their differences and their separate developments. This is the route to self-apartheid, and it is sometimes accompanied by the claim that Western cultural values and institutions are the preserve of white male Europeans or Anglo-Americans and have nothing to do with the identity of other groups living in the same territory. What is advocated in this way is total segregationism, the mere opposition

Ernesto Laclau

of one particularism to another. Now, it is true that the assertion of any particular identity involves, as one of its dimensions, the affirmation of the right to a separate existence. But it is here that the difficult questions start, because the separation—or better, the right to difference—has to be asserted within a global community—that is, within a space in which that particular group has to coexist with other groups. Now, how could that coexistence be possible without some shared universal values, without a sense of belonging to a community larger than each of the particular groups in question? Here people say, sometimes, that any agreement should be reached through *negotiation*. Negotiation, however, is an ambiguous term that can mean very different things. One of these is a process of mutual pressures and concessions whose outcome depends only on the balance of power between antagonistic groups. It is obvious that no sense of community can be constructed through that type of negotiation. The relation between groups can only be one of potential war. *Vis pacis para bellum.* This is not far away from the conception of the nature of the agreements between groups implicit in the Leninist conception of class alliances: the agreement concerns only circumstantial matters, but the identity of the forces entering it remains uncontaminated by the process of negotiation. Translated into the cultural field, this affirmation of an extreme separatism led to the sharp distinction between bourgeois science and proletarian science. Gramsci was well aware that, in spite of the extreme diversity of the social forces that had to enter into the construction of a hegemonic identity, no collective will and no sense of community could result from such a conception of negotiation and alliances. The dilemma of the defenders of extreme particularism is that their political action is anchored in a perpetual incoherence. On the one hand, they defend the right to difference as a *universal* right, and this defence involves their engagement in struggles for the change of legislation, for the protection of minorities in courts, against the violation of civil rights, and so forth. That is, they are engaged in a struggle for the internal reform of the present institutional setting. But as they assert, at the same time, that this setting is necessarily rooted in the cultural and political values of the traditional dominant sectors of the West, *and that they have nothing to do with that tradition,* their demands cannot be articulated into any wider hegemonic operation to reform that system. This condemns them to an ambiguous peripheral relation with the existing institutions, which can have only paralyzing political effects.

This is not, however, the only possible course of action for those engaged in particularistic struggles—and this is our second conclusion. As we have seen before, a system of oppression (that is, of closure) can be combatted in two different ways—either by an operation of inversion which performs a new closure, or by negating in that system its universal dimension: the principle of closure as such. It is one thing to say that the universalistic values of the West are the preserve of its traditional dominant groups; it is very different to assert that the historical link between the two is a contingent and unacceptable fact which can be modified through political and social struggles. When Mary Wollstonecraft, in the wake of the French Revolution, defended the rights of women, she did not present the exclusion of women from the declaration of rights of man and citizen as a proof that the latter are intrinsically male rights, but tried, on the contrary, to deepen the democratic revolution by showing the incoherence of establishing universal rights which were restricted to particular sectors of the population. The democratic process in present-day societies can be considerably deepened and expanded if it is made accountable to the demands of large sections of the population—minorities, ethnic groups and so on—who traditionally have been excluded from it. Liberal democratic theory and institutions have in this sense, to be deconstructed. As they were originally thought for societies which were far more homogeneous than the present ones, they were based on all kinds of unexpressed assumptions which no longer obtain in the present situation. Present-day social and political struggles can bring to the fore this game of decisions taken in an undecidable terrain, and help us to move in the direction of new democratic practices and a new democratic theory which is fully adapted to the present circumstances. That political participation can lead to political and social integration is certainly true, but for the reasons we gave before, political and cultural segregationism can lead to exactly the same result. Anyway, the decline of the integrationist abilities of the Western states make political conformism a rather unlikely outcome. I would argue that the unresolved tension between universalism and particularism opens the way to a movement away from Western Eurocentrism, through an operation that we could call a systematic decentering of the West. As we have seen, Eurocentrism was the result of a discourse which did not differentiate between the universal values that the West was advocating and the concrete social agents that were incarnating them. Now, however, we can proceed to a separation of these two aspects.

If social struggles of new social actors show that the concrete practices of our society restrict the universalism of our political ideals to limited sectors of the population, it becomes possible to retain the universal dimension while widening the spheres of its application—which, in turn, will define the concrete contents of such universality. Through this process, universalism as a horizon is expanded at the same time as its necessary attachment to any particular content is broken. The opposite policy—that of rejecting universalism *in toto* as the particular content of the ethnia of the West—can only lead to a political blind alley.

This leaves us, however, with an apparent paradox—and its analysis will be my last conclusion. The universal, as we have seen, does not have a concrete content of its own (which would close it in itself), but is the always receding horizon resulting from the expansion of an indefinite chain of equivalent demands. The conclusion seems to be that universality is incommensurable with any particularity and, however, cannot exist apart from the particular. In terms of our previous analysis: if only particular actors, or constellations of particular actors can actualize at any moment the universal, in that case the possibility of making visible the nonclosure inherent to a post-dominated society—that is, a society that attempts to transcend the very form of domination—depends on making permanent the asymmetry between the universal and the particular. The universal is incommensurable with the particular, but cannot, however, exist without the latter. How is this relation possible? My answer is that this paradox cannot be solved, but that its non-solution is the very precondition of democracy. The solution of the paradox would imply that a particular body would have been found, which would be the *true* body of the universal. But in that case, the universal would have found its necessary location, and democracy would be impossible. If democracy *is* possible, it is because the universal has no necessary body and no necessary content; different groups, instead, compete between themselves to temporarily give to their particularisms a function of universal representation. Society generates a whole vocabulary of empty signifiers whose temporary signifieds are the result of a political competition. It is this final failure of society to constitute itself as society—which is the same thing as the failure of constituting difference *as* difference—which makes the distance between the universal and the particular unbridgeable, and, as a result, burdens concrete social agents with that impossible task that makes democratic interaction achievable.

Notes

1. Gilles Deleuze, *Difference et repetition* (Paris, 1989), p. 2.
2. It is at this point that, in my recent work, I have tried to complement the idea of radical antagonism—which still involves the possibility of a radical representability—with the notion of dislocation which is previous to any kind of antagonistic representation. Some of the dimensions of this duality have been explored by Bobby Sayyid and Lilian Zac in a short written presentation to the Ph.D. seminar in Ideology and Discourse Analysis, University of Essex, December 1990.
3. Aletta J. Norval, "Letter to Ernesto," in E. Laclau, *New Reflections on the Revolution of our Time* (London, 1990), p. 157.
4. *Cf.* Walter Benjamin, "Zur Kritik der Gewalt," in *Gesammelte Schriften,* 179, R. Tiedemann and H. Schweppenhauser eds., 1977. See a commentary on Benjamin's text in Werner Hamacher, "Afformative, Strike," *Cardozo Law Review,* vol. 13, No. 4, December 1991.

Ernesto
Laclau

DEBATE

Stanley Aronowitz

Reflections on Identity

The Cold War, which dominated nearly all US public life for most of the latter half of this century, interrupted a debate about the crisis in modernity that had erupted at the turn of the century and occupied much of philosophical and social thought until World War II. Most anti-Stalinist intellectuals were fiercely committed to modernity's putative achievements—individualism, democracy and social (if not always cultural) pluralism—which had their basis in ideas as old as the era of revolution that accompanied the rise of the middle class in the seventeenth century, and reached their apogee with the liberal revolutions during the following two centuries. For both socialist intellectuals and the modern liberals who presupposed them, these values were typically framed in terms ineluctably connected to universalism and its cardinal principle, faith in progress.

According to this doctrine, the history of humankind was, in Croce's felicitous phrase, "the story of liberty."[1] Featured in this narrative were the beneficent effects of industrialism, driven by scientific and technological knowledge and the division of labor, which stood alongside liberal democracy and individual rights as goals whose achievement was as inevitable as the eventual eradication of poverty and hunger. At the center of progressivism—the political expression of modernity—was the striving individual. Yet one of the perplexing questions for Anglo-American philosophy was how to establish the ground for individuality in an increasingly complex social world dominated by the growth of large economic enterprises protected by a centralized state.

The proposition that the individual is identical with itself is one about which Locke had no doubt. For even if identity cannot be established by the positing of unique substance, the agency of *reflexive consciousness,* of which memory is the crucial faculty, unites past and present.[2] Locke's doctrine of consciousness was meant to solve the problem of demarcation between man and animals, and the more difficult issue of how individuality is possible in progressively more complex urban environments where identities are constantly buffeted by what he calls Laws: those of "God . . . politic societies . . . and the law of fashion or private censure." The laws of God provide the basis for morality, but the rules of civil law and the "law of opinion or reputation" are, from the standpoint of individual identity, more troubling; for these are the procedures whereby humans govern themselves, and they have, at best, an ambivalent relation to the tenets of divine law. But Locke himself recognized that what passes for virtue in one place may be considered vice in another. The aporias of civil law are unsettling enough, but Locke's uneasiness is most apparent in his discussion of the formation of the self within the private spheres—within the spheres of everyday encounters and everyday life. For most of us never seriously reflect on "the penalties that attend the breach of God's law," and "flatter ourselves" that we may attain "impunity" with respect to the laws of the commonwealth. Yet "no man escapes the punishment of their censure and dislike who offends against the fashion and opinion of the company he keeps," and thus brings on himself the "condemnation of his own club."[3]

In this way, Locke offers one of the earlier dialectical theories of socialization: a self constituted both by consciousness and by the external environment, in which conformity to the current fashions of one's own "club" is the most powerful interest. Identity, which cannot rely on such "innate principles" as substance, is confronted by the rules laid down by divine and civil law, and especially by the private sphere, where personal identity becomes a social self. In this theory we see the ground for later formulations of the problematic of the human psyche in terms of the conflict between individual and society, a formulation put forth notably by Freudian psychoanalysis and by the social psychology of William James and George Herbert Mead.[4]

By the turn of the twentieth century, nearly two hundred years after the appearance of Locke's *Essay,* William James based his own theory of the social self on Locke's ruminations. Responding, however, to the evidence of social and cultural fragmentation that appeared to pervade modern life in every industrial society, James carried the argument a step further:

> Properly speaking, a man has as many social selves as there are individuals who recognize him and carry an image of him in their mind. To wound any one of these images is to wound him. But as the individuals who carry the images fall naturally into classes, we may practically say that he has as many different social selves as there are distinct *groups* of persons about whose opinion he cares. He generally shows a different side of himself to each of these different groups . . . from this there results what practically is a division of the man into several selves; and this may be a discordant splitting . . . or it may be a perfectly harmonious division of labor.[5]

Locke's conception of social pressure exerted by a person's immediate "club" is here transmuted into the influence of the many groups to which the individual is related. The long process by which social identity has been fractured—first by the refutation of the Aristotelian concept of substance as the basis of identity and difference, and then by the perception that modern identity is constituted both by the "material self" and by an indeterminate multiplicity of social selves—is challenged by James, who even deconstructs the notion of the material self by pointing out that the very clothes in which the self presents itself are more than mediations, being, instead, fundamentally constitutive.[6]

Only under special circumstances can we speak of a "spiritual self," since, for James, consciousness is no longer given. Few of us are capable of reflection, but all are subject to feelings that, after the vagaries of the soul have been sorted out, may be the content of the "I."[7] For James, then, our various selves are arranged hierarchically, and a "certain amount of bodily selfishness is required as a basis for all the other selves." Lest pleasure overcome responsibility, however, James distinguishes between the "immediate and actual and the remote and potential." In the end, James argues, "most of us" strive to achieve recognition by the highest possible interlocutors, the "religious men," who, for him, are those charged with preserving the moral standard.[8]

This position is a meditation both on ways for the self to escape the vicissitudes of everyday life, and on the self's need to create its own "image" of propriety by reaching for a spiritual and moral existence. Yet the hope for transcendence remains just that; the burden of James's scientific and philosophic argument is the dominance of the bodily and *social* self, in the light of which the spiritual self is, at best, a vanishing horizon reserved for the few. Although for James there is an irreducible "I" that thinks, remembers and reflects, it remains uncertain of itself, precisely because of its dependence on the body and on the multiplicity of social relations. Group life is inevitably the home of individual identity.

It remained for George Herbert Mead to break from the spiritual positings of Locke and James. For Mead, the social contradiction between the "I"—the individual ego that remains the ideological *a priori* of all liberal thought—and the "me"—the social self—is resolved outside the ethical appeal to a higher authority. There is, for Mead, only a biological self that is mediated by a social self formed by the interaction between the individual and "significant" others—family members, civil authorities, peers—all of whom underdetermine what we mean by the individual. Like Freud's superego, these together constitute a generalized other—the totality of values, beliefs and, even more important, rules of conduct—by which individuals live. And, like Freud's concept of introjection, Mead's notion of *internalization* describes how society and its constitutive institutions, including Locke's "club," *determine* individuality: "The environment of living organisms is constantly changing, is constantly invaded with other and different things. The assimilation of what occurs and that which recurs with what is elapsing and what has elapsed is called 'experience'."[9]

Experience, then, is a process of "assimilation" of the environment, but one which is understood to be inescapably part of the self. Mead's notion of the social self entails two moments: the continually changing environment, and its assimilation by a living organism. The two terms are constantly in motion, and their relation is always indeterminate from the point of view of the subject.[10]

In his "Fragments" that deal with both Whitehead and relativity, Mead states that the theory of relativity has abolished absolute space and absolute time, substituting relative spaces and times within which objects move.

Stanley Aronowitz

Each object has its own space/time, which is constantly in motion. The relation of any two bodies is always a four-way interaction, so that even the object (self) is never identical to itself. Its identity can be apprehended only in relation to its own space/time and the space/times with which it intersects. "Identity" is the name we give the product of this intersection, and it is, necessarily, always temporary and relative to the process—or, more specifically, to the "events" that constitute it. We can speak of identity only in terms of what Marx calls the "ensemble" of social relations, a set of relations whose historicity is a fundamental aspect of identity's existence.

From this perspective we may apprehend some of the aporias of the present-day "politics of identity." Put directly, the argument—which is more indebted to a two-centuries-long discussion than it has yet admitted—states that there can be no "essential" identity. While in some contexts it appears that oppression is firmly situated in skin color, sexual practices or national origins (in which cases identity appears anchored in the human condition), in other contexts the sources for oppression may appear entirely different. In a supposition akin to the assumption of Newtonian physics that if one object in space is in motion the other is at rest, the older theories of identity have tended to posit "society" and the "individual" as fixed: when one is in motion the other is at rest. Now, however, the sociological theory according to which individuals are crucially formed by a fixed cultural system containing universal values that become internalized through the multiplicity of interactions between the "person" and her external environment has come under radical revision. We may now regard the individual as a process constituted by its multiple and *specific* relations, not only to the institutions of socialization such as family, school and law, but also to significant others, all of whom are in motion and constantly changing. The ways in which individuals and the groups to which they affiliate were constituted as late as a generation earlier may now be archaic. New identities arise; old ones pass away (at least temporarily).

For example, it was likely that a migrant male youth from Puerto Rico in the late 1920s could live through the thirties without being crucially identified as a Puerto Rican—not only by himself, but by social and economic institutions and by others. He saw himself instead as a worker, a Communist or a trade unionist of Puerto Rican nationality, much as Jewish-Americans, Italian-Americans and Finnish-Americans of the same spatiotemporal location may have adopted "ethnic" identities as a part of their *strategic* political and social arsenal without confusing this with anything but a relatively small part of the "self."

By the late 1940s, the massive postwar Puerto Rican migration combined with a new cultural and economic environment to produce the event of Puerto Rican "racial" formation. By 1950, buffeted by the Cold War, which caused, among other things, the expelling of thousands of suspected leftists from the unions, especially in industries that were considered vital to US security, a similar left-wing trade unionist would now discover that his primary identity and his frame of group reference had shifted to "Puerto Rican," and this was accompanied by a shift in political discourse from class to "oppressed minority." In the 1930s and forties, his frames of reference had been those of industrial labor, especially that of the transportation industries of New York, and the left-wing movement within which some trade unions played a crucial role, whereas his frame was now El Barrio (East Harlem), where he became an unpaid tenant organizer. He no longer spoke English in daily life, except at his job, and when he represented "his people" to city and state agencies and Anglo politicians. Among members of the generation of migrants who came to New York and other large cities after the war, Spanish was the privileged language. And, equally important, the key word "community," in part a term of distinction, became a euphemism for this new frame of reference. By 1957, on the heels of the breakup of the Communist movement and the dramatic shrinking of its institutions and organizational sites in the United States, the political identities of thousands of its once loyal adherents had been transformed. At the same time, since these identities were intimately linked to "personal" identity, these activists in some respects assumed new identities as their networks of group associations were radically altered.

From the perspective of identity-formation, Communism and socialism are viewed as universals, although counterhegemonic ones to those of prevailing liberalism. These were movements for fundamental change that contributed significantly to the altered economic discourse, politics and institutional matrix of late capitalism (even if only incrementally), but that also presented themselves as a counter*culture* within which the personal identities and, from the perspective of its leading concepts, the anomalous idea of community became part of the lived experience of its adherents. For the Socialist and Communist parties were also social movements, insofar as they both pressed for changes in the external social environment, and

Stanley
Aronowitz

demanded radical transformations in identities. The activists could not expect to "change the world" unless they underwent a profound personal transformation, unless they ultimately shed the old, habitual structure of capitalist social relations. To be in the "movement" signified, despite all its political limitations, that one had adopted, as a matter of principle, the proposition that one's life had world-historical meaning. Especially in the early days of the Communist movement, the concept of the inextricable link between personal and political transformation was more than an article of faith: bourgeois character was poor material for forging a cadre of professional revolutionaries.

The decline of the ideological Left over the past forty years—not only in the United States, but in Western Europe as well—signals that one of the more powerful alternative means by which identity-formation promises to overcome the vicissitudes of the "primal" identities acquired through family, school and the market is no longer available. At the same time, neither are individuals obliged to subject themselves to a privatized existence in which political identity is, at best, episodic. Instead, new social and cultural formations—nationality, race, gender and sexuality, among others—have provided the basis for group and individual identities.

Although it is not entirely accurate to claim that the social movements which provide the context for these social selves can be reduced to instances of *particularity*—that is, binary opposites to the universality of either liberalism (with its global individual as the basis for political and cultural agency) or Marxism (whose discourse of power is rooted in the discourse of class, historically considered)—in the terms defined by the problematic of the bourgeois revolutions of the eighteenth and nineteenth centuries, these new identities may be found lacking in philosophic depth. They can thereby be accused of providing vehicles for the amelioration of grievances within the existing system or, alternatively, of reifying identities on the basis of partial totalization.

Any social movement of consequence attracts a spectrum of tendencies whose subject-positions span amelioration, reform and the quest for fundamental historical transformation. Indeed, the movement's identity as a collective *moral* as well as political agent depends on the universality of its claims; that is, it presents itself as a movement united not only by a list of grievances, but also by a specific identity that may be said to challenge *everyone* (at least in democratic societies) to examine her or his own commitment to justice, equality, freedom and other ethical precepts. More profoundly, intellectuals within these social movements invariably generate historical and philosophic accounts of the privileged identity itself, refusing the purely contingent characterizations of detractors. For example, everyone knows this hypothetical comment: "Yes, gays and lesbians suffer discrimination, but their status as cultural and political identities can be doubted. After all, what is at stake is merely the issue of the 'right' to privacy, one that articulates quite well with the general appeal to civil liberties for individuals. Hence, the movement is inherently liberal, not oppositional." And this claim is also applied to feminism. The constellation of oppressions suffered by women may be grouped under a variety of headings: discrimination in employment and other public sites; rape and other acts of violence against the person of individual women; and, of course, cultural barriers to equality or, at least, equality of opportunity.

Missing in these accounts, however, is one fundamental dimension of the second wave of feminist politics. This feminist politics has been constituted not only by the history of exclusions, violence, and discrimination against women, but also by the economic exigencies of postwar US economic expansion. The period between the mid-1950s and the late 1980s produced a pull to recruit women labor reserves that required the reversal of the "normal" ideology that a woman's place was in the home. It is not surprising that the contradiction between the ideology of women's "place" and their massive entrance into the paid workforce helped generate affirmative identities that resulted in new feminist cultural formations that protested, among other grievances, the "double shift" to which women were now subjected. But these formations also consist of the development of unique political and cultural institutions: organizations for the improvement of women's social and economic position, and informal sites such as social clubs and other gathering places. By the late 1970s one sees a new, culturally and politically powerful community of women that consists of these sites, but is not limited to them. Women's identity is forged by the collective perception—women's as well as men's—that they have become a politically potent social category. Of course, as this identity becomes historical, that is, begins to become a frame of reference for politics and culture, it cannot help but produce a global counterattack that realigns hitherto "fixed" political and ideological identities.

In the course of identity development, feminism, at least in its more radical manifestations, acquired the elements of a social theory that explained the position of women in their contemporary situation and also in history. The theory of patriarchy as the root explanation for women's oppression was buttressed by anthropological, historical and philosophical arguments. Critics examined canonical literary texts to tease out patriarchy in action; psychologists and sociologists demonstrated that femininity was itself "socially" constructed. In short, notwithstanding the attack against foundational thinking, essentialism and so forth, it is one of the aporias of our current situation that *theory* was inextricably linked to the formation of gender identities in the postmodern era.

Like the participants in Black and gay and lesbian movements, feminist intellectuals have generated a powerful tradition of writing and speech that provides the *universal* signifiers by which the movement retains its solidarity. Historians, philosophers and literary critics have formed themselves as a kind of collective "organic intellectual" of the movement. Their work consists chiefly in erasing the erasure: contesting the moral and intellectual hegemony of male domination of legitimate knowledge.[11] The power of this movement toward the creation of a counter public sphere of feminist discourse may be indicated by the remarkable explosion of the readership for feminist writing—fiction and nonfiction—and, simultaneously, by the extent to which feminists have succeeded in implanting themselves in universities, thereby providing a basis for the claim that this mode of scholarship is legitimate intellectual knowledge. Whereas an older generation of women and gay intellectuals were, under the sign of subordination, more or less successfully integrated within the disciplines, observing the canons and producing traditional scholarship in sciences and the humanities, it is today more typical that intellectuals affiliated with feminist standpoints have chosen to orient their work, both in its content and its reception, to people who occupy similar social spaces. Without such a shift, the successful dissemination of these standpoints would be inconceivable.[12]

Yet, the creation of a self-enclosed universe of identity discourse has its dangers, particularly in periods like our own, when the tenets of modern liberalism—pluralism, democracy and intellectual freedom—are under severe attack from the Right. The Right was defined during the New Deal period as "reactionary," presenting itself as a stubborn but minoritarian defender of the past that stands in the way of "progress." In the 1970s, however, the Right forged a new identity. No longer isolationist, quaintly liberal in its economics, and antimodernist, it armed itself with "something old, something new." Now the Right has become the staunch proponent of internationalism, powerfully statist and clearly modernist while paradoxically (but only from the standpoint of reason) maintaining both a refurbished (and convincing) economic liberalism, and a peculiar but extremely effective version of populism that has, incidentally, revealed one more time its racist and sexist core.

The conjuncture of the politics of difference with this development has produced an intellectual crisis for the social movements that have embodied them. Having rejected Marxism (and, indeed, all universalist claims), the discourses of the most ubiquitous of the antiestablishment social movements—feminist, gay and lesbian, and ecological—respond to the changing frames of reference by adopting three alternative strategies. The first involves some return to modern liberalism, to the discourse of human rights and social justice, which substitutes ethics for social and historical theory and so brings universalism back, but through the side door. Second, in a renewed resolve for community-building, some abjure all politics except cultural separatism or, in the most virulent form, try to impose on the polity their own particularist ideology, cloaked as a universal moral imperative. And third, in the wake of the vigorous right-wing attack against ecological gains, abortion rights and freedom of sexual association, some of these movements acknowledge the need for entering coalitions with others on the basis of common minimum interests.

But as urgent as these coalitions are in the context of the current emergency, they cannot hope to regain the offensive unless they develop a *theory*, or at least a broader explanation for the current state of affairs from which an overall program and series of policies may emerge. For one thing, can these movements afford to ignore the degree to which right-wing discourse has captured the hearts and minds of large sections of middle- and working-class people? As the 1992 Democratic presidential primaries amply demonstrate, the old New Deal slogans are woefully inadequate for the contemporary situation, but as long as the opposition not only lacks but abjures a convincing theory that can speak to the economic crisis as, in part, a cultural and political crisis, coalition politics will almost certainly fail to stem the conservative tide.

Stanley Aronowitz

Evident in the past decade is the lesson of Mead's appropriation of relativity theory. As the frame of reference shifts, so do positions forged in other spatiotemporal contexts. Yesterday's answers become today's obstacles to finding new answers. Postmodernism effectively subdued, if not defeated, modernism's most virulent, universalist aspects, but in a period of counterrevolution, this same postmodernist insistence on the particular is unarmed. Since countercultural formations are crucial for the survival of subaltern identities, the agony of addressing the fact of the simultaneity of the changes in the relation of the movement and its environment leads in two directions. Mindful of the disastrous consequences—common to Marxism and Christianity—of imposing a universal discourse and set of rules of political conduct, these countercultural movements thus lack even a secure strategic referent from which alliances can emerge, and one tendency is to move steadily toward accommodation with the dominant discourses. " 'We' have to take liberalism seriously again" is a response often heard in all social movements. Here the attraction is born not only of the retreat and defeat of the historic Left, but also of the equally distressing assessment that freedom has only flourished, even in deformed terms, within liberal-democratic formations.

A second tendency is to batten down the hatches and reproduce Hegel's unhappy consciousness by asserting identity even more fiercely. Faced with an increasingly hostile political and cultural environment, people in subordinate positions frequently choose separatist directions. Accordingly, the Left and the remnants of the labor movement cannot be trusted, in the light of their penchant for master discourses, unprincipled programs and tactical opportunism. Of course these charges are entirely justified. Yet community-building may have its own authoritarian implications, whether intended or not. One example can be found in the cultural feminist proposals in Minneapolis and some other cities to ban the sale or purchase of pornography, and the subsequent congressional legislation written by Catharine MacKinnon and sponsored by Strom Thurmond and other right-wing senators, to punish publishers of pornography for the criminal acts of pornography's users. Here, cultural feminism makes an overt alliance with the Victorian Right's effort to subvert First Amendment guarantees, presumably arguing that, as the most abject of oppressed groups, it has the moral sanction to take such action.

The best that some have offered is a third alternative: the hope for tactical alliances among social movements that share, in one degree or another, the space of subordination as victims of the seemingly unceasing onslaught of prevailing domination. These putative alliances would be based, for the most part, on the underlying approach of coalition politics: unification around single issues, based upon self-interest, rather than the consideration of the possibility that there can emerge a common perspective that takes the history of subalternity as a "universal" cultural as well as political basis for a political *strategy*. Coalitions are safer, for they cannot challenge hard-won fundamental identities, nor can they impose a master discourse on a movement. The politics of difference cannot, however, admit of the possibility of forging either a paradigm of explanation, or a theory that is inclusive of a plurality of identities. The idea of *difference* becomes, in effect, the new universal that cannot be overcome, but must, instead, be celebrated. Some have even suggested a politics based upon a hierarchy of oppressions: the more abject the identity, the more privileged its claims among others who may experience a degree of oppression, but not to a degree sufficient to challenge the underlying premises of the cultural order.[13] In these circumstances, a discourse of the self is possible only in terms of "others," who are identical with it through their reduction to the most abject characteristic. In this framework, identity entails a metonymic selection of certain characteristics—race, gender or whatever—that are taken as *irreducible* and privileged over all competitive claims.

The underlying justification for this position is well known: identity politics arises not only on the ruins but within the perfidy of the universalist discourses—both Left and liberal—and within the political apparatuses that sustain them. Politically and intellectually, the prevailing master discourses have, throughout history, denied the validity of difference as both a philosophical warrant and a series of social and cultural practices, and have thwarted its exercise. In this century, particularly since the 1960s, difference has enjoyed a wide variety of theoretical justifications. From Theodor Adorno's negative dialectics and Memmi and Fanon's graphic discussions of Otherness, to Jacques Derrida's critique of logocentrism, and especially to Giles Deleuze's profound materialization of difference, the ineluctable character of difference provides the intellectual unity from which, paradoxically, the politics of identity has received crucial sustenance. The grip of the old Stalinist Left over the French intelligentsia was broken in part by this work. After 1968, Marxism was discredited as a master discourse of revolution. And by the late 1980s, the same fate befell state socialism.

Yet, as in the case of the recent outpourings of influential work within this tradition of the affirmation of difference, it must be acknowledged that the conditions of emergence—namely the revolt of an entire generation of French intellectuals against the corrupt and overbearing discourse of party Marxism—have been surpassed, just as the belated embrace of orthodoxy by the New Left in the United States belongs to historical rather than contemporary politics. The emergence of identity politics was a breath of fresh air compared to the stifling environments of liberal and Marxist hegemonies, but has the moment arrived when this politics, while necessary, is no longer sufficient during a time when the Right has everywhere moved swiftly into a power vacuum, closing the spaces for the play of difference?

Faced with the delegitimation of the old universalisms, must we remain in positions where the infinite regress of binary oppositions continues to hold us in thrall? Or can we envision a new radical democratic polity, where citizenship is constituted by cultural difference but is, at the same time, "identical" insofar as there is a shared sense that it defines itself by what it faces as its own erasure: the patriarchies of power? Of course such a radical democracy awaits specification, especially if it hopes to go beyond the invocation of an indefinite future and instead propose itself as a politics, as an ideology that takes freedom seriously both for individuals and communities.

Radical democracy as a political identity may be viewed as an expression of both the pragmatic and the psychoanalytic refutations of a substantialist self-identity. It recognizes the temporality of all possible subject positions, their ineluctable internal differences, and, most of all, their contingency. But the synthetic abstraction, *radical democracy*, corresponds to no existing group identity, and, on principle, refuses fixed positions.

To be sure, overcoming the fragmentation of political discourse that attends differential subject-positions is no small matter. Such a constellation of radical democracy would require considerable openness and criticism among its participants, and would be required to abjure "political correctness"—the moralism that did not die with the Old Left but is alive and well in its displacements (nationalism, cultural feminism, Earth Firstism and so forth). For one thing, we must stop pretending that there is no possible class discourse, even as we firmly reject its antecedent expressions. Rethinking class is plainly a necessary step in any social movement, and in any political discourse that takes among its leading premises both equality and autonomy. And we must come to terms with the plain fact that the renunciation of solidarity is a formula for the eternal recurrence of fragmentation among us, and an invitation for the inheritors of the old universalisms to maintain their hold. We were right to throw out the reductionist "class analysis" that was the theoretical basis of both the Old Left and, with variations, much of the New Left. This version of social and political theory virtually excluded all other considerations, or regarded them as displacements of the class struggle. In the course of this rightful rejection, however, class was occluded from the lexicon of radical terms on the basis of its pernicious history. Yet, in the light of the current debate between and among the two major parties concerning what is euphemistically called the "working middle class"(more precisely the middle working class), how can questions of class remain outside the discourse of opposition? To say that there are no longer master discourses of history precludes neither history nor its agents.

The traditional Left presents itself as the latter-day Enlightenment, engaged in a fierce battle against mass "false consciousness," which it regards as an anachronistic but potent holdover from feudal society. This is the foundation of political correctness. Armed with the science of Marxism (a rough analogy to the truth of Christian doctrine), the Left is appointed (by history) to judge political virtue, just as its counterparts are anointed gatekeepers of morally approved personal behavior. Political correctness and moral correctness are twins, but the latter seems more acceptable, since it draws on the certainties of the cultural system, while the former can only draw on its own arrogance.

We are obliged to live the irony of needing theory and explanation even as we distance ourselves from comprehensive formulaic paradigms. A solution is to offer theoretical formulations as *strategic*. That is, we can adopt the philosophical position that generalization is always subject to revision, and we can see the relation of theories to the spatiotemporal dimension within which they function as fundamental to their validity. Moreover, agents would acknowledge that all explanation is relative to standpoint: their universality is contradictorily mediated by changing circumstances.

You will have noticed that we are inevitably drawn to a perspective that relies, at least at its conclusion, on the position that instances of subalternity have a claim to ethical stature that overrides that of dominant groups. This standpoint cannot obliterate the aporias of the politics of difference. But neither would this position be satisfied by the minimalist notion of coalitions of convenience. The argument for theory and strategy does not depend merely on the power of the Right; it relies on the view that oppressions cannot be reduced to their relative quantitative measures because they are incommensurable with respect to their development. But even if there is no synchrony, neither are we condemned to be exclusively attentive to nonsynchrony. Between synchrony and nonsynchrony lies a political problematic in which the struggle for social space is shared by those who have experienced, day by day, the progressively narrowing possibility of dissident public voices. To recover these voices requires both a coherent explanation for why they are made objects of exclusion, and an alternative in which the art and politics of identity/difference create spaces where dialogue without rancor is possible between them.

NOTES

1. Benedetto Croce, *History as the Story of Liberty* (New York: W. W. Norton, 1937).
2. Locke writes: "Thus it is always as to our present sensations and perceptions: and by this every one is to himself that which he calls *self*: it not being considered in this case, whether the same self be continued in the same or diverse substances. For, since consciousness always accompanies thinking; and thereby distinguishes himself from all other thinking things, in this alone consists personal identity, i.e. the sameness of a rational being: and as far as this consciousness can be extended backwards to any past action of thought, so far reaches the identity of the person; it is the same self now it was then; and it is by the same self with this present one that now reflects on it, that that action was done" (John Locke, *An Essay Concerning Human Understanding, Vol 1* [New York: Dover Publications, 1959], p. 449).
3. *Ibid.*
4. Eighteenth- and nineteenth-century political and economic philosophy was deeply influenced by Locke's penetrating discovery of the social constitution of individuality, but the emphasis of social theorizing has decisively shifted to concepts such as "society," "history" and "progress." Although nineteenth-century German philosophies pay some tribute to the notion of the individual, this category became, especially in Hegel, the outcome of a long dialectical process in which

the state is the material embodiment of the unity of a humankind otherwise mired in conflict at the level of the family and economic relations. For Hegel—and Marx—false, or, more accurately, partial individuality is produced by the evolution of private property and the universal marketplace in which, as possessors of commodities, individuals confront each other. Yet, criticizing the widespread view that the development of this "civil society" is the final arbiter of human affairs, Hegel stands in opposition to Adam Smith's assurance that the hidden hand of God can make whole the otherwise incessant war of all against all. Yet, as Marx and other critics point out, everyday life remains a battlefield in Hegel's account of universalism; the contradiction between the individual and the state remains. See Karl Marx, "A Contribution to the Critique of Hegel's Philosophy of Right," in *Early Writings,* trans. Rodney Livingstone and Gregor Benton (New York: Vintage Books, 1974).

5. William James, *Principles of Psychology, Vol. 1* (New York: Henry Holt and Co., 1890), p. 295.

6. James writes, "We so appropriate our clothes and identify ourselves with them that there are few of us who, if asked to choose between having a beautiful body clad in raiment perpetually shabby and unclean, and having an ugly and blemished form always spotlessly attired would not hesitate a moment before making a decisive reply" (*Ibid.*, p. 292).

7. Concluding these observations, James writes: "It is difficult for me to detect in the activity any purely spiritual element at all. Whenever my introspective glance succeeds in turning round quickly enough to catch one of these manifestations of spontaneity in the act, all it can ever feel distinctly is some bodily process, for the most part taking place in the head" (*Ibid.*, p. 301).

8. *Ibid.*, p. 315.

9. George Herbert Mead, *The Philosophy of the Act* (Chicago: University of Chicago Press, 1938), p. 53.

10. For Mead, the past is present as memory. And the environment is present in the distinction between "I" and "me," where the former is immediate consciousness and the latter is the mediated representation of the environment, both the physical resistance of things and the significant others, including the generalized other. Our conversations are consequently not only with external others, but also with their repre-

sentations in the form of the "self." The formulation is Mead's appropriation of Hegel's concept that consciousness takes itself as its own object. But in Mead's formulation, "consciousness" is no innate entity, and has already passed through a process of transformation as a result of its interpenetration with the other.

11. See, especially, Sandra Harding, *The Science Question in Feminism* (Ithaca: Cornell University Press, 1986), and Donna Haraway, *Primate Visions: Gender, Race, and Nature in the World of Modern Science* (New York: Routledge, 1989).

12. Witness the proliferation, during the past two decades, of both feminist journals, and feminist scholarship within traditional disciplinary journals. Before 1970, there were almost no significant feminist scholarly journals, and the subject of "women" was treated exclusively within the parameters established by the disciplines. Women writers were simply excluded from the literary canon, and there was little distinctly feminist social and cultural theory. Today there is a vast readership for feminist fiction and poetry, as well as for feminist approaches to the humanities and the social sciences.

13. Judith Butler, among others, has attempted to establish a hierarchy of abjectness upon which to ground ethical claims. See Judith Butler, *Gender Trouble: Feminism and the Subversion of Identity* (New York: Routledge, 1990).

DEBATE

Discussion

JUDITH BUTLER: A few comments. I am not sure, Stanley, that what I proposed, and actually what Ernesto proposed, entails the *surpassing* of particularity. I would disagree that this is a historical movement in which particularity has been surpassed. In fact, I think that particular identities are being produced as contested zones within political discourse all the time, and this is being done in part by right-wing political forces. As a result, it would be perilous at this historical moment to claim or call for the surpassing of particular identities on the Left, since that would be to give over such identities to a reactionary constitution. In the face of the prospective silencing or erasure of gender, race or sexual-minority identities by reactionary political forces, it is important to be able to articulate them, and to insist on these identities as sites of valuable cultural contest. My own view is that it is imperative to assert identities, at the same time that it is crucial to interrogate the exclusionary operations by which they are constituted. So what I'm calling for is not the surpassing of particularity, but rather a double movement: the insistence on identity and the subjection of identity-terms to a contestation in which the exclusionary procedures by which those identity-terms are produced are called into question. This seems to me to be the necessary and contingent place of identity within a radical democratic culture.

I also want to make a point about how the term essentialism is circulating here. There is a great deal of feminist theory that has been reconsidering essentialism. Although I'm not a defender of this position, I do think that this is a movement within recent feminist theory that is important to consider. The conventional way of understanding essentialism is as a position that accepts the notion of a pregiven or preconstituted identity. Diana Fuss, Naomi Schor and Gayatri Spivak have spoken about the rhetorical use of the essentialist claim, sometimes in terms of "strategic essentialism." Spivak underscores the necessity of insisting on culturally specific differences over and against the theoretical and political efforts to erase or subordinate them. But this is not a question of offering an adequate representation in language of a preconstituted group; in a sense, it is the performative invocation of an identity for the purposes of political *resistance* to a hegemonic threat of erasure or marginalization.

STANLEY ARONOWITZ: I agree with Judith Butler. When I used the word *surpassed*, I was referring to particularity as a political position that was exclusionary. I didn't mean to say that what's surpassed is everything. It has to be defended in the way she says. The other thing I want to say about essentialism, however, is that I think we're about to rediscover essentialism. I think the position that social construction displaces is itself an essentialist position. Foucault says somewhere—I think it's in *Power/Knowledge*—that we can't know the biological because it's really too deeply hidden, and those layers of discourse are simply too dense. I think that's a dangerous position. At some point we have to rediscover the biological. There is a whole discussion within biology—by Gould, by Levins, by Lewontin, by Ernst Mayer—which tries to work at the play of the two signifiers of social and historical construction, of context dependency, and of the biological itself. And it's really terribly important that we do not give this up. Secondly, the problem of strategic essentialism has something to do with a blindness, especially a blindness about the question of the ecological crisis we're in. How do we theorize the ecological crisis from the perspective of social construction? We can theorize the *discourse* of ecology from that perspective, but at some point we need a historical perspective, and that historical perspective is something quite different.

ERNESTO LACLAU: I just want to make two points concerning Judith's intervention. First, concerning the notion of essentialism. In the way I use the term, I only mean self-referentiality. For instance, in German idealism after Kant, there is the notion of an absolute subsumption of the real in the rational, that something can be thought independently of any external reference. When we reach that point, determination by the class system, by the economy or by any other movement of history is not far away. Essentialism in the strong sense means that. There are other forms of essentialism, however—I could say that, for instance, a philosophy like Aristotle's could be essentialist. But insofar as you accept that a form can be corrupted, these are not essences in the strong sense of the term. Secondly, I want to say that I both like and dislike the notion of strategic essentialism. The aspect I like is the notion that you cannot simply say, "I'm outside essentialism," in the same way that one cannot say that one is entirely outside metaphysics. The only thing that one can do is to play new and different games with metaphysical and essentialist categories, games that both posit them and weaken them, and thus make possible language games far more complicated than those that were possible in the past. This is what I like. What I don't entirely like is the idea of strategy. Because strategy assumes two things: first, that the essence of something is there to be manipulated; and second, that I'm outside this essence doing the manipulating. I would say that today there are many essentialist forms that we no longer conceive as grounds but as horizons. And to construct such horizons—to use this old phenomenological category that can be reformulated in a new way—conceives essentialism in an entirely different way. I don't know if you agree with that.

JUDITH BUTLER: As I said, it's not my position. I prefer to think about the invocation of identity as a strategic provisionality, using the term, but knowing when to let it go, living its contingency, and subjecting it to a political challenge concerning its usefulness. And I agree with you that the notion of an instrumental subject, who can somehow wield an essence at a distance, is problematic. The one who would "use" the term is also established as a "one" by the term. What I want to suggest, however, is that in Naomi Schor's work—and in Diana Fuss's as well—the feminist question has been one of figuring out how to replay the games by which "one" has been enacted. Schor's notion of essentialism relies on the notion of miming mimesis, deploying the metaphysical categories by which the feminine has itself been constituted and constrained. This is not the instrumental wielding of a metaphysical category at a distance, but the mobilizing or miming of a category by which the feminine is itself entered into discourse. In this sense, then, it is an essentialism that mimes the category which is, for better or worse, the discursive condition of agency. In Schor's notion of miming mimesis, of refiguring the feminine, there is something at work not unlike your antiessentialist notion of a political signifier or subject-position as a *site* of rearticulation. It would be very useful to consider the points of theoretical convergence between rhetorical essentialism in feminism, which makes no claims about the content of the "feminine," but redeploys the categories by which the feminine has been constituted, and the notion of *rearticulation* in your own antiessentialist position. I think there is a similar emphasis on the rhetoricity, if not the performativity, of the political signifier in your own work. It also seems important to me to rethink performativity, as Derrida suggests, *as* citationality, for the invocation of identity is always a *re*invocation, and both Schor and you—and Chantal Mouffe, and Slavoj Žižek— invest some promise in the iterability of the signifier.

As for Stanley's remark that "we" are about to discover essentialism: the "we" who is about to discover essentialism is not a feminist "we," and is not a gay "we," and is not a "we" that has been working in ethnic studies in this country, if essentialism has not yet been discovered. I would suggest that it is important to read in these literatures, where the debates over essentialism are quite thorough and engaging. Some of the discussions we're having here could be shown to be at cross-purposes with the theoretical work on identity in these areas. That's all I'll say.

AUDIENCE: I'd like to query a point raised by Judith Butler. She addressed the ambiguity of the queer identity, and there's something there that perhaps could be developed a bit more—the kind of "I hate straights" element of it—which has parallels in ethnic and feminist politics. It seems to me that what is consistent with those others in "I hate straights" is an antiassimilationist-type politics. A lot of things we see, such as outing, which focus precisely on those gays or lesbians who are "straight-identified," have parallels in terms of the way the women's movement focuses on those women who are "male-identified," and so on. Now I'd like to think about this not just as a gay man but also because I've been teaching high school for eight years in Crown Heights. I came there with an understanding consistent with what's being voiced here, namely, that you could take words that were words of oppression and turn their meanings around. Yet the fact is, I have never heard the word *nigger* used in that high school in any sense other than self-deprecation. And so I was very quickly forced to arrive at the decision that I had to use my authority to say, "This is a term we do not use in my room"; because that was the only way I could find to challenge it. And I think the use of the term *queer* incorporates stereotypes of what gay people are, just as use of the term *nigger* incorporates stereotypes of African-American people.

JUDITH BUTLER: In fact a number of people have difficulty with "queer" politics, because the term *queer* has been used in such derogatory ways. The question of how and when a term becomes available for political reinscription is a difficult one. And it may be that in the incipient moments of that process of reinscription, the very abjection associated with the term, associated with *queer*—which has carried its own specific form of sexualized abjection—becomes reenacted and relived. This is not to claim that every repetition or reinscription of the term remains within abjection or recapitulates abjection, since the collective *re*usage effectively brings new valuations to bear on the term, those which are defiant and affirmative. But this is a difficult question, because I would think that *nigger* and *kike* are not words I would want to see subjected to a reinscription. Or rather, I cannot see within this political climate a way for such words to signify in any way other than the most derogatory one. I don't think there is a formula that can predict when and how a term is open to a reinscription and a displacement of the originally derogatory valence, the displacement of the abjection that has sustained a term like *queer*, and which the term itself has sustained. But insofar as the term *queer* has been taken up—and we repeatedly see public displays in which *queer* is taken up as a signifier of pride—then the signifier becomes to some extent detached from its traditional articulations, and becomes the site of a set of revaluations. Recently, we are seeing, reading *queer* in performances of political rage that insist on an affirmative visibility, but also on the power of a self-naming which is a reworking of the way in which a group has been named and constituted. These repeated theatrics have had the power to open up the term as a site of contest, to return to Denise Riley's formulation, which is to dislodge the term from its traditional moorings in abjection.

AUDIENCE: I'm confused by Judy Butler's talk, because the second part seemed to show how subjects could engage in transgressive performances that were generative in nature—that is, that subjects can generate performances—whereas the first part seemed to rely on a Lacanian semiotic machinery where there's a world of signifiers, but there are no referents, there are no signifieds, where its agents other than language have no experience, no generative capacity. So it seems like language was being reified, because agents could only act within a linguistic framework where there was structural predetermination.

JUDITH BUTLER: What links the first and the second parts of the talk is the notion of citationality. I *never* suggested, in my reading of *Paris Is Burning*, that there was a subject who generates its performances, and if you heard that, I would like to correct that. What I did suggest, however, was that it is only through the citing of a norm, a citing which instantiates and institutes the norm, that a subject is produced. So the subject is an effect of a citational practice. In the first part I lay out how that citing functions within the symbolic; and in the second, I read the "performance" of Venus Xtravaganza in *Paris Is Burning*, but I never indicated in any way that Venus's performance is *transgressive*. In fact, I do not use that word, and I would not concur with that reading. I suggested instead that one could read Venus's performance as a *reiteration* of norms. Whereas I did write in *Gender Trouble* about parodic and subversive performance, I explicitly did not refer to subversion in this context, because *Paris Is Burning* has forced a rethinking of my notion of parodic subversion, for clearly some forms of parody are not subversive. In Venus's performance, I read an ambivalent site of power and sexuality. We witness the *renaturalization* of certain hegemonic norms of race and gender, a reconsolidation of those norms *through* parody. And at the same time, there is a displacement of those norms, to the extent that Venus was never supposed to occupy them in quite that way.

AUDIENCE: Is the ambivalence in the language or is it in the subject? I'm a little lost here.

JUDITH BUTLER: In the language or in the subject? Toward the end of my paper, I suggested that the subject is a kind of crossroads of identification, identifications that are carried by language, and that Gloria Anzaldúa's notion of a crossroads is no longer the notion of the subject, certainly not a subject who stands outside of language. My position is that subjects are constituted in language, but that language is also the site of their destabilization.

AUDIENCE: My question is addressed to Dr. Judith Butler and Dr. Joan Scott, and probably to Mr. Stanley Aronowitz as well. Butler and Scott both gave very convincing analyses of how progressive thought, and particularly feminist thought, partakes of what they would identify as dangerous. Western individualism and Western humanism. I would suggest, however, that some of their poststructuralism participates in dangerous discourses. In Butler's paper I would identify that in the use, for example, of the substitution of "classism" for class structure or capitalism. That's a substitution that's prominent now in identity politics in the list of *isms*. It's never capitalism, it's classism. And also in your economy metaphor as well, which I think partakes of that. Another point that leads into two further questions is that some of the coherence of the conception of identity that you're critiquing, and rightly so, derives from a radical analysis of the structures of oppression and exploitation. So that some of the coherent identity of woman posited by those conceptions is not just organized about a biological given, but has to do with the forces of patriarchy, just as some of the nonexistent, fantasmatic identity of the worker can only be focused in relation to a critique of capitalism. These analyses ask questions about the social relations involved in producing and governing identities, but not just identities—practices and institutions. And these analyses also claim to be able to measure and discriminate between unequal and different positions: not everybody benefits from these systems in the same way. So understanding that you're poststructuralist, it remains unclear, as an earlier speaker asked of Joan Scott, how power is operating in your analyses, besides the overarching power of discourse. And here's where your economy metaphor really erases power—because it suggests an equivalence. By using the neoclassical kind of metaphor of economy, you're suggesting that there's an equivalence between a lesbian feminist constructing her identity and a straight, White male constructing a queer identity. And one last question. It remains unclear what your sense of scale is, of how it is possible to have a perspective on power in the absence of a system. How can you, or do you, or are you interested in mapping—without ordinances—hierarchy, inequality and non-equivalence of positions?

JUDITH BUTLER: Yes, except that in the paper I gave I was slightly disloyal to the position you're ascribing to me. I would agree with you that one needs a very complex map of power to read, one which accounts for the differential constitution of subject positions. And I think Joan Scott said that as well this morning. And what is involved in that complex configuration of power would be also economic structures. I have no problem with that, nor with calling a structure or a condition "capitalist." So if capitalism appeared elided in my remarks, that is not a necessary elision. It is simply that in this context, I was not offering a full sense of a political agenda—no one could. I did state explicitly, however, that there is no equivalence between, on the one hand, a heterosexual who articulates a fictive coherence to his own identity and a lesbian feminist who articulates a fictive coherence to hers. In fact, I stated that it was extremely important to mark those positions differentially. I would add that there is a dimension of power that works through language, but is not reducible to language. In other words, power is not a pure effect of language. I'm not a linguistic monist, and I do not take poststructuralism to be an example of linguistic monism (indeed, its difference from linguistic constructivism is a departure from that possibility). I do not think it is enough to claim that any given act of naming is internally upset by a fissure that is purely or exclusively linguistic, and that this naming of an identity is at once the failure to totalize what is named. My own sense is that there are very specific historical acts of naming which stabilize or destabilize identity according to the sites of power in which they occur. And insofar as I'm willing to make this latter move, I acknowledge a domain of power that operates through language, but is not reducible to it.

JOAN SCOTT: I just want to return a question, which is, how do you define power? What is missing in the analyses of power you think you heard from us that you're not getting, that you want? And second, what will class structure do for you as an analytical tool that's not working somehow for us? What's at stake for you in those terms and what do you mean by those terms?

AUDIENCE: I called you Doctor constitutively because I'm not so.

JOAN SCOTT: Well, in fact, I don't think those honorifics are necessary because you're setting up a power relationship in using them.

AUDIENCE: Actually it was a response to the use of "Judy." I'm not sure about people's intimacy with Judith Butler, and so it was a response to that. I would say, I have no answers, but I share a wariness, a wariness felt by some nonhumanities and slightly more structurally inclined theorists, of what I would identify as a poststructuralist move, an abandoning of a sense of system in which you can place people. To me, the shift from class structure to "classism" is indicative.

JOAN SCOTT: But what does class structure give you that "classism" doesn't?

AUDIENCE: I'd like to problematize this notion of essentialism, and I'm going to direct this mostly at Stanley, Chantal, and Cornel West. When Stanley Aronowitz brings up theorists like Gould or Lewontin, and says that we're going to bring in the biological again, I don't think they would say that we're having recourse to essentialism, but another kind of realism, which doesn't necessarily imply essentialism. Theorists like those would want to problematize the biological by setting up a dialectic between social construction and the biological that doesn't necessarily imply essentialism. I think Cornel West brought that up in an interesting way by bringing in bodies and actual deaths that we could all identify with. And I think that this space—where we have this notion of socially constructed identities, but then all of the sudden we get something like death—suggests that there is some play of the natural that we can all identify with. I want to relate this to that point in Chantal Mouffe's discussion when she brought up something—which I disagree with, really—which was the notion of the common good as a vanishing point with which we could all identify. Although Professor

Mouffe declares herself an antiessentialist, I think that the positing of this vanishing point of an ideal is to project a sort of essence.

CHANTAL MOUFFE: I don't see how the common good as a vanishing point—as I say, as a horizon of meaning, as a discursive surface of inscription—can be an essence. The very idea of defending that is to say—this is my position—that we should not give up the idea of the common good completely, but rather we should think of it in terms which are nonessentialist. In French we say, *"visée de la politique,"* and I think that that's what I translated by vanishing point; I don't like that so much, but I think that *visée,* which never exists, or exists only as a horizon of meaning, cannot possibly be conceived of as an essence.

But in addition, I want to say something concerning what Judith said about strategic essentialism. Because I think theories of strategic essentialism build on a misunderstanding of certain critiques of essentialism and certainly Ernesto's and my critique of essentialism. Because they believe that if you are antiessentialist, then you are necessarily left with pure dissemination, with no identities at all. And they say—and I think rightly—that therefore you can't have any politics. But this is a misunderstanding of the antiessentialist critique, because such a critique doesn't issue into the position that therefore there is pure dissemination and no possibility of speaking of politically constructed categories. So why call that strategic essentialism? I don't think that term is very helpful.

JUDITH BUTLER: It's not my term.

CHANTAL MOUFFE: Perhaps not your term; but basically I think the position is the same, and it is a problematic understanding of what the essentialist critique implies.

CORNEL WEST: I'd like to make three quick points. One, when we use terms like essentialism and poststructuralist critiques, and so forth, we are operating on a certain level of discourse. It's the level of philosophical discourse; it has to do with justification and skeptical challenges to various forms of epistemic foundationalism. But it's very, very different from analysis or explanation. And a lot of times we conflate and confuse these and commit a category mistake. Essentialism had to do with certain notions of the *I* and the *ego* in consciousness, which already means that your discourse is predicated against a Cartesian backdrop. But if you begin with organisms and bodies, then the starting point is already called into question. If you have a body-subject, you have body-in-pleasure, you have bodies bumping against other bodies struggling for resources in order to stay alive before they die. That's different from Cartesian consciousness serving as a foundation. So that then, when you pull the foundations out from under them, you think you've done something radical. So the important point here is to try to situate the very philosophical discourse you're trying to undermine historically. The crucial role that class plays, for example—that's a kind of implicit response to what sister Joan has said—is that we have to begin with the fact that in 1991 there's been seventy-six billion dollars transferred from working people to the well-to-do. It's the most massive upward redistribution of wealth in the history of America. Now that has something to do with resources, something to do with the way identity politics is articulated, given this tremendous sense of desperation and despair among people who are victims of cutbacks and slowdowns and taxes taken out of their pockets. Now of course there's a cultural dimension. This is where poststructuralists can teach us much. But we have to begin with talk about resources and the way they are linked to cultural identities, the conditions under which Black identities are articulated, for example. Can you imagine the attempt to talk about the articulation of Black identities versus upper-class identities without talking about resources? It makes no sense. It's radically ahistorical. That doesn't mean it privileges Black identity; it simply means that when you talk about identity it's got to be linked to material conditions in terms of what kind of assets and resources people have. The same is true about the struggle over AIDS. Everyone knows that if there were the proper distribution of resources, Magic Johnson and millions of others around the world would be on the road to recovery. They just don't provide money for it because they don't give a damn. You can articulate your identity all you want; you need the damn resources in order to respond to the concrete problems of bodies in pain. So this is in no way an attempt to trash poststructuralism, but it is an attempt to circumscribe it. It's a tradition that teaches us much; it's part of the intellectual weaponry for freedom fighters; but it has its limitations too, and if we don't talk about the material resources, and bodies and land and labor and corporations, then we remain inscribed within a very, very narrow kind of discourse, one that chimes well with professional managerial space. Of course there's a politics of professional managerial space that's important, but it's got to be linked to something beyond it. In fact the massive redistribution of resources actually privileges us. Because who has benefited from this redistribution of wealth? Professional managers—executives and so forth. That's the kind of analysis that ought to be the starting point for any reflection about identity politics, and what some of the emancipatory politics are. Now it's unfair of me to say that and leave—another professional manager on the plane, you know. But I think that this is important in terms of this debate about identity politics and ways in which we can use different discourses to tease out crucial elements and not miss other elements from other discourses and traditions.

JUDITH BUTLER: I wanted briefly to respond to Cornel's remark, which is very impassioned and very persuasive. And yet, I want to suggest that the conditions and the resources under which identities are produced are also constantly in the process of being delimited. And some of those identities are not merely produced through delimitation, but also erased through delimitation. What is to count as a "resource"? What counts as a "condition"? If we look at how the FDA and the NIH take stock of their resources and decide which and how many of those resources are to be made available to deal with the AIDS epidemic on a national basis, then we see that there is a practice of delimitation within public policy with life-threatening consequences. When one looks for a resource, one must first have defined it as such. And Simon Watney reports that the most sociological research—the educational site which might be expected to delimit resources and enumerate priorities—is concerned with protecting health professionals, rather than tracking the spread of the disease and the communities it affects differentially. In other words, if what is being "produced" is the notion of a disease and the notion of a "saveable" or "worthy" life, then these are discursive acts which both produce and erase life. In other words, there is no jettisoning of the question of discourse or, for that matter, of poststructuralism, because AIDS has produced a crisis in discourse precisely at the moment at which the delimitation of "resources" has extremely important consequences for the production and the annihilation of "gay identity" in this country.

STANLEY ARONOWITZ: The class/knowledge problematic has disappeared, however. The knowledge problematic is there, but it's linked to language. And the class/knowledge problematic has got to be revived. We can't abandon it, we simply have to relativize it and not make it essentialist.

AUDIENCE: It's hard to bring up the question of resources as concretely as Cornel did, but I've been wanting to bring together two strains that have been emerging today. One is the important question that Andreas Huyssen brought up about reexamining nationalism as something the Left must do. You talked about this too, Stanley. And I notice that in the speakers who addressed that, there was an absence of attention to feminism. I also noticed that the feminist speakers tended to stay away from the international. I think of Cynthia Enlo's slogan, "The international is personal," as something that feminists have to remember. And in your formulation of the libidinal and imaginary power of nationalism, I think of Benedict Anderson, and his idea that Marxism has overlooked some of the power of nationalism. Anderson returns to things that we're born into, things—like nation, like family, like gender— which create some of the very strongest libidinal and imaginary fields. I wonder whether the feminists on the panel could talk about how we might begin to reclaim the discourse of nationalism for the Left, and by that I don't mean to revivify nationalism, because it's a new idea for me to think from anything but an antinationalist position. But I think if we're going to do that, we need to bring feminism and other discourses together and speak to each other on this point.

JOAN SCOTT: I guess my feeling is that, rather than spell out a positive program for feminism, I would like to claim feminism's traditional position—in relation to politics, to nationalism—as a critical one. That is, I think it's important to look at these questions, or for feminists to analyze what's going on at the national and the international level as well as locally, but it seems to me that it would be a mistake to launch now into a discussion of the positive role we could play in nation-building in a general way.

AUDIENCE: I didn't mean that.

JOAN SCOTT: But there is that dimension. There are feminists in South Africa who are very involved in talking about how a postapartheid society would be organized, and they are at once contributing to political discussions and providing that kind of critical foil that feminism necessarily provides to any discussions of liberal democracy. My argument would be that feminism is constituted both within and against liberal democracy, and that that's a position it ought to stay in—the sort of critical reader of, interlocutor of, what else is going on.

AUDIENCE: Someone brought up the polemic, whether the personal is political, whether the political is personal. I personally feel it's both. And looking at the panel, you have six men, three women, seven European and White. There are no voices of women of color. None of the speakers recognizes his or her own power position. Whether it's race or class or gender, there was no recognition that the people speaking here have certain privileges. As a matter of fact, one person said that it wasn't good for someone to speak about his personal life. But I think it's necessary to recognize where you're coming from. I think that when you don't raise issues like, "Why aren't there any women of color here?," you're participating in the exclusion. It's great to talk about how White men are fucking us over; but quite frankly Bush knows that he needs Clarence Thomas, Bush knows that he needs White women, and Bush knows that he needs women of color. So it's not just as simple as White men oppressing me. There's the whole question of speaking for. One person said that we should be able to speak for other people. Quite frankly, that argument, coming from people who are perceived to be my allies, makes me a little nervous, because when we talk about who should be able to speak for others, it's usually White women—White, straight women—and men. I don't happen to believe that everybody has the right to speak for everybody else. What I would like to hear from the panelists is, do they have any feelings about there being no women of color here? Have they thought about it during the entire day we've spent here? What do they think they will do next time they're invited to a panel and there are no women of color there?

ERNESTO LACLAU: I just want to say that I am Latin-American, not European.

JUDITH BUTLER: I think this is an important point, and I think this panel has tried to do something problematic. The point of this conference—if I'm right—was both to call into question identity politics, but also to recognize some of its enduring values. I believe that the woman who just spoke is asking us to think more about its values, and to think about the importance of having a woman of color address the question of identity, to be visible and vocal, and to be legitimated. And here I would add that it is not only the inclusion of a woman of color on the panel, but what does the exclusion say about the focus and project of the conference as a whole, and whether race and gender have been brought together in a central way? Although there are some important differences among the speakers today, there has also been the reconstitution of hegemony at the level of knowledge. I think this is true, and even while it is not fully Eurocentric, it is nevertheless weighted in that direction. So, yes, that makes me uncomfortable.

HOMI BHABHA: Could I just say that, as is obvious, I'm not a woman of color. But given that limitation, my talk not only foregrounded the question of race in very specific power situations, but also most of the texts I dealt with are actually by women of color. And I think that within that context, it was not done to make a symbolic point. It was done because of the immense importance of those works, as they actually make one rethink a number of issues to do with identity, history, culture. The question of having a woman of color on the panel is obviously a very important one—but I do want to say that the understanding of posing positions and posing questions and seeing the value of works is not limited either by one's disciplinary or gender boundary.

AUDIENCE: I appreciate that people quoted Spivak and brought up more . . .

HOMI BHABHA: That's not what I said, no, that's not what I said. My talk was not to do with quoting or citing. It was centrally about Sonia Sanchez, Walcott, Toni Morrison, because that work is immensely valuable and that happens to be work that comes from a certain perspective of gender as it interacts with history and language.

AUDIENCE: Fine. I believe that is so. But what I'm saying is that you're all invited here, I assume, in part in recognition that you have contributed to the issues at hand. But if there are no women of color here, the implication is that women of color have not. Gloria Anzaldúa, Michelle Wallace, bell hooks, are all people who have contributed substantially and are within train distance of this conference. I think it is important to talk about power and how much power is invested in you as speakers.

ELABORATIONS

Cornel West

The New Cultural Politics of Difference

In these last few years of the twentieth century, there is emerging a significant shift in the sensibilities and outlooks of critics and artists. In fact, I would go so far as to claim that a new kind of cultural worker is in the making, associated with a new politics of difference. These new forms of intellectual consciousness advance reconceptions of the vocation of critic and artist, attempting to undermine the prevailing disciplinary divisions of labor in the academy, museum, mass media and gallery networks, while preserving modes of critique within the ubiquitous commodification of culture in the global village. Distinctive features of the new cultural politics of difference are: to trash the monolithic and homogeneous in the name of diversity, multiplicity and heterogeneity; to reject the abstract, general and universal in light of the concrete, specific and particular; and to historicize, contextualize and pluralize by highlighting the contingent, provisional, variable, tentative, shifting and changing. Needless to say, these gestures are not new in the history of criticism or art, yet what makes them novel—along with the cultural politics they produce—is how and what constitutes difference; the weight and gravity it is given in representation; and the way in which highlighting issues like exterminism, empire, class, race, gender, sexual orientation, age, nation, nature and region at this historical moment acknowledges some discontinuity and disruption from previous forms of cultural critique. To put it bluntly, the new cultural politics of difference consists of creative responses to the precise circumstances of our present moment—especially those of marginalized First World agents who shun degraded self-representations, articulating instead their sense of the flow of history in light of the contemporary terrors, anxieties and fears of highly commercialized North Atlantic capitalist cultures (with their escalating xenophobias against people of color, Jews, women, gays, lesbians and the elderly). The thawing, yet still rigid, Second World ex-Communist cultures (with increasing nationalist revolts against the legacy of hegemonic party henchmen), and the diverse cultures of the majority of inhabitants on the globe smothered by international communication cartels and repressive postcolonial elites (sometimes in the name of Communism, as in Ethiopia), or starved by austere World Bank and IMF policies that subordinate them to the North (as in free-market capitalism in Chile), also locate vital areas of analysis in this new cultural terrain.

The new cultural politics of difference are neither simply oppositional in contesting the mainstream (or *male*stream) for inclusion, nor transgressive in the avant-gardist sense of shocking conventional bourgeois audiences. Rather, they are distinct articulations of talented (and usually privileged) contributors to culture who desire to align themselves with demoralized, demobilized, depoliticized and disorganized people in order to empower and enable social action and, if possible, to enlist collective insurgency for the expansion of freedom, democracy and individuality. This perspective impels these cultural critics and artists to reveal, as an integral component of their production, the very operations of power within their immediate work contexts that is, academy, museum, gallery, mass media. This strategy, however, also puts them in an inescapable double bind—while linking their activities to the fundamental structural overhaul of these institutions, they often remain financially dependent on them (so much for "independent" creation). For these critics of culture, theirs is a gesture that is simultaneously progressive *and* co-opted. Yet without social movement or political pressure from outside these institutions (extraparliamentary and extracurricular actions like the social movements of the recent past), transformation degenerates into mere accommodation or sheer stagnation, and the role of the "co-opted progressive"—no matter how fervent one's subversive rhetoric—is rendered more difficult. There can be no artistic breakthrough or social progress without some form of crisis in civilization—a crisis usually generated by organizations or collectivities that convince ordinary people to put their bodies and lives on the line. There is, of course, no guarantee that such pressure will yield the result one wants, but there is a guarantee that the status quo will remain or regress if no pressure is applied at all.

The new cultural politics of difference faces three basic challenges—intellectual, existential and political. The intellectual challenge—usually cast as methodological debate in these days in which academicist forms of expression have a monopoly on intellectual life—is how to think about representational practices in terms of history, culture and society. How does one understand, analyze and enact such practices today? An adequate answer to this question can be attempted only after one comes to terms with the insights and blindnesses of earlier attempts to grapple with the question in light of the evolving crisis in different histories, cultures and societies. I shall sketch a brief genealogy—a history that highlights the contingent origins and often ignoble outcomes—of exemplary critical responses to the question. This genealogy sets forth a historical framework that characterizes the rich yet deeply flawed Eurocentric traditions which the new cultural politics of difference build upon, yet go beyond.

THE INTELLECTUAL CHALLENGE

An appropriate starting point is the ambiguous legacy of the Age of Europe. Between 1492 and 1945, European breakthroughs in oceanic transportation, agricultural production, state consolidation, bureaucratization, industrialization, urbanization and imperial dominion shaped the makings of the modern world. Precious ideals like the dignity of persons (individuality) or the popular accountability of institutions (democracy) were unleashed around the world. Powerful critiques of illegitimate authorities—of the Protestant Reformation against the Roman Catholic Church, the Enlightenment against state churches, liberal movements against absolutist states and feudal guild constraints, workers against managerial subordination, people of color and Jews against White and gentile supremacist decrees, gays and lesbians against homophobic sanctions—were fanned and fuelled by these precious ideals refined within the crucible of the Age of Europe. Yet the discrepancy between sterling rhetoric and lived reality, glowing principles and actual practices loomed large.

By the last European century—the last epoch in which European domination of most of the globe was uncontested and unchallenged in a substantive way—a new world seemed to be stirring. At the height of England's reign as the major imperial European power, its exemplary cultural critic, Matthew Arnold, painfully observed in his "Stanzas From the Grand Chartreuse" that he felt some sense of "wandering between two worlds, one dead / the other powerless to be born." Following his Burkean sensibilities of cautious reform and fear of anarchy, Arnold acknowledged that the old glue—religion—that had tenuously and often unsuccessfully held together the ailing European regimes could not do so in the mid-nineteenth century. Like Alexis de Tocqueville in France, Arnold saw that the democratic temper was the wave of the future. So he proposed a new conception of culture—a secular, humanistic one—that could play an integrative role in cementing and stabilizing an emerging bourgeois civil society and imperial state. His famous castigation of the immobilizing materialism of the declining aristocracy, the vulgar philistinism of the emerging middle classes and the latent explosiveness of the working-class majority was motivated by a desire to create new forms of cultural legitimacy, authority and order in a rapidly changing moment in nineteenth-century Europe.

For Arnold, (in *Culture and Anarchy*, 1869) this new conception of culture:

> seeks to do away with classes; to make the best that has been thought and known in the world current everywhere; to make all men live in an atmosphere of sweetness and light. . . .
>
> This is the *social idea* and the men of culture are the true apostles of equality. The great men of culture are those who have had a passion for diffusing, for making prevail, for carrying from one end of society to the other, the best knowledge, the best ideas of their time, who have laboured to divest knowledge of all that was harsh, uncouth, difficult, abstract, professional, exclusive; to humanize it, to make it efficient outside the clique of the cultivated and learned, yet still retaining the best knowledge and thought of the time, and a true source, therefore, of sweetness and light.

As an organic intellectual of an emergent middle class—as the inspector of schools in an expanding educational bureaucracy, Professor of Poetry at

Oxford (the first noncleric and the first to lecture in English rather than Latin) and an active participant in a thriving magazine network—Arnold defined and defended a new secular culture of critical discourse. For him, this discursive strategy would be lodged in the educational and periodical apparatuses of modern societies as they contained and incorporated the frightening threats of an arrogant aristocracy and especially of an "anarchic" working-class majority. His ideals of disinterested, dispassionate and objective inquiry would regulate this new secular cultural production, and his justifications for the use of state power to quell any threats to the survival and security of this culture were widely accepted. He aptly noted, "Through culture seems to lie our way, not only to perfection, but even to safety."

This sentence is revealing in two ways. First, it refers to "our way" without explicitly acknowledging who constitutes the "we." This move is symptomatic among many bourgeois, male, Eurocentric critics whose universalizing gestures exclude (by guarding a silence around) or explicitly degrade women and peoples of color. Second, the sentence links culture to safety—presumably the safety of the "we" against the barbaric threats of the "them," that is, those viewed as different in some debased manner. Needless to say, Arnold's negative attitudes toward British working-class people, women and especially Indians and Jamaicans in the Empire clarify why he conceives of culture as, in part, a weapon for bourgeois, male, European "safety."

For Arnold, the best of the Age of Europe—modeled on a mythological mélange of Periclean Athens, late Republican/early Imperial Rome and Elizabethan England—could be promoted only if there was an interlocking affiliation among the emerging middle classes, a homogenizing of cultural discourse in the educational and university networks, and a state advanced enough in its policing techniques to safeguard it. The candidates for participation and legitimation in this grand endeavor of cultural renewal and revision would be detached intellectuals willing to shed their parochialism, provincialism and class-bound identities for Arnold's middle-class-skewed project: "Aliens, if we may so call them—persons who are mainly led, not by their class spirit, but by a general *humane* spirit, by the love of human perfection." Needless to say, this Arnoldian perspective still informs much of the academic practices and secular cultural attitudes today—dominant views about the canon, admission procedures and collective self-definitions of intellectuals. Yet Arnold's project was disrupted by the collapse of nineteenth-century Europe—World War I. This unprecedented war brought to the surface the crucial role and violent potential not of the masses Arnold feared but of the state he heralded. Upon the ashes of this wasteland of human carnage—some of it the civilian European population—T.S. Eliot emerged as the grand cultural spokesman.

Eliot's project of reconstituting and reconceiving European highbrow culture—and thereby regulating critical and artistic practices—after the internal collapse of imperial Europe can be viewed as a response to the probing question posed by Paul Valéry in "The Crisis of the Spirit" after World War I:

> This Europe, will it become *what it is in reality*, i.e., a little cape of the Asiatic continent? Or will this Europe remain rather what it seems, i.e., the priceless part of the whole earth, the pearl of the globe, the brain of a vast body?

Eliot's image of Europe as a wasteland, a culture of fragments with no cementing center, predominated in postwar Europe. And though his early poetic practices were more radical, open and international than his Eurocentric criticism, Eliot posed a return to and revision of tradition as the only way of regaining European cultural order and political stability. For Eliot, contemporary history had become, as James Joyce's Stephen declared in *Ulysses* (1922), "a nightmare from which he was trying to awake"—"an immense panorama of futility and anarchy" as Eliot put it in his renowned review of Joyce's modernist masterpiece. In his influential essay, "Tradition and the Individual Talent," (1919) Eliot stated:

> Yet if the only form of tradition, of handing down, consisted in following the ways of the immediate generation before us in a blind or timid adherence to its successes, "tradition" should positively be discouraged. We have seen many such simple currents soon lost in the sand; and novelty is better than repetition. Tradition is a matter of much wider significance. It cannot be inherited, and if you want it you must attain it by great labour.

Eliot's fecund notion of tradition is significant, in that it promotes a historicist sensibility in artistic practice and cultural reflection. This historicist sensibility—regulated in Eliot's case by a reactionary politics—produced a powerful assault on existing literary canons (in which, for example, Romantic poets were displaced by the Metaphysical and Symbolist ones) and unrelenting attacks on modern Western civilization (such as the liberal ideas of democracy, equality and freedom). Like Arnold's notion of culture, Eliot's idea of tradition was part of his intellectual arsenal, to be used in the battles raging in European cultures and societies.

Eliot found this tradition in the Church of England, to which he converted in 1927. Here was a tradition that left room for his Catholic cast of mind, Calvinistic heritage, puritanical temperament and rebullient patriotism for the old American South (the place of his upbringing). Like Arnold, Eliot was obsessed with the idea of civilization and the horror of barbarism (echoes of Joseph Conrad's Kurtz in *Heart of Darkness*) or more pointedly, the notion of the decline and decay of European civilization. With the advent of World War II, Eliot's obsession became a reality. Again unprecedented human carnage (fifty million dead)—including an indescribable genocidal attack on Jewish people—throughout Europe as well as around the globe, put the last nail in the coffin of the Age of Europe. After 1945, Europe consisted of a devastated and divided continent, crippled by a humiliating dependency on and deference to the USA and USSR.

The second historical coordinate of my genealogy is the emergence of the USA as *the* world power. The USA was unprepared for world power status. However, with the recovery of Stalin's Russia (after losing twenty million dead), the USA felt compelled to make its presence felt around the globe. Then with the Marshall Plan to strengthen Europe against Russian influence (and provide new markets for US products), the 1948 Russian takeover of Czechoslovakia, the 1948 Berlin blockade, the 1950 beginning of the Korean War and the 1952 establishment of NATO forces in Europe, it seemed clear that there was no escape from world power obligations.

The post-World War II era in the USA, or the first decades of what Henry Luce envisioned as "The American Century," was not only a period of incredible economic expansion but of active cultural ferment. In the classical Fordist formula, mass production required mass consumption. With unchallenged hegemony in the capitalist world, the USA took economic growth for granted. Next to exercising its crude, anti-communist, McCarthyist obsessions, buying commodities became the primary act of civic virtue for many American citizens at this time. The creation of a mass middle class—a prosperous working class with a bourgeois identity—was countered by the first major emergence of subcultures of American non-WASP intellectuals: the so-called New York intellectuals in criticism, the Abstract Expressionists in painting and the bebop artists in jazz music. This emergence signaled a vital challenge to an American, male, WASP elite loyal to an older and eroding European culture.

The first significant blow was dealt when assimilated Jewish-Americans entered the higher echelons of the cultural apparatuses (academy, museums, galleries, mass media). Lionel Trilling is an emblematic figure. This Jewish entrée into the anti-Semitic and patriarchal critical discourse of the exclusive institutions of American culture initiated the slow but sure undoing of the male WASP cultural hegemony and homogeneity. Lionel Trilling's project was to appropriate Matthew Arnold for his own political and cultural purposes—thereby unraveling the old male WASP consensus, while erecting a new, post-World War II, liberal, academic consensus around Cold War, anti-Communist renditions of the values of complexity, difficulty, variousness and modulation. In addition, the postwar boom laid the basis for intense professionalization and specialization in expanding institutions of higher education—especially in the natural sciences that were compelled to somehow respond to Russia's successful ventures in space. Humanistic scholars found themselves searching for new methodologies that could buttress self-images of rigor and scientific seriousness. For example, the close reading techniques of New Criticism (severed from their conservative, organicist, anti-industrialist ideological roots), the logical precision of reasoning in analytic philosophy and the jargon of Parsonian structural-functionalism in sociology helped create such self-images. Yet towering cultural critics like C. Wright Mills, W.E.B. Du Bois, Richard Hofstadter, Margaret Mead and Dwight MacDonald bucked the tide. This suspicion of the academicization of knowledge is expressed in Trilling's well-known essay "On the Teaching of Modern Literature":

Can we not say that, when modern literature is brought into the classroom, the subject being taught is betrayed by the pedagogy of the subject? We have to ask ourselves whether in our day too much does not come within the purview of the academy. More and more, as the universities liberalize themselves, turn their beneficent imperialistic gaze upon what is called life itself, the feeling grows among our educated classes that little can be experienced unless it is validated by some established intellectual discipline. . . .

Trilling laments the fact that university instruction often quiets and domesticates radical and subversive works of art, turning them into objects "of merely habitual regard." This process of "the socialization of the anti-social, or the acculturation of the anti-cultural, or the legitimization of the subversive" leads Trilling to "question whether in our culture the study of literature is any longer a suitable means for developing and refining the intelligence." Trilling asks this question not in the spirit of denigrating and devaluing the academy but rather in the spirit of highlighting the possible failure of an Arnoldian conception of culture to contain what he perceives as the philistine and anarchic alternatives becoming more and more available to students of the sixties—namely, mass culture and radical politics.

This threat is partly associated with the third historical coordinate of my genealogy—the decolonization of the Third World. It is crucial to recognize the importance of this world-historical process if one wants to grasp the significance of the end of the Age of Europe and the emergence of the USA as a world power. With the first defeat of a Western nation by a non-Western nation—in Japan's victory over Russia (1905), revolutions in Persia (1905), Turkey (1908), China (1912), Mexico (1911–12) and much later the independence of India (1947) and China (1948) and the triumph of Ghana (1957)—the actuality of a decolonized globe loomed large. Born of violent struggle, consciousness-raising and the reconstruction of identities, decolonization simultaneously brings with it new perspectives on that long-festering underside of the Age of Europe (of which colonial domination represents the *costs* of "progress," "order" and "culture"), as well as requiring new readings of the economic boom in the USA (wherein the Black, Brown, Yellow, Red, female, elderly, gay, lesbian and White working class live the same *costs* as cheap labor at home as well as in US-dominated Latin American and Pacific Rim markets).

The impetuous ferocity and moral outrage that motors the decolonization process is best captured by Frantz Fanon in *The Wretched of the Earth* (1961):

Decolonization, which sets out to change the order of the world, is obviously, a program of complete disorder. . . . Decolonization is the meeting of two forces, opposed to each other by their very nature, which in fact owe their originality to that sort of substantification which results from and is nourished by the situation in the colonies. Their first encounter was marked by violence and their existence together—that is to say the exploitation of the native by the settler—was carried on by dint of a great array of bayonets and cannons. . . .

In decolonization, there is therefore the need of a complete calling in question of the colonial situation. If we wish to describe it precisely, we might find it in the well-known words: "The last shall be first and the first last." Decolonization is the putting into practice of this sentence.

The naked truth of decolonization evokes for us the searing bullets and bloodstained knives which emanate from it. For if the last shall be first, this will only come to pass after a murderous and decisive struggle between the two protagonists.

Fanon's strong words, though excessively Manichaean, still describe the feelings and thoughts between the occupying British Army and colonized Irish in Northern Ireland, the occupying Israeli Army and subjugated Palestinians on the West Bank and Gaza Strip, the South African Army and oppressed Black South Africans in the townships, the Japanese police and Koreans living in Japan, the Russian Army and subordinated Armenians and others in the Southern and Eastern USSR. His words also partly invoke the sense many Black Americans have toward police departments in urban centers. In other words, Fanon is articulating century-long, heartfelt, human responses to being degraded and despised, hated and hunted, oppressed and exploited, marginalized and dehumanized at the hands of powerful, xenophobic, European, American, Russian and Japanese imperial countries.

During the late fifties, sixties and early seventies in the USA, these decolonized sensibilities fanned and fueled the Civil Rights and Black Power movements, as well as the student antiwar, feminist, gray, brown, gay, and lesbian movements. In this period we witnessed the shattering of male, WASP, cultural homogeneity and the collapse of the short-lived liberal consensus. The inclusion of African-Americans, Latino/a-Americans, Asian-Americans, Native Americans and American women into the culture

Cornel West

of critical discourse yielded intense intellectual polemics and inescapable ideological polarization that focused principally on the exclusions, silences and blindnesses of male, WASP, cultural homogeneity and its concomitant Arnoldian notions of the canon.

In addition, these critiques promoted three crucial processes that affected intellectual life in the country. First is the appropriation of the theories of postwar Europe—especially the work of the Frankfurt school (Marcuse, Adorno, Horkheimer), French/Italian Marxisms (Sartre, Althusser, Lefebvre, Gramsci), structuralisms (Lévi-Strauss, Todorov) and poststructuralisms (Deleuze, Derrida, Foucault). These diverse and disparate theories—all preoccupied with keeping alive radical projects after the end of the Age of Europe—tend to fuse versions of transgressive European modernisms with Marxist or post-Marxist Left politics and unanimously shun the term "postmodernism." Second, there is the recovery and revisioning of American history in light of the struggles of White male workers, women, African-Americans, Native Americans, Latino/a-Americans, gays and lesbians. Third is the impact of forms of popular culture, such as television, film, music videos and even sports, on highbrow literature culture. The Black-based hip-hop culture of youth around the world is one grand example.

After 1973, with the crisis in the international world economy, America's slump in productivity, the challenge of OPEC nations to the North Atlantic monopoly of oil production, the increasing competition in high-tech sectors of the economy from Japan and West Germany and the growing fragility of the international debt structure, the USA entered a period of waning self-confidence (compounded by Watergate), and a nearly contracting economy. As the standards of living for the middle classes declined, owing to runaway inflation, and the quality of living fell for most, due to escalating unemployment, underemployment and crime, religious and secular neoconservatism emerged with power and potency. This fusion of fervent neonationalism, traditional cultural values and "free-market" policies served as the groundwork for the Reagan-Bush era.

The ambiguous legacies of the European Age, American preeminence and decolonization continue to haunt our postmodern moment as we come to terms with both the European, American, Japanese, Soviet, and Third World *crimes against* and *contributions to* humanity. The plight of Africans in the New World can be instructive in this regard.

By 1914 European maritime empires had dominion over more than half of the land and a third of the peoples in the world—almost seventy-two million square kilometers of territory and more than 560 million people under colonial rule. Needless to say, this European control included brutal enslavement, institutional terrorism and cultural degradation of Black diaspora people. The death of roughly seventy-five million Africans during the centuries-long transatlantic slave trade is but one reminder, among others, of the assault on Black humanity. The Black diaspora condition of New World servitude—in which they were viewed as mere commodities with production value, who had no proper legal status, social standing or public worth—can be characterized as, following Orlando Patterson, natal alienation. This state of perpetual and inheritable domination that diaspora Africans had at birth produced the *modern Black diaspora problematic of invisibility and namelessness.* White-supremacist practices—enacted under the auspices of the prestigious cultural authorities of the churches, printed media and scientific academics—promoted Black inferiority and constituted the European background against which Black diaspora struggles for identity, dignity (self-confidence, self-respect, self-esteem) and material resources took place.

An inescapable aspect of this struggle was that the Black diaspora peoples' quest for validation and recognition occurred on the ideological, social and cultural terrains of other non-Black peoples. White-supremacist assaults on Black intelligence, ability, beauty and character required persistent Black efforts to hold self-doubt, self-contempt and even self-hatred at bay. Selective appropriation, incorporation and rearticulation of European ideologies, cultures and institutions alongside an African heritage—a heritage more or less confined to linguistic innovation in rhetorical practices, stylizations of the body in forms of occupying an alien social space (hairstyles, ways of walking, standing, hand expressions, talking) and means of constituting and sustaining camaraderie and community (for instance, antiphonal, call-and-response styles, rhythmic repetition, risk-ridden syncopation in spectacular modes in musical and rhetorical expressions)—were some of the strategies employed.

The modern Black diaspora problematic of invisibility and namelessness can be understood as the condition of *relative lack of Black power to represent themselves to themselves and others as complex human beings, and thereby to contest the bombardment of negative, degrading stereotypes put forward by White-supremacist*

Cornel West

ideologies. The initial Black response to being caught in this whirlwind of Europeanization was to resist the misrepresentation and caricature of the terms set by uncontested non-Black norms and models and fight for self-representation and recognition. Every modern Black person, especially cultural disseminators, encounters this problematic of invisibility and namelessness. The initial Black diaspora response was a mode of resistance that was *moralistic in content* and *communal in character.* That is, the fight for representation and recognition highlighted moral judgments regarding Black "positive" images over and against White-supremacist White stereotypes. These images "re-presented" monolithic and homogeneous Black communities, in a way that could displace past misrepresentations of these communities. Stuart Hall has talked about these responses as attempts to change "the relations of representation."

These courageous yet limited Black efforts to combat racist cultural practices uncritically accepted non-Black conventions and standards in two ways. First, they proceeded in an *assimilationist manner* that set out to show that Black people were really like White people—thereby eliding differences (in history, culture) between Whites and Blacks. Black specificity and particularity was thus banished in order to gain White acceptance and approval. Second, these Black responses rested upon a *homogenizing impulse* that assumed that all Black people were really alike—hence obliterating differences (class, gender, region, sexual orientation) between Black peoples. I submit that there are elements of truth in both claims, yet the conclusions are unwarranted, owing to the basic fact that non-Black paradigms set the terms of the replies.

The insight in the first claim is that Blacks and Whites are in some important sense alike—that is, in their positive capacities for human sympathy, moral sacrifice, service to others, intelligence and beauty, or negatively, in their capacity for cruelty. Yet the common humanity they share is jettisoned when the claim is cast in an assimilationist manner that subordinates Black particularity to a false universalism, that is, non-Black rubrics or prototypes. Similarly, the insight in the second claim is that all Blacks are in some significant sense "in the same boat"—that is, subject to White-supremacist abuse. Yet this common condition is stretched too far when viewed in a *homogenizing* way that overlooks how racist treatment vastly differs owing to class, gender, sexual orientation, nation, region, hue and age.

The moralistic and communal aspects of the initial Black diaspora responses to social and psychic erasure were not simply cast into simplistic binary oppositions of positive/negative, good/bad images that privileged the first term in light of a White norm so that Black efforts remained inscribed within the very logic that dehumanized them. They were further complicated by the fact that these responses were also advanced principally by anxiety-ridden, middle-class, Black intellectuals (predominantly male and heterosexual), grappling with their sense of double-consciousness— namely their own crisis of identity, agency and audience—caught between a quest for White approval and acceptance and an endeavor to overcome the internalized association of Blackness with inferiority. And I suggest that these complex anxieties of modern, Black, diaspora intellectuals partly motivate the two major arguments that ground the assimilationist moralism and homogeneous communalism just outlined.

Kobena Mercer has talked about these two arguments as the *reflectionist* and the *social engineering* arguments. The reflectionist argument holds that the fight for Black representation and recognition must reflect or mirror the real Black community, not simply the negative and depressing representations of it. The social engineering argument claims that since any form of representation is constructed—that is, selective in light of broader aims— Black representation (especially given the difficulty of Blacks gaining access to positions of power to produce any Black imagery) should offer positive images of themselves in order to inspire achievement among young Black people, thereby countering racist stereotypes. The hidden assumption of both arguments is that we have unmediated access to what the "real Black community" is and what "positive images" are. In short, these arguments presuppose the very phenomena to be interrogated, and thereby foreclose the very issues that should serve as the subject matter to be investigated.

Any notions of "the real Black community" and "positive images" are value-laden, socially loaded and ideologically charged. To pursue this discussion is to call into question the possibility of such an uncontested consensus regarding them. Stuart Hall has rightly called this encounter "the end of innocence or the end of the innocent notion of the essential Black subject . . . the recognition that 'Black' is essentially a politically and culturally *constructed* category." This recognition—more and more pervasive among the postmodern Black diaspora intelligentsia—is facilitated in part by the slow but sure dissolution of the European Age's maritime empires, and the unleashing of new political possibilities and cultural articulations among ex-colonialized peoples across the globe.

One crucial lesson of this decolonization process remains the manner in which most Third World, authoritarian, bureaucratic elites deploy essentialist rhetorics about "homogeneous national communities" and "positive images" in order to repress and regiment their diverse and heterogeneous populations. Yet in the diaspora, especially among First World countries, this critique has emerged not so much from the Black male component of the Left but rather from the Black women's movement. The decisive push of postmodern Black intellectuals toward a new cultural politics of difference has been made by the powerful critiques and constructive explorations of Black diaspora women (for example, Toni Morrison). The coffin used to bury the innocent notion of the essential Black subject was nailed shut with the termination of the Black male monopoly on the construction of the Black subject. In this regard, the Black, diaspora, womanist critique has had a greater impact than the critiques that highlight exclusively class, empire, age, sexual orientation or nature.

This decisive push toward the end of Black innocence—though prefigured in various degrees in the best moments of W.E.B. Du Bois, Anna Cooper, C.L.R. James, James Baldwin, Claudia Jones, the later Malcolm X, Frantz Fanon, Amiri Baraka and others—forces Black diaspora cultural workers to encounter what Hall has called the "politics of representation." The main aim now is not simply access to representation in order to produce positive images of homogeneous communities—though broader access remains a practical and political problem. Nor is the primary goal here that of contesting stereotypes—though contestation remains a significant though limited venture. Following the model of the Black diaspora traditions of music, athletics and rhetoric, Black cultural workers must constitute and sustain discursive and institutional networks that deconstruct earlier modern Black strategies for identity formation, demystify power relations that incorporate class, patriarchal and homophobic biases, and construct more multivalent and multidimensional responses that articulate the complexity and diversity of Black practices in the modern and postmodern world.

Furthermore, Black cultural workers must investigate and interrogate the other of Blackness Whiteness. One cannot deconstruct the binary oppositional logic of images of Blackness without extending it to the contrary condition of Blackness/Whiteness itself. However, a mere dismantling will not do—for the very notion of a deconstructive social theory is oxymoronic. Yet social theory is what is needed to examine and *explain* the historically specific ways in which "Whiteness" is a politically constructed category parasitic on "Blackness," and thereby to conceive of the profoundly hybrid character of what we mean by "race," "ethnicity" and "nationality." For instance, European immigrants arrived on American shores perceiving themselves as "Irish," "Sicilian," "Lithuanian" and so on. They had to learn that they were "White" principally by adopting an American discourse of positively valued Whiteness and negatively charged Blackness. This process by which people define themselves physically, socially, sexually and even politically in terms of Whiteness or Blackness has much bearing not only on constructed notions of race and ethnicity but also on how we understand the changing character of US nationalities. And given the Americanization of the world, especially in the sphere of mass culture, such inquiries—encouraged by the new cultural politics of difference—raise critical issues of "hybridity," "exilic status" and "identity" on an international scale. Needless to say, these inquiries must traverse those of "male/female," "colonizer/colonized," "heterosexual/homosexual" and others, as well.

In light of this brief sketch of the emergence of our present crisis—and the turn toward history and difference in cultural work—four major historicist forms of theoretical activity provide resources for how we understand, analyze and enact our representational practices: Heideggerian *destruction* of the Western metaphysical tradition, Derridean *deconstruction* of the Western philosophical tradition, Rortian *demythologization* of the Western intellectual tradition and Marxist, Foucaultian, feminist, antiracist or antihomophobic *demystification* of Western cultural and artistic conventions.

Despite his abominable association with the Nazis, Martin Heidegger's project is useful in that it discloses the suppression of temporality and historicity in the dominant metaphysical systems of the West from Plato to Rudolph Carnap. This is noteworthy in that it forces one to understand philosophy's representational discourses as thoroughly historical phenomena. Hence, they should be viewed with skepticism, as they are often flights from the specific, concrete, practical and particular. The major problem with Heidegger's project—as noted by his neo-Marxist student, Herbert Marcuse—is that he views history in terms of fate, heritage and destiny. He dramatizes the past, and present as if it were a Greek tragedy with no tools of social analyses to relate cultural work to institutions and structures or antecedent forms and styles.

Jacques Derrida's version of deconstruction is one of the most influential schools of thought among young academic critics. It is salutary in that it focuses on the political power of rhetorical operations—of tropes and metaphors in binary oppositions such as white/black, good/bad, male/female, machine/nature, ruler/ruled, reality/appearance—showing how these operations sustain hierarchical worldviews by devaluing the second terms as something subsumed under the first. Most of the controversy about Derrida's project revolves around this austere epistemic doubt that unsettles binary oppositions while undermining any determinate meaning of a text, that is, book, art object, performance, building. Yet his views about skepticism are no more alarming than those of David Hume, Ludwig Wittgenstein or Stanley Cavell. He simply revels in it for transgressive purposes, whereas others provide us with ways to dissolve, sidestep or cope with skepticism. None, however, slide down the slippery, crypto-Nietzschean slope of sophomoric relativism as alleged by old-style humanists, be they Platonists, Kantians or Arnoldians.

The major shortcoming of Derrida's deconstructive project is that it puts a premium on a sophisticated ironic consciousness that tends to preclude and foreclose analyses that guide action with purpose. And given Derrida's own status as an Algerian-born, Jewish leftist marginalized by a hostile French academic establishment (quite different from his reception by the youth in the American academic establishment), the sense of political impotence and hesitation regarding the efficacy of moral action is understandable—but not justifiable. His works and those of his followers too often become rather monotonous, Johnny-one-note rhetorical readings that disassemble texts with little attention to the effects and consequences these dismantlings have in relation to the operations of military, economic and social powers.

Richard Rorty's neopragmatic project of demythologization is insightful in that it provides descriptive mappings of the transient metaphors—especially the ocular and specular ones—that regulate some of the fundamental dynamics in the construction of self-descriptions dominant in highbrow European and American philosophy. His perspective is instructive because it discloses the crucial role of narrative as the background for rational exchange and critical conversation. To put it crudely, Rorty shows why we should speak not of History, but histories, not of Reason, but historically

constituted forms of rationality, not of Criticism or Art, but of socially constructed notions of criticism and art—all linked but not reducible to political purposes, material interests and cultural prejudices.

Rorty's project nonetheless leaves one wanting, owing to its distrust of
social analytical explanation. Similar to the dazzling new historicism of
Stephen Greenblatt, Louis Montrose and Catherine Gallagher—inspired by
the subtle symbolic-cum-textual anthropology of Clifford Geertz and the
powerful discursive materialism of Michel Foucault—Rorty gives us mappings and descriptions with no explanatory accounts for change and conflict. In this way, he gives us an aestheticized version of historicism in which
the provisional and variable are celebrated at the expense of highlighting
who gains, loses or bears what costs.

Demystification is the most illuminating mode of theoretical inquiry for
those who promote the new cultural politics of difference. Social structural
analyses of empire, exterminism, class, race, gender, nature, age, sexual orientation, nation and region are the springboards—though not landing
grounds—for the most desirable forms of critical practice that take history
(and herstory) seriously. Demystification tries to keep track of the complex
dynamics of institutional and other related power structures in order to dis-
close options and alternatives for transformative praxis; it also attempts to
grasp the way in which representational strategies are creative responses to
novel circumstances and conditions. In this way, the central role of human
agency (always enacted under circumstances not of one's choosing)—be it
in the critic, artist or constituency and audience—is accented.

I call demystificatory criticism "prophetic criticism"—the approach
appropriate for the new cultural politics of difference—because while it
begins with social structural analyses it also makes explicit its moral and
political aims. It is partisan, partial, engaged and crisis-centered, yet always
keeps open a skeptical eye to avoid dogmatic traps, premature closures, formulaic formulations or rigid conclusions. In addition to social structural
analyses, moral and political judgments and sheer critical consciousness,
there indeed is evaluation. Yet the aim of this evaluation is neither to pit
art objects against one another like racehorses nor to create eternal canons
that dull, discourage or even dwarf contemporary achievements. We listen
to Ludwig Beethoven, Charlie Parker, Luciano Pavarotti, Laurie Anderson,
Sarah Vaughan, Stevie Wonder or Kathleen Battle, read William Shakespeare, Anton Chekhov, Ralph Ellison, Doris Lessing, Thomas Pynchon,

Toni Morrison or Gabriel García Márquez, see works of Pablo Picasso, Ingmar Bergman, Le Corbusier, Martin Puryear, Barbara Kruger, Spike Lee, Frank Gehry or Howardena Pindell—not in order to undergird bureaucratic assents or enliven cocktail party conversations, but rather to be summoned by the styles they deploy for their profound insight, pleasures and challenges. Yet all evaluation—including a delight in Eliot's poetry despite his reactionary politics, or a love of Zora Neale Hurston's novels despite her Republican Party affiliations—is inseparable from, though not identical or reducible to, social structural analyses, moral and political judgments and the workings of a curious critical consciousness.

The deadly traps of demystification—and any form of prophetic criticism—are those of reductionism, be it of the sociological, psychological or historical sort. By reductionism I mean either one-factor analyses (that is, crude Marxisms, feminisms, racialisms and so on) that yield a one-dimensional functionalism, or a hypersubtle analytical perspective that loses touch with the specificity of an artwork's form and the context of its reception. Few cultural workers of whatever stripe can walk the tightrope between the Scylla of reductionism and the Charybdis of aestheticism—yet demystificatory (or prophetic) critics must.

THE EXISTENTIAL CHALLENGE

The existential challenge to the new cultural politics of difference can be stated simply: how does one acquire the resources to survive and the cultural capital to thrive as a critic or artist? By cultural capital (Pierre Bourdieu's term), I mean not only the high-quality skills required to engage in critical practices but, more important, the self-confidence, discipline and perseverance necessary for success without an undue reliance on the mainstream for approval and acceptance. This challenge holds for all prophetic critics, yet it is especially difficult for those of color. The widespread, modern, European denial of the intelligence, ability, beauty and character of people of color puts a tremendous burden on critics and artists of color to "prove" themselves in light of norms and models set by White elites whose own heritage devalued and dehumanized them. In short, in the court of criticism and art—or any matters regarding the life of the mind—people of color are guilty, that is, not expected to meet standards of intellectual achievement, until "proven" innocent, that is, acceptable to "us."

This is more a structural dilemma than a matter of personal attitudes. The profoundly racist and sexist heritage of the European Age has bequeathed to us a set of deeply ingrained perceptions about people of color including, of course, the self-perceptions that people of color bring. It is not surprising that most intellectuals of color in the past exerted much of their energies and efforts to gain acceptance and approval by "White normative gazes." The new cultural politics of difference advises critics and artists of color to put aside this mode of mental bondage, thereby freeing themselves both to interrogate the ways in which they are bound by certain conventions and to learn from and build on these very norms and models. One hallmark of wisdom in the context of any struggle is to avoid knee-jerk rejection and uncritical acceptance.

Self-confidence, discipline and perseverance are not ends in themselves. Rather they are the necessary stuff of which enabling criticism and self-criticism are made. Notwithstanding inescapable jealousies, insecurities and anxieties, one telling characteristic of critics and artists of color linked to the new prophetic criticism should be their capacity for and promotion of relentless criticism and self-criticism—be it the normative paradigms of their White colleagues that tend to leave out considerations of empire, race, gender and sexual orientation, or the damaging dogmas about the homogeneous character of communities of color.

There are four basic options for people of color interested in representation—if they are to survive and thrive as serious practitioners of their craft. First, there is the Booker T. Temptation, namely the individual preoccupation with the mainstream and its legitimizing power. Most critics and artists of color try to bite this bait. It is nearly unavoidable, yet few succeed in a substantive manner. It is no accident that the most creative and profound among them—especially those with staying power beyond mere flashes in the pan to satisfy faddish tokenism—are usually marginal to the mainstream. Even the pervasive professionalization of cultural practitioners of color in the past few decades has not produced towering figures who reside within the established White patronage system that bestows the rewards and prestige for chosen contributions to American society.

It certainly helps to have some trustworthy allies within this system, yet most of those who enter and remain tend to lose much of their creativity, diffuse their prophetic energy and dilute their critiques. Still, it is unrealistic for creative people of color to think they can sidestep the White patronage system. And though there are indeed some White allies conscious of the tremendous need to rethink identity politics, it is naive to think that being comfortably nestled within this very same system—even if one can be a patron to others—does not affect one's work, one's outlook and, most important, one's soul.

The second option is the Talented Tenth Seduction, namely, a move toward arrogant group insularity. This alternative has a limited function—to preserve one's sanity and sense of self as one copes with the mainstream. Yet it is, at best, a transitional and transient activity. If it becomes a permanent option it is self-defeating, in that it usually reinforces the very inferior complexes promoted by the subtly racist mainstream. Hence, it tends to revel in a parochialism and encourage a narrow radialist and chauvinistic outlook.

The third strategy is the Go-It-Alone option. This is an extreme rejectionist perspective that shuns the mainstream and group insularity. Almost every critic and artist of color contemplates or enacts this option at some time in their pilgrimage. It is healthy in that it reflects the presence of independent, critical and skeptical sensibilities toward perceived constraints on one's creativity. Yet it is, in the end, difficult if not impossible to sustain if one is to grow, develop and mature intellectually; as some semblance of dialogue with a community is necessary for almost any creative practice.

The most desirable option for people of color who promote the new cultural politics of difference is to be a critical organic catalyst. By this I mean a person who stays attuned to the best of what the mainstream has to offer—its paradigms, viewpoints and methods—yet maintains a grounding in affirming and enabling subcultures of criticism. Prophetic critics and artists of color should be exemplars of what it means to be intellectual freedom-fighters, that is, cultural workers who simultaneously position themselves within (or alongside) the mainstream while clearly aligned with groups who vow to keep alive potent traditions of critique and resistance. In this regard, one can take clues from the great musicians or preachers of color who are open to the best of what other traditions offer, yet are rooted in nourishing subcultures that build on the grand achievements of a vital heritage. Openness to others—including the mainstream—does not entail wholesale co-optation, and group autonomy is not group insularity. Louis Armstrong, W.E.B. Du Bois, Ella Baker, Jose Carlos Mariatequi, M. M. Thomas, Wynton Marsalis, Martin Luther King, Jr., and Ronald Takaki have understood this well.

The new cultural politics of difference can thrive only if there are communities, groups, organizations, institutions, subcultures and networks of people of color who cultivate critical sensibilities and personal accountability—without inhibiting individual expressions, curiosities and idiosyncrasies. This is especially needed given the escalating racial hostility, violence and polarization in the USA. Yet this critical coming-together must not be a narrow closing-ranks. Rather it is a strengthening and nurturing endeavor that can forge more solid alliances and coalitions. In this way, prophetic criticism—with its stress on historical specificity and artistic complexity—directly addresses the intellectual challenge. The cultural capital of people of color—with its emphasis on self-confidence, discipline, perseverance and subcultures of criticism—also tries to meet the existential requirement. Both are mutually reinforcing. Both are motivated by a deep commitment to individuality and democracy—the moral and political ideals that guide the creative response to the political challenge.

THE POLITICAL CHALLENGE

Adequate rejoinders to intellectual and existential challenges equip the practitioners of the new cultural politics of difference to meet the political ones. This challenge principally consists of forging solid and reliable alliances of people of color and White progressives guided by a moral and political vision of greater democracy and individual freedom in communities, states and transnational enterprises, for instance, corporations, information and communications conglomerates.

Jesse Jackson's Rainbow Coalition is a gallant yet flawed effort in this regard—gallant due to the tremendous energy, vision and courage of its leader and followers, yet flawed because of its failure to take seriously critical and democratic sensibilities within its own operations. In fact, Jackson's attempt to gain power at the national level is a symptom of the weakness of US progressive politics, and a sign that the capacity to generate extraparliamentary social motion or movements has waned. Yet given the present organizational weakness and intellectual timidity of Left politics in the USA, the major option is that of multiracial, grass-roots, citizens' participation in credible projects in which people see that their efforts can make a difference. The salutary revolutionary developments in Eastern

Europe are encouraging and inspiring in this regard. Ordinary people organized can change societies.

The most significant theme of the new cultural politics of difference is the agency, capacity and ability of human beings who have been culturally degraded, politically oppressed and economically exploited by bourgeois liberal and Communist illiberal status quos. This theme neither romanticizes nor idealizes marginalized peoples. Rather it accentuates their humanity and tries to attenuate the institutional constraints on their life-chances for surviving and thriving. In this way, the new cultural politics of difference shuns narrow particularisms, parochialisms and separatisms, just as it rejects false universalisms and homogeneous totalisms. Instead, the new cultural politics of difference affirms the perennial quest for the precious ideals of individuality and democracy by digging deep in the depths of human particularities and social specificities in order to construct new kinds of connections, affinities and communities across empire, nation, region, race, gender, age and sexual orientation.

The major impediments to the radical libertarian and democratic projects of the new cultural politics are threefold: the pervasive processes of objectification, rationalization and commodification throughout the world. The first process—best highlighted in Georg Simmel's *The Philosophy of Money* (1900)—consists of transforming human beings into manipulable objects. It promotes the notion that people's action have no impact on the world, that we are but spectators not participants in making and remaking ourselves and the larger society. The second process—initially examined in the seminal works of Max Weber—expands bureaucratic hierarchies that impose impersonal rules and regulations in order to increase efficiency, be they defined in terms of better service or better surveillance. This process leads to disenchantment with past mythologies of deadening, flat, banal ways of life. The third and most important process—best examined in the works of Karl Marx, Georg Lukács and Walter Benjamin—augments market forces in the form of oligopolies and monopolies that centralize resources and powers and promote cultures of consumption that view people as mere spectatorial consumers and passive citizens.

These processes cannot be eliminated, but their pernicious effects can be substantially alleviated. The audacious attempt to lessen their impact—to preserve people's agency, increase the scope of their freedom and expand the operations of democracy—is the fundamental aim of the new cultural politics of difference. This is why the crucial questions become: What is the moral content of one's cultural identity? And what are the political consequences of this moral content and cultural identity?

In the recent past, the dominant cultural identities have been circumscribed by immoral patriarchal, imperial, jingoistic and xenophobic constraints. The political consequences have been principally a public sphere regulated by and for well-to-do White males in the name of freedom and democracy. The new cultural criticism exposes and explodes the exclusions, blindnesses and silences of this past, calling from it radical libertarian and democratic projects that will create a better present and future. The new cultural politics of difference is neither an ahistorical Jacobin program that discards tradition and ushers in new self-righteous authoritarianisms, nor a guilt-ridden, leveling, anti-imperialist liberalism that celebrates token pluralism for smooth inclusion. Rather, it acknowledges the uphill struggle of fundamentally transforming highly objectified, rationalized and commodified societies and cultures in the name of individuality and democracy. This means locating the structural causes of unnecessary forms of social misery (without reducing all such human suffering to historical causes), depicting the plight and predicaments of demoralized and depoliticized citizens caught in market-driven cycles of therapeutic release—drugs, alcoholism, consumerism—and projecting alternative visions, analyses and actions that proceed from particularities and arrive at moral and political connectedness. This connectedness does not signal a homogeneous unity or monolithic totality but rather a contingent, fragile coalition-building in an effort to pursue common radical libertarian and democratic goals that overlap.

In a world in which most of the resources, wealth and power are centered in huge corporations and supportive political elites, the new cultural politics of difference may appear to be solely visionary, utopian and fanciful. The recent cutbacks of social service programs, business take-backs at the negotiation tables of workers and management, speedups at the workplace and buildups of military budgets reinforce this perception. And surely the growing disintegration and decomposition of civil society—of shattered families, neighborhoods and schools—adds to this perception. Can a civilization that evolves more and more around market activity, more and more around the buying and selling of commodities, expand the scope of freedom and democracy? Can we simply bear witness to its slow decay and doom—a painful denouement prefigured already in many poor Black and Brown

Cornel West

communities and rapidly embracing all of us? These haunting questions remain unanswered, yet the challenge they pose must not remain unmet. The new cultural politics of difference tries to confront these enormous and urgent challenges. It will require all the imagination, intelligence, courage, sacrifice, care and laughter we can muster.

The time has come for critics and artists of the new cultural politics of difference to cast their nets widely, flex their muscles broadly, and thereby refuse to limit their visions, analyses and praxis to their particular terrains. The aim is to dare to recast, redefine and revise the very notions of "modernity," "mainstream," "margins," "difference," "otherness." We have now reached a new stage in the perennial struggle for freedom and dignity. And while much of the First World intelligentsia adopts retrospective and conservative outlooks that defend the crisis-ridden present, we promote a prospective and prophetic vision with a sense of possibility and potential, especially for those who bear the social costs of the present. We look to the past for strength, not solace; we look at the present and see people perishing, not profits mounting; we look toward the future and vow to make it different and better.

To put it boldly, the new kind of critic and artist associated with the new cultural politics of difference consists of an energetic breed of New World *bricoleurs* with improvisational and flexible sensibilities that sidestep mere opportunism and mindless eclecticism; persons from all countries, cultures, genders, sexual orientations, ages and regions with protean identities who avoid ethnic chauvinism and faceless universalism; intellectual and political freedom-fighters with partisan passion, international perspectives and, thank God, a sense of humor that combats the ever-present absurdity that forever threatens our democratic and libertarian projects and dampens the fire that fuels our will to struggle. Yet we will struggle and stay, as those brothers and sisters on the block say, "out there"—with intellectual rigor, existential dignity, moral vision, political courage and soulful style.

ELABORATIONS

Etienne Balibar
translated by J. Swenson

Culture and Identity
(Working Notes)

I. Cultural Identity, National Identity

How are we to evaluate the role that the notion of cultural identity plays today?[1] I would be tempted to say: the role that the notion of cultural identity plays *in culture*. I will approach the question here by way of the use made of the notion of cultural identity in the official documents of international cultural organisms, representatives of a wider discourse, for the very reasons that make these institutions privileged sites of reception and emission of "commonplaces." And it is preeminently in culture that the problem of the "commonplace," in all the senses of the term, is posed.[2]

The multiple problems posed by these discourses—such as those of the "cultural rights" of individuals and of peoples; of "cultural democracy"; of "cultural development" and of the relations between "culture" and "development"; of the "promotion of national languages"; of the relation between "conservation of the cultural heritage" and "creation" or "innovation"; of "communication" in relation to freedom of expression or the reinforcement of peace and so on—whether envisaged in their theoretical aspects or in their political implications, are formulated in terms fundamentally structured by four major categorical polarities:

1. Objective and subjective

Cultural identity appears as a collection of traits, of objective structures (as such spontaneously thought of in the dimension of the collective, the social and the historical) *and* as a principle or a process of subjectivation (spontaneously thought of in the dimension of "lived experience," of "conscious" or "unconscious" individuality). Between these poles there would normally be correspondence or reciprocity, following the models of exteriorization and interiorization; but in certain cases there may also be conflict. The idea can then be formed that a discrepancy translates situations or moments of "crisis" (even "pathological" moments), but also, by a classic reversal, so can the idea that discrepancy is in fact the rule. The correspondence that would allow for a perfect recognition of individual subjectivities in an objective cultural identity, or the perfect realization of the norms of collective culture in the identity of subjects, then appears as a limit, which it is not certain that we can or should attain.

2. Universal and singular

Cultural identity is often described as being what expresses the singularity of "groups," peoples or societies, what forbids conflating them in a uniformity of thought and practice or purely and simply erasing the "borders" that separate them and that translate the at least tendential correlation between linguistic facts, religious facts, facts of kinship, aesthetic facts in the broad sense (for there are styles of life just as there are musical or literary styles) and political facts. But at the same time cultural identity poses the question of universality or universalization. First of all, because cultures cannot be thought in their social or anthropological diversity except by comparison with universals (whether natural or logical). Next, because this very diversity induces a communication "between cultures" or between "bearers" of singular cultures which at least potentially crosses all borders. Finally and above all, because the identity of each culture would have to be recognized as containing a *value* that, as such, is universal.

This last aspect has repercussions on the preceding ones. It is what permits, for example, a distinction to be proposed between a "good" and a "bad" concept of cultural diversity, from an ethical and political standpoint (to put it schematically, an egalitarian concept and a hierarchical one). It is

Etienne Balibar

what allows a discussion of the "good" and "bad" forms of communication: those that tend to institute the universal *in* respect for singularities or that find a "balanced" way to combine them, as opposed to those that crush singularity under uniformity (currently such an effect is often feared to result from the contemporary evolution of "mass communications" and the worldwide diffusion of certain hegemonic models) or that, going to the opposite extreme, exacerbate singularity to the point of isolationism. The median, desirable path would put communication in the service of the reproduction of differences, that is, it would affirm singularity *by the mediation* of the universal. And, reciprocally, it would affirm the reality of the universal by the mediation of singularities.

3. Elite and masses (or high and popular)

This third polarity is omnipresent, but it finds different expressions, between which there reigns a relation of analogy. It is first of all a formalization of the classical (at least since the nineteenth century) distinction between *culture* (scientific, technical, literary) and *cultures* expressive of social groups (or better, of individuals' belonging to groups), and in this sense it is simply a projection of the preceding "dialectic" of universal and singular into the historico-sociological field. But it also adds new connotations to it, notably by authorizing *educational* institutions and activities (in practice, schools) to be considered as the preeminent site in which to seek a resolution to historical tensions between scientifico-technical culture and aesthetic culture, between the practice of languages of international communication and that of irreducibly "maternal" idioms, between the conservation of traditions and cultural innovation, and finally between the arts of the body and the development of the intellect or the mind. Which leads us directly to a fourth polarity.

4. Permanent and evolving

Here the notion of cultural identity in some sense reflects upon itself in the privileged dimension of time. With or without explicit reference to "progress," with or without a critique of the pertinence or limits of this notion or of the modes of historical temporality presupposed by any thesis bearing on the historicity of culture, it seems that we can recognize a postulate that takes the form of a unity of opposites: cultural identity *resists time* as simple change, it is identical to itself as the constant underlying every transformation (which is why it authorizes the recognition, the "proper" nomination of collective subjects) *and* nevertheless it only exists by *its incessant transformation* (called creation, life, development, but which in the end appears as a requirement of the very notion of "culture").

There exists a "weak" version of this postulate, which tries to systematically locate and compare the traits or structures of permanence (the "long term") and the traits of history, of evolution or of dissemination of the "personality" of groups. And there exists a "strong" version, which pushes the unity beyond juxtaposition to a point that we can call, in Hegelian terms, the identity of identity and difference (if need be valorizing conflict for its own sake, for example by positing that the permanence of a culture, constantly threatened with dissolution, needs to be continually recreated by a conscious or unconscious effort of individuals).[3]

Without wanting to pass judgment here on the subtle or crude, complex or summary use that can be made of these categories (which in any case are classical ones in philosophy), I will draw two questions from the fact that they organize down to the very details the institutional discourse on cultural identity, arranging in advance the different forms of argument possible.

In the first place, a formal question.

Is culture indeed the pregiven or preconstituted "object" to which such categories are applied? One might doubt this merely by observing the repetition of negative observations of the type: "culture," "cultural identity" cannot be grasped *except* by articulating objective and subjective dimensions, universal and singular, not sacrificing popular (or mass) culture to the high culture of the elite or vice versa, and so on. It might clarify matters to treat the notions of culture and even more of cultural identity *functionally*, as terms that today designate a form rather than a content or an object. Better still: as terms that designate an *empty place*, vacant for a multiplicity of contents and objects, and determined by the intersection of discourses that are in turn structured by the categories we have singled out. It is clear that this would amount to saying that *anything* that can be thought with the help of such categorical polarities, and above all of their combination, can be taken as stemming from the realm of culture.

We should notice that each of these polarities, whether directly or obliquely, delimits a different field in which to think the "human": the psychological (or sociopsychological) field, the logical (or logico-metaphysical) field, the political field and the historical field. The question of identity, at least for the last two centuries, has implied an attempt to define identity *either* psychologically, *or* logically, *or* politically *or* historically. But once one wants to combine or superimpose these different pertinencies, once one is no longer willing to sacrifice any of them, is it not inevitable—today, in any case—that "identity" should be designated precisely as "cultural"? Or, reciprocally, that "culture" should be designated as the most general element in which *to identify identity*?

In the second place, a historical question.

What is called cultural identity is constantly compared to and at the limit conflated with *national identity*, and nevertheless is in some sense "sheltered" from the empirical existence of nations, their borders, their politico-military history.[4] Thus we constantly speak of "French culture," "Italian culture," "American culture," "Chinese culture" and so on, and even use this translation of identity into terms of nationality in order to evaluate the degree of reality and well-foundedness of national constructions (does there exist an Israeli culture? a Soviet culture? a Palestinian culture? a Congolese culture?). But at the same time we are always careful not to *reduce* cultural identity to a "national character" or, *a fortiori*, to the normative traits that the institutions of the national state give it. This is in particular the model for many discussions of the relation between "cultural identity" and "ethnic identity," more or less insistent according to the degree of coincidence, in a given historical situation, between ethnicity and nationality.

Doubtless this sort of ambivalent proximity of the discourses of cultural identity and of national identity is particularly visible and marked when the frame of these discourses is provided by international institutions whose natural destiny would seem to be to seek out the identity (and their own identity along with it), between "nation" and "culture." This is all the more understandable given that these institutions were founded and have been used in order to confront social and political problems such as decolonization, underdevelopment or peaceful coexistence between blocs of nations *by means of culture*. But this emphasis has a more general import. It seems to me that three kinds of problems are at stake:

(a) The problem of the relation *between the nation and the state*: culture is the distinctive element that allows us to avoid conflating the nation with the state, even as, in practice, individuals "encounter" the nation through the state (through an at least *possible* state) that "represents" it, through the state's institutions. Culture is thus the name to be given to the "essential nation"; it designates the pure difference between the nation as national state and the other "nation" that is to be distinguished from any state, just as an "internal" or intrinsic "community" is to be distinguished from an artificial community (following the paradigm opposing *Kulturnation* and *Staatsnation*). In this capacity it can either anticipate the state, resist it or figure the "ultimate" goal of its constitution. But, being indebted to culture for the national identity that founds it, the first duty of the state is to "give" to the nation its cultural identity and above all to work to "develop" it.

(b) The problem of the relation *between the historical nation*, more or less closely tied to the formation of a political unity, *and the transhistorical ensembles* (generally supranational) for which the name of "*civilizations*" has come to be reserved. The permanent traits of its culture are what attaches a nation, whether "old" or "young," to the models (not to say the archetypes) of the civilization of which it would be both an incarnation and a variant.

We should note here that this very general dependence can be evoked completely independently of the choice that one might make in favor of any particular *theory* of "civilization" (even if the political implications of such a choice are anything but negligible): civilization as the manifestation of a spirit or as the superstructure of a material base; civilization as the heritage of an archaic origin or as the product of diffusions and crossings; civilization thought of above all as a set of ethnic, religious or geographical traits (whence discussions about whether there is a "European civilization," an "African civilization," an "Arab-Islamic civilization" or a "Mediterranean civilization" and so on). But above all, this reference to the idea of civilization is at the heart of the whole reflection on the articulation—within a national space—between the "two cultures," or if you prefer *between two concepts of* "culture," one of which refers to a group's traditional identity and the expressions of its singularity, and the other to instruction (*Bildung*) and the development of the intellectual forms of art and knowledge. Civilization (*a* civilization of reference, whether attested or simply conceivable) is the mediation without which it would be impossible to reconcile the two aspects of culture as the quest for "self" and the quest for the "universal."[5]

(c) Finally, the problem of the relation *between the nation and nonnational* "communities." This relation can be conflictual or not, and it can concern—

in confrontation with the nation, which in practice means in confrontation with the state, which presents itself as a national state—either transnational communities (for example, communities of religious affiliation), or prenational or antinational communities (for example, ones that contest the state's borders, or which are struggling against political or economic oppression on an "ethnic" basis, demanding recognition of rights, autonomy or independence). What is striking here is the generalization in the world today of the discourse of culture in order to characterize both identity and nonidentity, both the principle of national hegemony and that of the autonomy of nonnational communities. Particularly when this relation takes on the form of a conflict, one sees cultural signs, despite their equivocal character and historical overdetermination, crystallize the demand that both sides address to individuals: to make a "choice," or at least to state a "preference" between several competing "belongings."

We then cannot not pose the question: *what if the notion of cultural identity were today nothing other than the metaphor of national identity?*

By metaphor we should understand translation, expression, representation, but also displacement, even "acting out," expressing an at least relative incapacity of national constructions to endow themselves and their "nationals" with an "identity" that is perfectly simple and univocal, and absolutely common and unified. This does not mean that such an identity is not desired or postulated by individuals who recognize the nation as "theirs," nor that it does not have collective effects, but rather that it always has to deal with its own contradictions, its internal and external divisions, and that it overcomes them only by projecting itself into the element of cultural unity. This cultural unity would be nothing other than a "double" of the historical nation situated *beside* it (as the essential *Kulturnation* is beside the *Staatsnation*), *beyond* it (as "civilizations" allow the past and future of a nation to overhang its present) or *beneath* it (as "communitarian" identities persist and arise within the national ensemble in order to contribute to its diversity or resist its uniformity).

It could then be understood that culture, while impossible to grasp theoretically as the "object" of a description or scientific definition, is impossible to bypass practically as the semantic "horizon" of all the discourses that try to signify identity in a world of nations (dominant and dominated, recognized or denied, in search of their unity or already showing signs of being integrated into larger ensembles). It could also be understood that *the very word* "culture," after a long prehistory and a period of crystallization at the turn of the eighteenth and nineteenth centuries, acquired the strategic function that it has today (including in philosophy) at the precise moment that the nation form definitively won out over other forms of state in Europe, and began to become generalized in the world. Thenceforth any collective appropriation of knowledge, rights or traditions has had to be thought of as "culture": either as the institution of a *cultural order*, or as the contestation of the existing order *by culture*. And all identity has had to be founded in a past cultural origin, or projected into a future of culture that is ceaselessly interrogated in the light of the origins.[6]

Such a situation is obviously suggestive of the function that was and still is in modern history that of religion, or of the great religions called, precisely, universalist. But how are we to handle this analogy? It can be explored in both directions—for example, by discussing what today tends to submit religious formations to the hegemony of culture (religious practices and symbols thought of as affirmations of cultural identity, or as privileged anchoring points for *imputing* a cultural identity *to the other*), but also by discussing what, in the universe of culture and cultures, translates the persistence of the religious model (here we need to think less of a "return of religion" than of culture as a religion of art, a religion of science, a religion of history, a religion of communication). Nevertheless, the most interesting way is doubtless to point out *the dissymmetry between the two models*.

Let us agree to call *hegemonic* or *total* those historical institutions that are capable, be it at the price of violent conflicts, of imposing a single "superior community" on all the individuals who recognize themselves as members of different collectivities (familial, linguistic, professional, local), and thereby conferring a universal ethical "end" on the multiplicity of practices and exchanges within which these same individuals conceive of themselves as subjects (in short, what, in another context, Ernest Gellner calls "a Terminal Court of Appeal").[7] Modern history then presents us with two great competing models of a total institution: the religious institution and the national institution. Each is authentically hegemonic, in the sense that it *does not suppress the multiplicity* of "belongings" (as opposed to a "totalitarian" institution, if one has ever existed), but succeeds for a longer or shorter time and within certain limits in hierarchizing and pacifying this multiplicity.[8] Each is also total in the sense that, leaving *virtually no* aspect of existence and thus no "reason to live" outside of its realm (at the price, no doubt, of appropriate

Etienne Balibar

distinctions and subordinations such as that of the temporal and the eternal or the public and the private), it can inscribe the existence of individuals within the horizon of death and thus give death a symbolic signification: not so much death *given* (although both religions and nations have found ways to legitimate collective murder, removing it from the domain of private vengeance) as death *accepted* (religions and nations are in a position to demand sacrifice and to obtain it in the name of the salvation of each and of all).

But the difference is clear: the nation as such, a political institution that is always virtually profane even when separation of church and state is not officially proclaimed, *is not sufficient* to totalize or hegemonize discourses, practices, forms of individuality ("language games" and "forms of life" in Wittgensteinian terminology), even though it has shown itself to be incomparably more efficient than any universal religion in the reduction of "communitarian belongings."[9] Would *what modern thought calls culture,* in the range of uses of the term, be *the analogue of religion in the national institution,* once it has become dominant? Would it not rather be the name that must be given, analogically, to all "national religions" *if they were religions, which is what they can never be?* Or again: would it not be the *antireligion* that national institutions or formations develop (and project into the past, into the whole "evolution of humanity") in order to affirm their hegemony *over religions* (but that certain balances of power can oblige us to think, once again, as the expression of a religious core, or the development of a religious tradition)?

Whatever the case may be, it is the site of an unceasing contradiction. The reference to the nation and the institutional comparison with religion would at least allow us to pose the question of why the reference to a "cultural identity" *oscillates around belief* (fact and concept): in a sense it is always much less than a belief—as imperative or "ought"—even if cultural identity is said to be normative; in another sense it is much more than a belief— as attribution or "being"—even if it is a matter of a participatory, acquired being.[10] In a similar way one might wonder why the philosophical discourse on cultural identity itself oscillates between a very powerful *spiritualism* (for the universalism of culture, present in each culture, presents itself as a reversal of nature, an inversion of its values, even when it does not make any specific reference to the mind) and a very powerful *naturalism* (for culture is at least analogically what institutes vertical and horizontal "species" within the *genus homo*).[11] But it seems that this sort of question needs to be held in reserve at the moment.

II. Identity and Identification in the Field of Culture

This problem is in a way complementary to the preceding one. But whereas we could at least formulate a hypothesis with respect to the first question, here we can only enumerate questions, which cannot claim to be exhaustive, and try to classify them. Each question would obviously call for a long discussion, and a choice will have to be made, particularly if other formulations seem preferable.[12]

1. From identity in culture to the place of the subject in the institution

A first question, entirely elementary, but which seems to me impossible to avoid: does it make any sense to speak of identity in the field of culture when, as we have just seen, the suspicion can be raised that the very notion of "culture" designates less a definite object than a place or a function that remains indeterminate? The addition of the epithet "cultural" to the term *identity* would not, in this case, have the result of qualifying the latter, but on the contrary of rendering it definitively problematic. The contemporary inflation of discourses that speak of a "crisis of cultural identity" as well as of "affirming identities" should rather incite us to take cognizance of this paradox. Who am I? Who are we? Who are they?—these implicit and explicit demands, the response to which ought to translate the knowledge of an identity, are not made more precise in any degree whatsoever by the reference to culture, because the mode according to which an "I," a "we" or a "they" belongs to or inheres in the field of a culture, or of culture as such, is absolutely enigmatic.

What generally functions as a guiding thread for resolving this enigma is either *the analogy of nature and culture* (identity "in culture" compared to identity "in nature," that is, classifiable, localizable singularity), or *the antithesis of nature and culture* (identity in culture conceived of as the negation of exteriority, of natural being: whence participation in a world of the Mind or of spirits). On one side a system of metaphors, on the other a system of negations. But there is no need to invoke contemporary reconceptualizations of the notion of a natural object in order to be sure that the signified sought by the question: Who am I? is precisely *neither* a given singularity *nor* a radical negation of objectivity. It

Etienne Balibar

would rather be the opening up of a problem—with or without a solution: How can I (how can we, how can they) receive from another or from a (potentially infinite) series of others *the objective sign of my (our, their) singularity?*

This question does not bear on what identity in the cultural field is, or on the way that culture determines identity, so much as on the very possibility of *constituting culture as a field of experience in which identities can be "recognized,"* in which various sorts of answers by philosophers become possible: existential, logical (or structural), transcendental. But here I will restrict myself to suggesting that, in any case, each of the terms involved (identity, culture) needs to be related to a more polyvalent notion, an original "variable" that it presupposes: on the one hand that of *subject*, on the other that of *institution* (or any other equivalent notion, but I do not see a better one in English). I will thus propose, as a minimal condition of clarification, the following double thesis:

1. There is identity only by and for subjects;
2. There is culture only by and for institutions.

Obviously this is meaningful only if "subject" is not just another word for identity (or self-identity) and "institution" not just another word for culture. It seems to me that we can say that "subject" is, first of all, a name for the possibility of assigning *a referent to the persons distinguished by the language,* thus of saying "I," "we" and "they" in context. As for "institution," it is generally a name signifying that any human practice involves a certain *distribution of statuses* (or obligations) *and functions* (utility, efficiency, communication), susceptible of being expressed and legitimated in discourses—whether they be codes, stories or programs. In this sense the question of identity is first of all posed in an entirely formal way, because "I," "we" and "they" are *equivocal* expressions of subjective position (of the position of the subject), because the subject as such is originally *no more* "I" than "we" or "they," and can never be definitively attributed to any of these persons, but continually "floats" or "circulates" between them. And the question of culture is posed because, in time and space, all societies (even all societies having the form of the national state in common) do not distribute statuses, obligations and function of production, reproduction, communication, memory, knowledge and so forth in the same way. But the subject moves from language to practice; the institution from practice to discourse.

Is it not necessary, before we begin to theorize about cultural identity, to ask what it means for the individual-collective (I would rather suggest: transindividual or multipersonal) subject to confront institutions, and what the modalities of this "encounter" can be, whether they are aleatory or prescribed long in advance? This problem is not so much a matter for a sociology or a psychology, even less for a "general" theory of individuality of or systems, as for a pragmatics of language and a political anthropology.

But is it not then necessary to *suspend*, as a matter of principle, the presupposition that sees culture as a "whole" (and consequently sees the relation of the individual to culture as "all or nothing," controlled by the logic of identity and difference, inclusion and exclusion)? What would we put in its place? Perhaps simply the idea that in the field of human practices, submitted to innumerable institutional variations, subjective positions give rise to *traits* of diversely distributed cultural identity. That these traits form a system or are totalized into mutually exclusive ensembles can only be a logically *secondary* phenomenon.

2. The experience of a language

One of the most widespread ideas of a spontaneous philosophy of cultural diversity is that languages form not only systems but *universes*. The reference to a language's universe, to its closure, to the "perilous leap" that any "exit" from this universe represents, has become the privileged mediation for designating the relation of individuals to the difference between cultures. A language—institution of institutions—is what determines an individual as belonging to *this* culture (he is "chosen" by it more than he chooses it), but also what serves to appropriate it; whence comes the possibility of designating the relation of each individual to "his" language as the very essence of the relation by which he appropriates culture. "Mastery" of the language promises mastery of culture: but only he whose mistress the language is from and by birth can truly master a language. As a counterpart, the defense of a culture whose identity, integrity or creativity is threatened would be above all the defense of the language (as official, autonomous, literary, popular). From this point there is a fairly natural transition to the idea that the subject recognizes himself as an autonomous being (reflexive sense of identity) exactly to the extent that his language and his culture are indiscernible from one another (logical sense of identity).

It indeed seems that a practical truth is expressed here. Nonetheless, at least two models are invoked. On the one hand there is the idea that a language's "borders" *circumscribe* a culture (at the limit they forbid the linguistic subject from moving from one culture to another without undergoing the irremediable loss of meaning said to occur in "translation"). On the other hand there is the idea that a "position" in language *inscribes* subjectivity in culture (at the limit it would open up the possibility of taking on as many distinct "cultural identities" as a subject could inhabit linguistic universes).

It is thus necessary to ask what the value of the representation of a language as a "universe" is. This question has never stopped recurring in contemporary philosophy, whether centrally or obliquely. It can be found in discussions of translatability and untranslatability: if there is an aspect of language that can never be reduced to its function as an instrument of communication, what in general can be called its poetic power, is it not something that essentially belongs to the *idiom*? But is the idiom a linguistic "identity"? Inversely the question can be found in discussions of the element of liberation or transcendence (ethical, logical, political) that the intention of communication would introduce into *each* language or idiom. Insofar as it serves to communicate (or better: that it intrinsically wills communication), the end of a maternal language would not be the closure of its universe but an at least virtual human universality. This discussion thereby cuts across reflection on "private language," a paradoxical notion about which it might be asked whether it has in view the limit-case of a subject for whom language would not be submitted to the rules of communication, or rather the ideal of a communicative sphere that would exactly coincide with the foundation of a community, even with its autarchy.

Jacques Derrida, for his part, has repeatedly suggested that the "sign" that represents the individual in the language, or better that presents him there, binding together, so to speak, the unicity of the subject and the unicity of the idiom, namely the proper name, is precisely not originarily *one of the language's signs*. On account of this fact it is not possible to say rigorously that the subject of the language "belongs" to the language linguistically. That he is constantly reinscribed there, for example in the form of the signature, testifies to the fact that the language operates as a power of dissemination of statements or indefinite transformation of meaning, in other terms as a generalized *écriture* and not as the "expression" of a universe of thought.[13]

In another order of ideas it can be observed that no experience of the maternal language (which forms the basis of the experience of the possibility or impossibility of translation, and of the greater or lesser degree of difficulty in "appropriating" a foreign culture) is in reality a simple experience of its stability, its univocity or closure. It always combines in a much more ambivalent way a plurality of more or less mutually incompatible uses of the "same" language (whether these uses are functionally or socially determined), and the presence ("normal" or "shocking," transparent or enigmatic) in one's "own" language of elements drawn from other languages. On this double heading the experience in question is not univocal but a problematic one in which a gap constantly arises between *language* in general and *a language* in particular: as a plurivocity of language *within* the univocity of the language (no two people speak identically the "French," "English" or "Arabic" that they nonetheless have "in common"), and as a decomposition and reconstitution of the opening of language on the basis of the plurality of languages (no one would speak at all if he spoke *only* pure "French," "English" or "Arabic.") Thus the experience of the foreign and of foreignness in the element of a language precisely does *not* have as its counterpart an assurance of belonging to an autarchic universe or of being able to circumscribe one. The sense of originality and familiarity that the language constantly reactivates for each subject does not have the form of interiority. And the identity that is *spoken* here is not given but "fictive," in the active sense of the word: it is made from elaborated differentiations and constructed communications.

3. Identity or identification(s)?

Is it not significant that the notion of cultural identity is invoked by predilection in conjunctures of conflict or "crisis"? Identity is never a peaceful acquisition: it is claimed as a guarantee against a threat of annihilation that can be figured by "another identity" (a foreign identity) or by an "erasing of identities" (a depersonalization). Should we not generalize what sociologists on the one hand and psychoanalysts on the other have described of contemporary "affirmations of identity" (whether ethnic or religious), namely that every identity that is *proclaimed* (with fanfare or in secret) is elaborated as a function of the Other, in response to his desire, his power and his discourse (which already represents a power over desire)?

At the limit it is the notion of a "traditional identity" (or of an inherited identity) that would be a contradiction in terms. It would be more precise to say that identity is a *discourse* of tradition. And one of the privileged names of tradition, in contemporary societies, is precisely "culture." In reality there are no identities, only identifications: either with the institution itself, or with other subjects by the intermediary of the institution. Or, if one prefers, identities are only the ideal goal of processes of identification, their point of honor, of certainty or uncertainty of their consciousness, thus their imaginary referent.

But doubtless this does not mean that processes of identification as such are *imaginary*. A simple description of their effects in constructing "representations" or the way they arrange places for the subject that will permit him to imagine himself as a "self" is insufficient. In practice some identifications "succeed" in a contradictory way and others "fail" and even become unlivable; something besides their common form must account for this difference! It does not purely and simply coincide with the difference between conformism and nonconformism, that is, adaptation or nonadaptation to the rituals, norms and beliefs prescribed by the "dominant" institution. It could be suggested that a construction of identity is not an imaginary process but a *processing of the imaginary:* a behavior, a history or a singular strategy of the subject in his relation to the imaginary ("his," that of "others"). Why, then, should this behavior, this strategy or this history "normally" culminate in a beatific identification (or an aggressive counteridentification) of individuals with a univocal and massive "we" (or with the symbols and emblems that represent it) defined as an all-or-nothing proposition? Is it enough, in this respect, to invoke the general idea of domination, or to think of the imaginary as a moment in and the instrument of a balance of power? Nothing tells us that its practical effectiveness, in every circumstance, depends on a lack of distinction of "I" and "we."[14]

4. The problem of belonging

Supposing that an identity is effective, does this mean that it has to be *unique*? The same discourse that makes every culture into a "whole" poses as an impossibility *belonging to several cultures*. Correlatively no instituted community—in particular no nation—could be "multicultural." But the critics of this position (generally inspired by political motives) hesitate simply and purely to take up an opposite position. And if they do risk it they still hesitate between several ways of doing so: must we posit that every individual always belongs to more than one culture?[15] Or rather must we posit that the expression "*a* culture," taken in isolation, is a contradiction in terms, so that belonging to *culture* means belonging to a network, to an *intersection* of cultures?[16] But this sort of dilemma cannot be resolved without asking how the "logic of belonging" that seems to tie identity(ies) and culture(s) together functions. Or better: that ties *identity, culture and community* together, for it is these *three* terms whose association and reciprocal implication we have constantly encountered.

Jean-Claude Milner[17] has proposed distinguishing between two types of "classes" or "collections": classes of the imaginary and classes of the symbolic. To which he adds, *après coup*, classes of a third type: "paradoxical classes" (which stand in for classes of the real in a Lacanian typology). The classes of the imaginary are founded upon the *attribution* of one or several "properties" common to individuals, supposed to be distinct and to exist independently of the act of attribution: in other words they are grouped together by the supposition of a visible resemblance (Black or White, naked or clothed), or more generally a representable resemblance (for it can be a "character," a moral resemblance) between their members. The classes of the symbolic are founded upon the irremediably nonrepresentable fact that subjects *respond* to the same name—a name by which they are interpellated and that interpellates them: thus "Frenchman," "Christian," "Communist."[18] Subjects are thus identified not as *similar* individuals, but as individuals *in solidarity* although absolutely dissimilar ("unique"). These are both modalities of identification of individuals by the mediation of a communitarian term, but they are logically irreducible to one another.

This distinction is quite illuminating, and its application could be extended, for example by showing how the integrative function of *rites* is situated on the "symbolic" side, whereas that of *typical behaviors* is situated on the "imaginary" side.[19] But it also poses several problems. Are classes of the imaginary and classes of the symbolic independent, or rather, do they function independently of one another? Milner himself speaks of the *imaginarization* of symbolic classes as a more or less finished process that nourishes the vicissitudes of politics and history. But he does not pose the inverse question of the symbolization of imaginary classes, which is preeminently what happens in institutions: for example when "races" are juridically, which is to say institutionally "defined" or, even more fundamentally (we will return to this point), when sexual identities are grouped (which is to say divided) under the mythical and juridical signifiers of essential Man and Woman.

Another question then arises, to which we should not be too hasty to respond. If we admit that the thesis (and the sentiment) of a *unique identity* has as its corollary the insertion of the individual into an *ultimate community* which would be both a finite "world" and a "worldview," is it not necessary to suppose that such a community rests—at least ideally—on the possibility of *hierarchizing* all "belongings"? Which means, first of all, making them compatible with one another. Is this not precisely how the total institutions or ideologies that we discussed above work? Thus "being French" does not mean being *only* "French," but being a "French Breton" or a "French Lorrainer" (impossible to be a "French Saxon" but not absolutely impossible to be a "French Berber"), a "French Catholic," a "French Jew" or a "French freethinker" (difficult to be a "French Muslim"), a "French worker," a "French capitalist" or a "French writer," a "French liberal" or a "French socialist," or more precisely it means being all that according to a "specifically French" modality (and at the limit it means being Man or Woman or Child *à la française*). In the same way "being a Muslim" does not mean merely seeking Allah by following the call of the Prophet, but being Arab or Black, or Turkish, Egyptian or Iranian, Sunni or Shi'ite in order to observe the law, and thus incorporating all these particularities into the community of believers.

Unicity of identity, *order* of compatibility and hierarchy of belongings, so as to constitute an *ultimate* community and only one: it indeed seems that these structural presuppositions form a system. But which sort of "class" subsumes the other, carrying out what could be called the collection of collections? Are imaginary classes subsumed under symbolic signifiers (thus individuals having all sorts of "properties," and mutually recognizing each other as having them, all respond to the call of a single name: Allah, République Française, Soviet Union.)? Or rather, in the last analysis, does the multiplicity of calls, allegiances, confessions need to be "bound" by an underlying communitarian representation (an imaginary substance or personality "proper" to all members of the community)? Or yet again is the question, in its generality, *undecidable*: because *it depends on the case* (religion and nation functioning in this respect, once again, inversely from one another, which does not prevent history from being made up of all the attempts to give national religions and religious nations flesh)?

What Milner calls "paradoxical classes" can serve as our counterproof here. Paradoxical classes should be to the *real* what the preceding two are to the symbolic and the imaginary. Milner takes the example of the categories of "neurotic," "perverse" and "obsessional" in psychoanalysis, that is classifications of psychiatric medicine whose naturalist form is *negated* by psychoanalysis in order to conjure away their effects of suggestion in the treatment:[20] a collection under a single name of subjects whom nothing binds to one another, except their always singular way of *being an exception*. But as soon as other examples are sought, one runs into the following question: Are paradoxical classes fundamentally constituted by the negation of one or more "common" properties? Or are they rather constituted by the negation of an instituted "allegiance"? What sort of *norm*, or *value*, is fundamentally threatened "in the real" here? Or to put it in other terms, what sort of *transgression* must appear as supremely incompatible with the proper order of belongings and, by its very reality, make the limits of that order apparent in a way that is unbearable for the passion of identity: Is it betrayal, crime, heresy, unbelief? Or is it rather abnormality, monstrosity, deviance, representable "difference"? And why has a whole literature continually—whether to stigmatize it or to valorize the paradox—sought to *translate* one of these forms into the other?

5. Cultural identity, sexual identity

Let us return once again to the equivocation presented by certain "paradoxical classes," that is, classes that manifest in the real a *nonbelonging*. It can be suggested that they are linked to all the forms of *exclusive inclusion*, or *interior exclusion*.

Such is, in certain historical circumstances, the case for oppressed or exploited social conditions. Such is, massively, the case of "races."[21] The prototype of interior exclusion, however, is *Geschlecht*, the difference between the sexes, or better the difference of "sex identities," insofar as it is instituted as a *division* (and also, in all known history, as a domination). But if one reflects upon it, it becomes clear that something other than a prototype is at stake. "Cultural identity" and "sexual identity" are two indissociable terms. The second, constantly referred to *nature*, seems to be the exact opposite of the first. It would not be difficult to introduce here the dialectical reversals of universal and particular: natural universality of sexual difference, particularity of cultures; but also access of cultures to the universal, irreducible particularity of sexual identity and in particular of femininity, which is the sex *"par excellence."*[22] But if one takes care not to erase the dissymmetry in fact covered up by the expression "sexual difference" or "difference of sexual identities," it can appear that the very notion of cultural identity, in its generality, depends upon this dissymmetry.

It may indeed be significant that the discourse of "culture," which has always tended to multiply cultures and subcultures according to all human groupings possible in time and space (thus we have ethnic cultures, aristocratic, bourgeois and proletarian class cultures,[23] "generational cultures" and so forth), *never invokes*—to my knowledge—the idea of a distinction *between "men's culture" and "women's culture"* (even if anthropology considers the greater or lesser degree of separation—formalized in statuses and rites—between the "world" of masculine activities and the "world" of feminine activities to be an essential variable of *the* culture "common" to both). As if *this* particular dividing line were the only one that could never give rise to a division of culture without overturning the very meaning of the word. It pokes through only at the limits, in the provocation of a woman of letters: "We can only help you to defend culture and intellectual liberty by defending our own culture and our own intellectual liberty,"[24] or in the almost mythical themes of a "feminist" history and anthropology that would seek, behind the subordination and public silence imposed on women by men, the traces of a "war of the sexes" analogous to that of two civilizations, two nations or two races. In every case it is more a matter of a metaphor of the conflict that all cultural identity would contain, and that would liberate the latent tension between the apparent neutrality of its formulation and the real masculinity of its hierarchical organization (and perhaps of the very notion of "belonging").

Here again, consequently, the model of a "dominant ideology" is doubtless too simple: it is better suited to designating what needs to be explained than what might explain the connection between the inequality of the sexes and the position of a subjective "identity" in culture. Invoking the universality of masculine domination and its inscription in objective structures or in collective mentalities comes close to tautology. Unless, precisely, one undertakes an analysis for each social formation of the role of kinship and of the family in the "totalization" of belongings, doubtless considering the regulation of marriages, but, above all, functions that are defined as belonging to men and to women in order to insure the collective control of the latter by the former. The fact is that in no "social order" that is part of what is called civilization does kinship as such constitute common identity. But it is also the fact that no totalization would seem to be possible if universal rules of kinship do not cut across *all* "belongings." Thus the cultural order of bourgeois nations was able to overcome the duality of "class cultures" in the nineteenth century, when the norms of the conjugal family and of domesticity were extended in the "same" way to owners and to workers. Or, in a more recent period, the historical compromise between the state and religion baptized "separation of church and state" was imperiled, and along with it the very notion of a "national culture," when these institutions split on the questions of divorce, abortion, artificial insemination and so on. To which can be added the fact that the family is one of the fundamental operative terms of the articulation between "high culture," which is necessarily the object of a public institution and public instruction, and "popular culture," which would seem to be a fall within the "private" sphere. Women are designated in a privileged way as conservators of traditions.[25]

How, then, in the statement of what is "proper" to a culture, is the recognition and misrecognition of feminine subjectivity instituted? Feminism will at least have allowed us to say that "our" historical "occidental" cultures (no doubt others too) practice a double negation of the speech and desire of women: attributing them with a purely generic nature or destiny tied to sex and reproduction, and measuring them according to the archetype of ideal Femininity. Thus women do not have an identity so much as they are identified with sexual difference as such. Which leads to a denial (as inessential) of all the singular differences among them to the benefit of an essential difference with men, as well as to a prohibition of their sharing, when they so desire, the identity of men.

The question which would begin to appear here would be the following: If there is a "class" or a "collection" of women, could it be anything but an ultraparadoxical class? A class whose permanent *dissolution* has as its exact counterpart the function that the community of men attributes to them: *binding* the community together in reality (by their labor as well as by their sentiments), *bearing* cultural identity (even exhibiting it to the eyes of others by an ostentatious "modesty"), and occasionally *symbolizing*, by their education and their talents, the "degree of civilization" that a culture has attained. Inversely cultures will stigmatize the foreignness of each other's identities by criticizing the place that "the others" grant women (following a model that was already at work between Greeks and barbarians). This projective mechanism of distancing the "other" or the "foreigner" seems to me in the end much more effective than the one that, after Lévi-Strauss, has been so much spoken of: the representation of the members of the other community under the features (or name) of animality.

But one can also ask, for this very reason, whether women will not acquire in today's world or tomorrow's the possibility of "circulating between cultures" in a way that does not exist for men: if only they succeed in overcoming the prohibition against communicating amongst themselves without authorization. The same question has already been posed in history with respect to other "paradoxical classes," but at a less fundamental level. Once interior exclusion is put back into question, will not those who are the bearers of the logic of belonging be able to initiate the logic of interculturalism?

Which poses more generally (following what is certainly a partial approach, but probably a privileged one) the question of knowing how the contemporary imperative of "communication" (and even of *global* communication) should be understood: As an encounter *between different cultures* (which concretely means between institutions)? Or as an encounter *between individuals of different cultures*, following the double gesture of using the means of communication that cultures furnish and struggling against the obstacles that they put in its way?

Notes

1. The following notes set out a research program. They were written in preparation for the Round Table on Identity and Culture organized at UNESCO on December 14 and 15, 1989, by the Division on Philosophy and the Human Sciences, which I am happy to be able to thank here.

2. *Cf.*, for example, UNESCO, *Final Report: World Conference on Cultural Policies*, Mexico City 1982 (Paris: UNESCO, 1982); UNESCO, *Blueprint for the Future: UNESCO's Medium Term Plan 1984–1989* (Paris: UNESCO, 1982), Section XI, "Culture and the Future."

*Culture and Identity
(Working Notes)*

3. It seems that we now—probably for political reasons—have left the historical phase in which history and anthropology associated the concept of "culture" with an overarching dichotomy between *cultures of permanence* and *cultures of change*, corresponding to two antagonistic types of "identity" (and thus of society). *Each culture* must contain the dialectic of these two aspects within itself. The dichotomy does nonetheless survive in the nostalgic form of an opposition between the "self-certainty" tied to permanence and the "loss of identity" tied to change (thus to modernity or even postmodernity, described as change for the sake of change and so on).

4. The same ambivalence could naturally be noted with respect to *languages* (and in fact it happens that people speak about linguistic identity), but it seems that there we are confronted with a particular case, both metonymic and metaphoric, of cultural identity.

5. This is valid when the "Occident," through a certain model of instruction, claims to integrate all cultures within its universalism, when nations struggling against the hegemony of the Occident oppose other universalisms to it, and even when one poses the question of the communication of all cultures in the framework of a "world civilization" in the course of being born.

6. I have tried to relate these questions to the problematic of "fictive ethnicity" in a series of essays collected in Etienne Balibar and Immanuel Wallerstein, *Race, Nation, Class: Ambiguous Identities*, trans. Chris Turner (London: Verso, 1991).

7. *Cf.* Ernest Gellner, "Tractatus Sociologico-philosophicus," in *Culture, Identity, and Politics* (Cambridge: Cambridge University Press, 1987).

8. This is why the establishment of peace between nations is emblematic of religious hegemony, just as the establishment of peace between confessions or churches is emblematic of national hegemony. In practice either one or the other is possible.

9. Whence comes the paradox that the nation's clerics do not form a caste in the way that a religion's clerics generally do; nonetheless the "intellectual" sphere of their activities seems to be separated from other practices by an even greater "distance" or "distinction."

10. Concerned with the specifically *modern* question of whether the Ancient Greek pantheon stemmed from the domain of "culture" or that of "religion," Paul Veyne has recently wondered "whether the Greeks believed

in their gods" (*Did the Greeks Believe in Their Myths*, trans. Paula Wissing (Chicago: University of Chicago Press, 1988)). This oscillation has been at work within modern philosophy from the beginning, not only with respect to the theme of "natural religion"—one of the ancestors of the idea of culture—but also whenever the relations between *belief* and *habit* are discussed (*cf.* Hume).

11. It is difficult not to think here of the *animality of mind* Hegel describes with respect to intellectuals.

12. I will justify my choice of these questions by saying that they all are intended to show the complexity of the problem of the "subject" as philosophy needs to rethink it after becoming conscious of the insufficiently critical element in "critical universalisms," as well as of the ahistorical element in "philosophies of history" (including historical materialisms).

13. *Cf.*, in particular, Jacques Derrida, "Signature-Event-Context," in *Margins of Philosophy*, trans. Alan Bass (Chicago: University of Chicago Press, 1982), pp. 307–330; *Signéponge/Signsponge*, trans. Richard Rand (New York: Columbia University Press, 1984); and most recently *Limited Inc.*, ed. Gerald Graff (Evanston: Northwestern University Press, 1988).

14. This is no more the case, it seems to me, when it is a matter of imposing a dominant order than when it is a matter of overturning one.

15. In the same way we suggested above that every individual always belongs to "more than one language." Such a statement, however, cannot immediately be translated by: belongs to several (two, three, etc.) languages.

16. We should note that the term "civilization," evoked above, can serve to "resolve" this sort of dilemma: cultures that interact with and influence one another will tendentially form a "single" civilization: the problem of belonging will thus be pushed back a notch (the notion of civilization almost always connotes a metacultural level).

17. Jean-Claude Milner, *Les noms indistincts* (Paris: Editions du seuil, 1983).

18. These names respond in turn to other names: France (or Republic), Christ (or Church), Revolution (or Party).

19. In many respects Georges Devereux's analysis of the difference between "ethnic personality" and "ethnic identity" intersects with Milner's. *Cf. Ethnopsychoanalysis: Psychoanalysis and Anthropology as Complementary Frames of Reference* (Berkeley: University of California Press, 1978).

20. In such a way, in particular, that no prognosis can ever *follow* from a diagnosis.

21. I do not believe, fundamentally, that the phenomenon called "self-racialization" is ever *primary*. The racialization of a "group" and the quest for indices or symptoms of belonging to a race is first of all projective, at least in the modern period. The Jew, the Arab, the Black are both types of criminal "refusal" of dominant values and types of "abnormality" that refer back to a naturalization of culture.

22. Lévi-Strauss's famous principle of the universality of the incest prohibition, "interpreted" differently by each culture, is situated at exactly this transitional point.

23. And even a specific culture of slaves and former slaves (voodoo, *candomblé*, etc.): in general a *culture of the dominant* and a *culture of the dominated*.

24. Virginia Woolf, *Three Guineas* (New York: Harcourt Brace Jovanovich, 1966), p. 88.

25. And the state or the school can only agree to participate in this process because there is no one else to do it, because of the "breakdown" of the family in the modern world, and with the constant fear of having left their competency and perverting the spontaneity of popular culture. As we have seen, however, this couple of high and popular is constitutive of the very notion of "culture."

ELABORATIONS

Wendy Brown

Wounded Attachments: Late Modern Oppositional Political Formations

> If something is to stay in the memory, it must be burned in: only that which never ceases to *hurt* stays in the memory.
>
> Friedrich Nietzsche

Taking enormous pleasure in the paradox, Jamaican-born cultural studies theorist Stuart Hall tells this story of the postwar, postcolonial "breakup" of English identity:

> in the very moment when finally Britain convinced itself it had to decolonize, it had to get rid of them, we all came back home. As they hauled down the flag [in the colonies], we got on the banana boat and sailed right into London. . . . [T]hey had ruled the world for 300 years and, at last, when they had made up their minds to climb out of the role, at least the others ought to have stayed out there in the rim, behaved themselves, gone somewhere else, or found some other client state. But no, they had always said that this [London] was really home, the streets were paved with gold, and bloody hell, we just came to check out whether that was so or not.[1]

In Hall's mischievous account, the restructuring of collective "First World" identity and democratic practices required by postcoloniality did not remain in the hinterlands but literally, restively, came home to roost. The historical "others" of colonial identity, cast free in their own waters, sailed in to implode the center of the postcolonial metropoles, came to trouble the last vestiges of centered European identity with its economic and political predicates. They came to make havoc in the master's house after the master relinquished his military-political but not his cultural and metaphysical holdings as *the* metonymy of man.

Hall's narrative of the palace invasion by the newly released subjects might also be pressed into service as metaphor for another historical paradox of late-twentieth-century collective and individual identity formation: in the very moment when modern liberal states fully realize their secularism (as Marx put it in "The Jewish Question"), just as the mantle of abstract personhood is formally tendered to a whole panoply of those historically excluded from it by humanism's privileging of a single race, gender and organization of sexuality, the marginalized reject the rubric of humanist inclusion and turn, at least in part, against its very premises. Refusing to be neutralized, to render the differences inconsequential, to be depoliticized as "life-styles," "diversity" or "persons like any other," we have lately reformulated our historical exclusion as a matter of historically produced and politically rich *alterity*. Insisting that we are not merely positioned but fabricated by this history, we have at the same time insisted that our very production as marginal, deviant or subhuman is itself constitutive of the centrality and legitimacy of the center, is itself what paves the center's streets with semiotic, political and psychic gold. Just when polite liberal (not to mention, correct leftist) discourse ceased speaking of us as dykes, faggots, colored girls or natives, we began speaking of ourselves this way. Refusing the invitation to absorption, we insisted instead upon politicizing and working into cultural critique the very constructions that a liberalism increasingly exposed in its tacit operations of racial, sexual and gender privilege was seeking to bring to a formal close.

These paradoxes of late-modern liberalism and colonialism, of course, are not a matter of simple historical accident—indeed, they are both incomplete and mutually constitutive to a degree which belies the orderly chronological scheme Hall and I have imposed on them in order to render them pleasurable ironies. Moreover, the ironies do not come to an end with the

Jamaican postcolonials sailing into London, nor with the historically marginalized constructing an oppositional political culture and critique out of their historical exclusion. Even as the margins assert themselves as margins, the denaturalizing assault they perform on coherent collective identity in the center turns back on them to trouble their own. Even as it is being articulated, circulated and, lately, institutionalized in a host of legal, political and cultural practices, identity is unravelling—metaphysically, culturally, geopolitically and historically—as rapidly as it is being produced. The same vacillation can be seen in the naturalistic legitimating narratives of collective identity as nationalism. Imploded within by the insurrectionary knowledges and political claims of historically subordinated cultures, and assaulted from without by the spectacular hybridities and supranational articulations of late-twentieth-century global capitalism as well as crises of global ecology—nation formation, loosened from what retrospectively appears as a historically fleeting attachment to states, is today fervently being asserted in politico-cultural claims ranging from Islamic to deaf, indigenous to Gypsy, Serbian to queer.

Despite certain convergences, articulations and parallels between such culturally disparate political formations in the late twentieth century, I shall not be considering the problematic of politicized identity on a global scale. Indeed, this essay is, among other things, an argument for substantial historical, geopolitical and cultural specificity in an exploration of the problematic of political identity. My focus in the following pages will be on selected contradictory operations of politicized identity *within* late-modern democracy, considering politicized identity as both a production and contestation of the political terms of liberalism, disciplinary-bureaucratic regimes, certain forces of global capitalism, and the demographic flows of postcoloniality which together might be taken as constitutive of the contemporary North American political condition. In recent years, enough stalemated argument has transpired about the virtues and vices of something named identity politics to suggest the limited usefulness of a discussion of identity, either in terms of the timeless metaphysical or linguistic elements of its constitution, or in terms of the ethical-political rubric of good and evil. Beginning instead with the premise that the proliferation and politicization of identities in the United States is not a moral or even political choice but a complex historical production, a more interesting contribution from scholars might consist in elucidating something of the nature of this production, in order to locate within it both the openings and the perils for a radically democratic or counterhegemonic political project.

Many have asked how, given what appear as the inherently totalizing and "othering" characteristics of identity in/as language, identity can avoid reiterating such investments in its ostensibly emancipatory mode.[2] I want to ask a similar question, but in a historically specific cultural-political register, not because the linguistic frame is unimportant, but because it is insufficient for discerning the character of contemporary politicized identity's problematic investments. Thus, the sets of questions framing the work of this essay are these: First, given the subjectivizing conditions of identity production in a late-modern capitalist, liberal and disciplinary-bureaucratic social order, how can reiteration of these production conditions be averted in identity's purportedly emancipatory project? In the specific context of contemporary liberal and bureaucratic disciplinary discourse, what kind of political recognition can identity-based claims seek—and what kind can they be counted on to want—that will not resubordinate the subject, itself historically subjugated through identity, through categories such as race or gender which emerged and circulated as terms of power to enact subordination? The question here is not *whether* denaturalizing political strategies subvert the subjugating force of naturalized identity formation, but *what kind* of politicization, produced out of and inserted into *what kind* of political context, might perform such subversion? Second, given the widely averred interest of politicized identity in achieving emancipatory political recognition in a posthumanist discourse, what are the logics of pain in the subject-formation processes of late-modern society that might contain or subvert this aim? What are the particular constituents—specific to our time yet roughly generic for a diverse spectrum of identities—of identity's desire for recognition that seem as often to breed a politics of recrimination and rancor, of culturally dispersed paralysis and suffering, a tendency to reproach power rather than aspire to it, to disdain freedom rather than practice it? In short, where do the historically and culturally specific elements of politicized identity's investments in itself, and especially in its own history of suffering, come into conflict with the need to give up these investments, to engage in something of a Nietzschean "forgetting" of this history, in the pursuit of an emancipatory democratic project?

I will approach these questions by first offering a highly selective account of the discursive historical context of identity politics' emergence in the

Wendy Brown

United States, and then elaborating, through reconsideration of Nietzsche's genealogy of the logics of *ressentiment*, the wounded character of politicized identity's desire within this context. This is not an essay about the general worth or accomplishments of "identity politics," nor is it a critique of that oppositional political formation. It is, rather, an exploration of the ways in which certain aspects of the specific genealogy of politicized identity are carried in the structure of its political demands, with consequences that include self-subversion.

I

The tension between particularistic "I's" and a universal "we" in liberalism is sustainable as long as the constituent terms of the "I" remain unpoliticized, indeed, as long as the "I" itself remains unpoliticized on one hand, and the state (as the expression of the ideal of political universality) remains unpoliticized on the other. That is, the latent conflict in liberalism between universal representation and individualism remains latent, remains unpoliticized, as long as differential powers in civil society remain naturalized, as long as the "I" remains politically unarticulated, as long as it is willing to have its freedom represented abstractly, in effect, to subordinate its "I-ness" to the abstract "we" represented by the universal community of the state. This subordination is achieved either by the "I" abstracting from itself in its political representation, thus trivializing its "difference" so as to remain part of the "we" (as in homosexuals who are "just like everyone else except for who we sleep with") or by accepting its construction as a supplement, complement or partial outsider to the "we" (as in the history of women being "concluded by their husbands," to use Blackstone's phrase, or homosexuals who are just "different," or Jews whose communal affiliations lie partly or wholly outside their national identity). The history of liberalism's management of its inherited and constructed "others" could be read as a history of variations on and vacillations between these two strategies.

The abstract character of liberal political membership and the ideologically naturalized character of liberal individualism together work against politicized identity formation.[3] A formulation of the political state and of citizenship which, as Marx put it in the "Jewish Question," abstracts from the substantive conditions of our lives, works to prevent recognition or articulation of differences *as* political—as effects of power—in their very construction and organization; they are at most the stuff of divergent political or economic *interests*.[4] Equally important, to the extent that political membership in the liberal state involves abstracting from one's social being, it involves abstracting not only from the contingent productions of one's life circumstances but from the *identificatory* processes constitutive of one's social construction and position. Whether read from the frontispiece of Hobbes' *Leviathan,* in which the many are made one through the unity of the sovereign, or from the formulations of tolerance codified by John Locke, John Stuart Mill and, more contemporaneously, George Kateb, in which the minimalist liberal state is cast as precisely what enables our politically unfettered individuality, we are invited to seek equal deference—equal blindness from—but not equalizing *recognition* from the state, liberalism's universal moment.[5] As Marx discerned in his critique of Hegel, the universality of the state is ideologically achieved by turning away from and thus depoliticizing, yet at the same time *presupposing* our collective particulars, not by embracing them, let alone emancipating us from them.[6] In short, "the political" in liberalism is precisely not a domain for social identification: expected to recognize our political selves in the state, we are not led to expect deep recognition there. Put slightly differently, in a smooth and legitimate liberal order, if the particularistic "I" must remain unpoliticized, so also must the universalistic "we" remain without specific content or aim, without a common good *other than* abstract universal representation or pluralism. The abstractness of the "we" is precisely what insists upon, reiterates and even enforces the depoliticized nature of the "I." In Ernesto Laclau's formulation, "if democracy *is* possible, it is because the universal does not have any necessary body, any necessary content."[7]

While this détente between universal and particular within liberalism is potted with volatile conceits, it is rather thoroughly unraveled by two features of late modernity, spurred by developments in what Marx and Foucault respectively reveal as liberalism's companion powers: capitalism and disciplinarity. On one side, the state loses even its guise of universality as it becomes ever more transparently invested in particular economic interests, political ends and social formations—as it transmogrifies from a relatively minimalist, "night watchman" state to a heavily bureaucratized, managerial, fiscally enormous and highly interventionist welfare-warfare state, a transmogrification occasioned by the combined imperatives of capital and the auto-proliferating characteristics of bureaucracy.[8] On the other side, the

Wendy Brown

liberal subject is increasingly disinterred from substantive nation-state identification, not only by the individuating effects of liberal discourse itself, but through the social effects of late twentieth-century economic and political life: deterritorializing demographic flows; the disintegration from within and invasion from without of family and community as (relatively) autonomous sites of social production and identification; consumer capitalism's marketing discourse in which individual (and sub-individual) desires are produced, commodified, and mobilized as identities; and disciplinary productions of a fantastic array of behavior-based identities ranging from recovering alcoholic professionals to unrepentant crack mothers. These disciplinary productions work to conjure and regulate subjects through classificatory schemes, naming and normalizing social behaviors as social positions. Operating through what Foucault calls "an anatomy of detail," "disciplinary power" produces social identities (available for politicization because they are deployed for purposes of political regulation) which cross-cut juridical identities based on abstract right. Thus, for example, the welfare state's production of welfare subjects—themselves subdivided through the socially regulated categories of motherhood, disability, race, age, and so forth—potentially produce political identity through these categories, produce identities *as* these categories.

In this story, the always imminent but increasingly politically manifest failure of liberal universalism to be universal—the transparent fiction of state universality—combines with the increasing individuation of social subjects through capitalist disinterments and disciplinary productions. Together, they breed the emergence of politicized identity, rooted in disciplinary productions, but oriented by liberal discourse toward protest against exclusion from a discursive formation of universal justice. This production, however, is not linear or even, but highly contradictory: while the terms of liberalism are part of the ground of production of a politicized identity which reiterates yet exceeds these terms, liberal discourse itself also continuously recolonizes political identity *as* political interest—a conversion which recasts politicized identity's substantive and often deconstructive cultural claims and critiques as generic claims of particularism endemic to universalist political culture. Similarly, disciplinary power manages liberalism's production of politicized subjectivity by neutralizing identity through normalizing practices. As liberal discourse converts political identity into essentialized private interest, disciplinary power converts interest into normativized social identity manageable by regulatory regimes. Thus, disciplinary power politically neutralizes entitlement claims generated by liberal individuation, while liberalism politically neutralizes rights claims generated by disciplinary identities.

In addition to the formations of identity which may be the complex effects of disciplinary and liberal modalities of power, I want to suggest one other historical strand relevant to the production of politicized identity, this one hewn more specifically to developments in recent political culture. Although sanguine to varying degrees about the phenomenon they are describing, many on the European and North American Left have argued that identity politics emerges from the demise of class politics attendant upon post-Fordism or pursuant to May '68. Without adjudicating the precise relationship between the breakup of class politics and the proliferation of other sites of political identification, I want to refigure this claim by suggesting that what we have come to call identity politics is partly dependent upon the demise of a *critique* of capitalism and of bourgeois cultural and economic values.[9] In a reading which links the new identity claims to a certain relegitimation of capitalism, identity politics concerned with race, sexuality and gender will appear not as a supplement to class politics, not as an expansion of Left categories of oppression and emancipation, not as an enriching complexification of progressive formulations of power and persons—*all of which they also are*—but as tethered to a formulation of justice which reinscribes a bourgeois (masculinist) ideal as its measure. If it is this ideal which signifies educational and vocational opportunity, upward mobility, relative protection against arbitrary violence and reward in proportion to effort, and if it is this ideal against which many of the exclusions and privations of people of color, gays and lesbians and women are articulated, then the political purchase of contemporary American identity politics would seem to be achieved in part *through* a certain renaturalization of capitalism which can be said to have marked progressive discourse since the 1970s. What this also suggests is that identity politics may be partly configured by a peculiarly shaped and peculiarly disguised form of class resentment, a resentment which is displaced onto discourses of injustice other than class, but a resentment, like all resentments, which retains the real or imagined holdings of its reviled subject as objects of desire. In other words, the enunciation of politicized identities through race, gender and sexuality may require—rather than incidentally produce—a limited identification through class, and may specifically abjure a critique of class power and class norms precisely insofar as these identities are established *vis-à-vis* a bourgeois norm of social acceptance, legal protection and relative material comfort. Yet, when not only economic stratification but other injuries to the human body and psyche enacted by capitalism—alienation, commodification, exploitation, displacement, disintegration of sustaining albeit contradictory social forms such as families and neighborhoods—when these are discursively normalized and thus depoliticized, other markers of social difference may come to bear an inordinate weight, indeed, all the weight of the sufferings produced by capitalism in addition to that attributable to the explicitly politicized marking.[10]

If there is one class which articulates and even politicizes itself in late modern US life, it is that which gives itself the name of the "middle class." But the foregoing suggests that this is not a reactionary identity in the sense, for example, that "White" or "straight" are in contemporary political discourse. Rather it is an articulation by the figure of the class which represents, indeed depends upon, the naturalization rather than the politicization of capitalism, the denial of capitalism's power effects in ordering social life, and the representation of the ideal of capitalism to provide the good life for all. Poised between the rich and poor, feeling itself to be protected from the encroachments of neither, the phantasmatic middle class signifies the natural and the good between, on one side, the decadent or the corrupt and on the other, the aberrant or the decaying. It is a conservative identity in the sense that it semiotically recurs to a phantasmatic past, an idyllic, unfettered and uncorrupted historical moment (implicitly located around 1955) when life was good again—housing was affordable, men supported families on single incomes, drugs were confined to urban ghettos. But it is not a reactionary identity in the sense of reacting to an insurgent politicized identity from below: rather, it precisely embodies the ideal to which non-class identities refer for proof of their exclusion or injury: homosexuals who lack the protections of marriage, guarantees of child custody or job security, and freedom from harassment; single women who are strained and impoverished by trying to raise children and hold paid jobs simultaneously; people of color disproportionately affected by unemployment, punishing urban housing costs, inadequate health care programs, and disproportionately subjected to unwarranted harassment and violence, figured as criminals, ignored by cab drivers. The point is not that these privations are trivial, but that, without recourse to the White, masculine, middle-class ideal, politicized identities would forfeit a good deal of their claims to injury and exclusion, their claims to the political significance of their difference. If they thus require this ideal for the potency and poignancy of their political claims, we might ask to what extent a critique of capitalism is foreclosed by the current configuration of oppositional politics, and not simply by the "loss of the socialist alternative" or the ostensible "triumph of liberalism" in the global order. In contrast with the Marxist critique of a social whole and Marxist vision of total transformation, to what extent do identity politics require a standard internal to existing society against which to pitch their claims, a standard which not only preserves capitalism from critique, but sustains the invisibility and inarticulateness of class, not accidentally, but endemically? Could we have stumbled upon one reason why class is invariably named but rarely theorized or developed in the multiculturalist mantra, "race, class, gender, sexuality"?

II

The story of the emergence of contemporary identity politics could be told in many other ways—as the development of "new social antagonisms" rooted in consumer capitalism's commodification of all spheres of social life, as the relentless denaturalization of all social relations occasioned by the fabrications and border violations of postmodern technologies and cultural productions, as a form of political consciousness precipitated by the Black Civil Rights Movement in the United States.[11] I have told the story this way in order to emphasize the *discursive political context* of its emergence, its disciplinary, capitalist and liberal parentage, and this in order to comprehend politicized identity's genealogical structure as comprised of and not only opposing these very modalities of political power. Indeed, if the ostensibly oppositional character of identity politics also renders it something of the "illegitimate offspring" of liberal, capitalist, disciplinary discourses, its absent fathers are not, as Donna Haraway suggests, "inessential," but installed in the very structure of *desire* fueling identity-based political claims: the psyche of the bastard child is hardly independent of its family of origin.[12] And if we are interested in developing the contestatory, subversive, potentially transformative elements of identity-based political claims, we need to know the implications of the particular genealogy and production conditions of identity's desire for recognition. We need to be able to ask: Given what produced it, given what shapes and suffuses it, what does politicized identity want?

We might profitably begin these investigations with a reflection on their curious elision by the philosopher who also frames them, Michel Foucault. For Foucault, the constraints of emancipatory politics in late-modern democracy pertain both to the ubiquity and pervasiveness of power—the impossibility of eschewing power in human affairs—as well as to the ways in which subjects and practices are always at risk of being resubordinated through the discourses naming and politicizing them. Best known for his formulation of this dual problem in the domain of sexual liberation, Foucault offers a more generic theoretical account in his discussion of the disinterment of the "insurrectionary knowledges," of marginalized populations and practices:

> Is the relation of forces today still such as to allow these disinterred knowledges some kind of autonomous life? Can they be isolated by these means from every subjugating relationship? What force do they have taken in themselves?. . . Is it not perhaps the case that these fragments of genealogies are no sooner brought to light, that the particular elements of the knowledge that one seeks to disinter are no sooner accredited and put into circulation, than they run the risk of re-codification, re-colonisation? In fact, those unitary discourses which first disqualified and then ignored them when they made their appearance, are it seems, quite ready now to annex them, to take them back within the fold of their own discourse and to invest them with everything this implies in terms of their effects of knowledge and power. And if we want to protect these only lately liberated fragments, are we not in danger of ourselves constructing, with our own hands, that unitary discourse . . . ?[13]

Foucault's caution about the annexing, colonizing effects of invariably unifying discourses is an important one. But the question of the emancipatory orientation of historically subordinated discourse is not limited to the risk of co-optation or resubordination by extant or newly formed unitary discourses—whether those of humanism on one side, or of cultural studies, multiculturalism, subaltern studies and minority discourse on the other.

Nor is it reducible to what has always struck me as an unexamined Frankfurt School strain in Foucault, the extent to which the Foucauldian subject, originally desirous of freedom, comes to will its own domination, or in Foucault's rubric, becomes a good disciplinary subject. Rather, I think that for Foucault, insofar as power always produces resistance, even the disciplinary subject is perversely capable of resistance, and in practicing it, practices freedom. Discernible here is the basis of a curious optimism, even volunteerism in Foucault, namely his oddly physicalist and insistently non-psychic account of power, practices and subject-formation. His removal of the "will to power" from Nietzsche's complex psychology of need, frustration, impotence and compensatory deeds is what permits Foucault to feature resistance as always possible and as equivalent to practicing freedom. In an interview with Paul Rabinow, Foucault muses:

> I do not think that it is possible to say that one thing is of the order of "liberation" and another is of the order of "oppression." . . . No matter how terrifying a given system may be, there always remain the possibilities of resistance, disobedience, and oppositional groupings.
>
> On the other hand, I do not think that there is anything that is functionally . . . absolutely liberating. Liberty is a *practice*. . . . The liberty of men is never assured by the institutions and laws that are intended to guarantee them. . . . Not because they are ambiguous, but simply because "liberty" is what must be exercised. . . . The guarantee of freedom is freedom.[14]

My quarrel here is not with Foucault's valuable insistence upon freedom as a practice, but with his distinct lack of attention to what might constitute, negate or redirect the desire for freedom.[15] Notwithstanding his critique of the repressive hypothesis and postulation of the subject as an effect of power, Foucault seems to tacitly assume the givenness and resilience of the desire for freedom, a givenness that arises consequent to his implicit conflation of the will to power in resistance with a will to freedom. Thus, Foucault's confidence about the possibilities of "practicing" or "exercising" liberty resides in a quasi-empirical concern with the relative *capacity* or space for action in the context of certain regimes of domination. But whether or not resistance is possible is a different question from what its aim is, what it is for, and especially whether or not it resubjugates the resisting subject. Foucault's rejection of psychoanalysis and his arrested reading of Nietzsche (his utter eclipse of Nietzsche's diagnosis of the culture of modernity as the triumph of "slave morality") combine to locate the problem of freedom for Foucault as one of domain and discourse, rather than the problem of "will" that it is for Nietzsche. Indeed, what requires for its answer a profoundly more psychological Nietzsche than the one Foucault embraces, is not a question about when or where the practice of freedom is possible but a question about *the direction of the will to power*, a will which potentially, but only potentially, animates a desire for freedom. Especially for the Nietzsche of *The Genealogy of Morals*, the modern subject does not simply cease to desire freedom, as is the case with Foucault's disciplinary subject, but much more problematically, loathes freedom.[16] Let us now consider why.

III

Contemporary politicized identity contests the terms of liberal discourse insofar as it challenges liberalism's universal "we" as a strategic fiction of historically hegemonic groups and asserts liberalism's "I" as social—both relational and constructed by power—rather than contingent, private or autarkic. Yet it reiterates the terms of liberal discourse insofar as it posits a sovereign and unified "I" that is disenfranchised by an exclusive "we." Indeed, I have suggested that politicized identity emerges and obtains its unifying coherence through the politicization of *exclusion* from an ostensible universal, as a protest against exclusion, a protest premised on the fiction of an inclusive/universal community, a protest which reinstalls the humanist ideal—and a specific White, middle-class, masculinist expression of this ideal—insofar as it premises itself upon exclusion from it. Put the other way around, politicized identities generated out of liberal, disciplinary societies, insofar as they are premised on exclusion from a universal ideal, require that ideal, as well as their exclusion from it, for their own perpetuity as identities.[17]

Politicized identity is also potentially reiterative of regulatory, disciplinary society in its configuration of a disciplinary subject. It is both produced by and potentially accelerates the production of that aspect of disciplinary society which "ceaselessly characterizes, classifies, and specializes," which works through "surveillance, continuous registration, perpetual assessment, and classification," through a social machinery "that is both immense and minute."[18] A recent example from the world of local politics makes clear politicized identity's imbrication in disciplinary power, as well as the way in which, as Foucault reminds us, disciplinary power "infiltrates" rather than replaces liberal juridical modalities.[19] Last year the city council of my town reviewed an ordinance, devised and promulgated by a broad coalition of identity-based political groups, which aimed to ban discrimination in employment, housing and public accommodations on the basis of: "sexual orientation, transsexuality, age, height, weight, personal appearance, physical characteristics, race, color, creed, religion, national origin, ancestry, disability, marital status, sex or gender."[20] Here is a perfect instance of the universal juridical ideal of liberalism and the normalizing principle of disciplinary regimes conjoined and taken up within the discourse of politicized identity. This ordinance—variously called the "purple hair ordinance" or the "ugly ordinance" by state and national news media— aims to count every difference as no difference, as part of the seamless whole, but also to count every potentially subversive rejection of culturally enforced norms as themselves normal, as normalizable, and as normativizable through law. Indeed, through the definitional, procedural and remedies sections of this ordinance (for instance, "sexual orientation shall mean known or assumed homosexuality, heterosexuality, or bisexuality") persons are reduced to observable social attributes and practices; these are defined empirically, positivistically, as if their existence were intrinsic and factual, rather than effects of discursive and institutional power; and these positivist definitions of persons as their attributes and practices are written into law, ensuring that persons describable according to them will now become regulated through them. Bentham could not have done it better. Indeed, here is a perfect instance of how the language of recognition becomes the language of unfreedom, how articulation in language, in the context of liberal and disciplinary discourse, becomes a vehicle of subordination through individualization, normalization and regulation, even as it strives to produce visibility and acceptance. Here, also, is a perfect instance of the way in which differences that are the effects of social power are neutralized through their articulation as attributes and their circulation through liberal administrative discourse: What do we make of a document which renders as juridical equivalents the denial of employment to an African-American, an obese man, and a White, middle-class youth festooned with tattoos and fuchsia hair?

Wendy Brown

What I want to consider, though, is why this strikingly unemancipatory political project emerges from a potentially more radical critique of liberal juridical and disciplinary modalities of power. For this ordinance, I want to suggest, is not simply misguided in its complicity with the rationalizing and disciplinary elements of late-modern culture, it is not simply naive with regard to the regulatory apparatus within which it operates. Rather, it is symptomatic of a feature of politicized identity's *desire* within liberal-bureaucratic regimes, its foreclosure of its own freedom, its impulse to inscribe in the law and in other political registers its historical and present pain rather than to conjure an imagined future of power to make itself. To see what this symptom is a symptom of, we need to return once more to a schematic consideration of liberalism, this time in order to read it through Nietzsche's account of the complex logics of *ressentiment*.

IV

Liberalism contains from its inception a generalized incitement to what Nietzsche terms *ressentiment*, the moralizing revenge of the powerless, "the triumph of the weak as weak."[21] This incitement to *ressentiment* inheres in two related constitutive paradoxes of liberalism: that between individual liberty and social egalitarianism, a paradox which produces failure turned to recrimination by the subordinated, and guilt turned to resentment by the "successful"; and that between the individualism that legitimates liberalism and the cultural homogeneity required by its commitment to political universality, a paradox which stimulates the articulation of politically significant differences on the one hand, and the suppression of them on the other, and which offers a form of articulation that presses against the limits of universalist discourse even while that which is being articulated seeks to be harbored within—included—in the terms of that universalism.

Premising itself on the natural equality of human beings, liberalism makes a political promise of universal individual freedom, in order to arrive at social equality, or achieve a civilized retrieval of the equality postulated in the state of nature. It is the tension between the promises of individualistic liberty and the requisites of equality that yields *ressentiment* in one of two directions, depending on the way in which the paradox is brokered. A strong commitment to freedom vitiates the fulfillment of the equality promise and breeds *ressentiment* as welfare-state liberalism—attenuations of the unmitigated license of the rich and powerful on behalf of the "disadvantaged." Conversely, a strong commitment to equality, requiring heavy state interventionism and economic redistribution, attenuates the commitment to freedom and breeds *ressentiment* expressed as conservative anti-statism, racism, charges of reverse racism and so forth.

However, it is not only the tension between freedom and equality but the prior presumption of the self-reliant and self-made capacities of liberal subjects, conjoined with their unavowed dependence on and construction by a variety of social relations and forces, which makes *all* liberal subjects, and not only markedly disenfranchised ones, vulnerable to *ressentiment*: it is their situatedness within power, their production by power, and liberal discourse's denial of this situatedness and production, which casts the liberal subject into failure, the failure to make itself in the context of a discourse in which its self-making is assumed, indeed, is its assumed nature. This failure, which Nietzsche calls suffering, must either find a reason within itself (which redoubles the failure) or a site of external blame upon which to avenge its hurt, and redistribute its pain. Here is Nietzsche's account of this moment in the production of *ressentiment*:

> For every sufferer instinctively seeks a cause for his suffering, more exactly, an agent; still more specifically a *guilty* agent who is susceptible to suffering—in short, some living thing upon which he can on some pretext or other, vent his affects, actually or in effigy.
> ... This ... constitutes the actual physiological cause of *ressentiment*, vengefulness, and the like: a desire to deaden pain by means of affects ... to deaden, by means of a more violent emotion of any kind, a tormenting, secret pain that is becoming unendurable, and to drive it out of consciousness at least for the moment: for that one requires an affect, as savage an affect as possible, and, in order to excite that, any pretext at all.[22]

Ressentiment in this context is a triple achievement: it produces an affect (rage, righteousness) which overwhelms the hurt; it produces a culprit responsible for the hurt; and it produces a site of revenge to displace the hurt (a place to inflict hurt as the sufferer has been hurt). Together these operations both ameliorate (in Nietzsche's terms, "anaesthetize") and externalize what is otherwise "unendurable."

Wendy
Brown

Now, what I want to suggest is that in a culture already streaked with the pathos of *ressentiment* for these reasons, there are several characteristics of late-modern post-industrial societies which accelerate and expand the conditions of its production. My listing will necessarily be highly schematic: first, the phenomenon William Connolly names "increased global contingency" combines with the expanding pervasiveness and complexity of domination by capital and bureaucratic state and social networks to create an unparalleled individual powerlessness over the fate and direction of one's own life, intensifying the experiences of impotence, dependence and gratitude inherent in liberal capitalist orders and constitutive of *ressentiment*.[23] Second, the steady desacralization of all regions of life—what Weber called disenchantment, what Nietzsche called the death of God—would seem to add yet another reversal to Nietzsche's genealogy of *ressentiment* as perpetually available to "alternation of direction." In Nietzsche's account, the ascetic priest deployed notions of "guilt, sin, sinfulness, depravity and damnation" to "direct the *ressentiment* of the less severely afflicted sternly back upon themselves . . . and in this way [exploited] the bad instincts of all sufferers for the purpose of self-discipline, self-surveillance, and self-overcoming."[24] However, the desacralizing tendencies of late modernity undermine the efficacy of this deployment and turn suffering's need for exculpation back toward a site of external agency.[25] Third, the increased fragmentation, if not disintegration, of all forms of association until recently not organized by the commodities market—communities, churches, families—and the ubiquitousness of the classificatory, individuating schemes of disciplinary society, combine to produce an utterly *unrelieved* individual, one without insulation from the inevitable failure, entailed in liberalism's individualistic construction. In short, the characteristics of late-modern secular society, in which individuals are buffeted and controlled by global configurations of disciplinary and capitalist power of extraordinary proportions, and are at the same time nakedly individuated, stripped of reprieve from relentless exposure and accountability for themselves, together add up to an incitement to *ressentiment* that might have stunned even the finest philosopher of its occasions and logics. Starkly accountable yet dramatically impotent, the late-modern liberal subject quite literally seethes with *ressentiment*.

Enter politicized identity, now conceivable in part as both product of and "reaction" to this condition, where "reaction" acquires the meaning Nietzsche ascribed to it, namely as an effect of domination that reiterates impotence, a substitute for action, for power, for self-affirmation that reinscribes incapacity, powerlessness and rejection. For Nietzsche, *ressentiment* itself is rooted in "reaction"—the substitution of reasons, norms and ethics for deeds—and suggests that not only moral systems but identities themselves take their bearings in this reaction. As Tracy Strong reads this element of Nietzsche's thought:

> Identity . . . does not consist of an active component, but is reaction to something outside; action in itself, with its inevitable self-assertive qualities, must then become something evil, since it is identified with that against which one is reacting. The will to power of slave morality must constantly reassert that which gives definition to the slave: the pain he suffers by being in the world. Hence any attempt to escape that pain will merely result in the reaffirmation of painful structures.[26]

If *ressentiment's* "cause" is suffering, its "creative deed" is the reworking of this pain into a negative form of action, the "imaginary revenge" of what Nietzsche terms "natures denied the true reaction, that of deeds."[27] This revenge is achieved through the imposition of suffering "on whatever does not feel wrath and displeasure as he does"[28] (accomplished especially through the production of guilt), through the establishment of suffering as the measure of social virtue, and through casting strength and good fortune ("privilege" as we say today) as self-recriminating, as its own indictment in a culture of suffering: "it is disgraceful to be fortunate, there is too much misery."[29]

But in its attempt to displace its suffering, identity structured by *ressentiment* at the same time becomes invested in its own subjection. This investment lies not only in its discovery of a site of blame for its hurt will, not only in its acquisition of recognition through its history of subjection (a recognition predicated on injury, now righteously revalued), but also in the satisfactions of revenge which ceaselessly reenact even as they redistribute the injuries of marginalization and subordination in a liberal discursive order which alternately denies the very possibility of these things or blames those who experience them for their own condition. Identity politics structured by *ressentiment* reverses without subverting this blaming structure: it

Wendy Brown

does not subject to critique the sovereign subject of accountability that liberal individualism presupposes, nor the economy of inclusion and exclusion that liberal universalism establishes. Thus, politicized identity which presents itself as a self-affirmation now appears as the opposite, as predicated on and requiring its sustained rejection by a "hostile external world."[30]

Insofar as what Nietzsche calls slave morality produces identity in reaction to power, insofar as identity rooted in this reaction achieves its moral superiority by reproaching power and action themselves as evil, identity structured by this ethos becomes deeply invested in its own impotence, even while it seeks to assuage the pain of its powerlessness through its vengeful moralizing, through its wide distribution of suffering, through its reproach of power as such. Politicized identity, premised on exclusion and fueled by the humiliation and suffering imposed by its historically structured impotence in the context of a discourse of sovereign individuals, is as likely to seek generalized political paralysis, to feast on generalized political impotence, as it is to seek its own or collective liberation through empowerment. Indeed, it is more likely to punish and reproach—"punishment is what revenge calls itself; with a hypocritical lie it creates a good conscience for itself"—than to find venues of self-affirming action.[31]

But contemporary politicized identity's desire is not only shaped by the extent to which the sovereign will of the liberal subject, articulated ever more nakedly by disciplinary individuation and capitalist disinternments, is dominated by late-twentieth-century configurations of political and economic powers. It is shaped as well by the contemporary problematic of history itself, by the late-modern rupture of history as a narrative, history as ended because it has lost its end, a rupture which paradoxically produces an immeasurable heaviness to history. As the grim experience of reading *Discipline and Punish* makes clear, there is a sense in which the gravitational force of history is multiplied at precisely the moment that history's narrative coherence and objectivist foundation is refuted. As the problematic of power in history is resituated from subject positioning to subject construction, as power is seen to operate spatially, infiltrationally, "microphysically," rather than only temporally—permeating every heretofore designated "interior" *space* in social lives and individuals—as the erosion of historical metanarratives takes with them both laws of history and the futurity such laws purported to assure, as the presumed continuity of history is replaced with a sense of its violent, contingent and ubiquitous *force*, history becomes that which has weight but no trajectory, mass but no coherence, force but no direction; it is war without ends or end. Thus, the extent to which "dead generations weigh like a nightmare on the brains of the living" is today unparalleled, even as history itself disintegrates as a coherent category or practice. We know ourselves to be saturated by history, we feel the extraordinary force of its determinations; we are also steeped in a discourse of its insignificance, and above all, we know that history will no longer (always already did not) act as our redeemer.

I raise the question of history because in thinking about late-modern politicized identity's structuring by *ressentiment*, I have thus far focused on its foundation in the sufferings of a subordinated sovereign subject. But Nietzsche's account of the logic of *ressentiment* is also tethered to that feature of the will which is stricken by history, which rails against time itself, which cannot "will backwards," which cannot exert its power over the past—either as a specific set of events or as time itself.

> Willing liberates but what is it that puts even the liberator himself in fetters? "It was"—that is the name of the will's gnashing of teeth and most secret melancholy. Powerless against what has been done, he is an angry spectator of all that is past. . . . He cannot break time and time's covetousness, that is the will's loneliest melancholy.[32]

Although Nietzsche appears here to be speaking of the will as such, Zarathustra's own relationship to the will as a "redeemer of history" makes clear that this "angry spectatorship" can, with great difficulty, be reworked as a perverse kind of mastery, a mastery that triumphs over the past by reducing its power, by remaking the present against the terms of the past—in short, by a project of self-transformation which arrays itself against its own genealogical consciousness. In contrast with the human ruin he sees everywhere around him—"fragments and limbs and dreadful accidents"—it is Zarathustra's own capacity to discern and to make a future which spares him from a rancorous sensibility, from crushing disappointment in the liberatory promise of his will:

> The now and the past on earth—alas, my friends, that is what *I* find most unendurable; and I should not know how to live if I were

not also a seer of that which must come. A seer, a willer, a creator, a future himself and a bridge to the future—and alas, also as it were, a cripple at this bridge: all this is Zarathustra.[33]

Nietzsche here discerns both the necessity and the near-impossibility—the extraordinary and fragile achievement—of formulating oneself as a creator of the future and a bridge to the future in order to appease the otherwise inevitable rancor of the will against time, in order to redeem the past by lifting the weight of it, by reducing the scope of its determinations. "And how could I bear to be a man if man were not also a creator and guesser of riddles and redeemer of accidents?"[34]

Of course, Zarathustra's exceptionality in what he is willing to confront and bear, in his capacities to overcome in order to create, is Nietzsche's device for revealing us to ourselves. The ordinary will, steeped in the economy of slave morality, devises means "to get rid of his melancholy and to mock his dungeon," means which reiterate the cause of the melancholy, which continually reinfect the narcissistic wound to its capaciousness inflicted by the past. "Alas," says Nietzsche, "every prisoner becomes a fool; and the imprisoned will redeems himself foolishly."[35] From this foolish redemption—foolish because it does not resolve the will's rancor but only makes a world in its image—is born the wrath of revenge:

> "that which was" is the name of the stone [the will] cannot move. And so he moves stones out of wrath and displeasure, and he wreaks revenge on whatever does not feel wrath and displeasure, as he does. Thus the will, the liberator, took to hurting; and on all who can suffer he wreaks revenge for his inability to go backwards. This . . . is what *revenge* is: the will's ill will against time and its "it was."[36]

Revenge as a "reaction," a substitute for the capacity to act, produces identity as both bound to the history which produced it and as a reproach to the present which embodies that history. The will that "took to hurting" in its own impotence against its past becomes (in the form of an identity whose very existence is due to heightened consciousness of the immovability of its "it was," its history of subordination) a will that makes not only a psychological but a political practice of revenge, a practice which reiterates the existence of an identity whose present past is one of insistently unredeemable injury. This past cannot be redeemed *unless* the identity ceases to be invested in it, and it cannot cease to be invested in it without giving up its identity as such, thus giving up its economy of avenging and at the same time perpetuating its hurt—"when he then stills the pain of the wound, he at the same time infects the wound. . . . "[37]

In its emergence as a protest against marginalization or subordination, politicized identity thus becomes attached to its own exclusion, both because it is premised on this exclusion for its very existence as identity, and because the formation of identity at the site of exclusion, as exclusion, augments or "alters the direction of the suffering" entailed in subordination or marginalization, by finding a site of blame for it. But in so doing, it installs its pain over its unredeemed history in the very foundation of its political claim, in its demand for recognition as identity. In locating a site of blame for its powerlessness over its past, as a past of injury, a past as a hurt will, and locating a "reason" for the "unendurable pain" of social powerlessness in the present, it converts this reasoning into an ethicizing politics, a politics of recrimination that seeks to avenge the hurt even while it reaffirms it, discursively codifies it. Politicized identity thus enunciates itself, makes claims for itself, only by entrenching, restating, dramatizing, and inscribing its pain in politics, and can hold out no future—for itself or others—which triumphs over this pain. The loss of historical direction, and with it the loss of futurity characteristic of the late-modern age, is thus homologically refigured in the structure of desire of the dominant political expression of the age—identity politics. In the same way, the generalized political impotence produced by the ubiquitous yet discontinuous networks of late-modern political and economic power is reiterated in the investments of late-modern democracy's primary oppositional political formations.

What might be entailed in transforming these investments in an effort to fashion a more radically democratic and emancipatory political culture? One avenue of exploration may lie in Nietzsche's counsel on the virtues of "forgetting," for if identity structured in part by *ressentiment* resubjugates itself through its investment in its own pain, through its refusal to make itself in the present, memory is the house of this activity and this refusal. Yet erased histories and historical invisibility are themselves such integral elements of the pain inscribed in most subjugated identities that the counsel of forgetting, at least in its unreconstructed Nietzschean form, seems inappropriate, if not cruel.[38] Indeed, it is also possible that we have reached a pass where we ought to part with Nietzsche, whose skills as diagnostician usually reach the limits of their political efficacy in his privileging of individual character and capacity over the transformative possibilities of collective political invention, in his remove from the refigurative possibilities of political conversation or transformative cultural practices. For if I am right about the problematic of pain installed at the heart of many contemporary contradictory demands for political recognition, all that such pain may long for more than revenge is the chance to be heard into a certain reprieve, recognized into self-overcoming, incited into possibilities for triumphing over, and hence, losing, itself. Our challenge, then, would be to configure a radically democratic political culture which can sustain such a project in its midst without being overtaken by it, a challenge which includes guarding against abetting the steady slide of political into therapeutic discourse, even as we acknowledge the elements of suffering and healing we might be negotiating.

What if it were possible to incite a slight shift in the character of political expression and political claims common to much politicized identity? What if we sought to supplant the language of "I am"—with its defensive closure on identity, its insistence on the fixity of position, its equation of social with moral positioning—with the language of "I want?" What if we were to rehabilitate the memory of desire within identificatory processes, the moment in desire—either "to have" or "to be"—prior to its wounding?[39] What if "wanting to be" or "wanting to have" were taken up as modes of political speech that could destabilize the formulation of identity as fixed position, as entrenchment by history, and as having necessary moral entailments, even as they affirm "position" and "history" as that which makes the speaking subject intelligible and locatable, as that which contributes to a hermeneutics for adjudicating desires? If every "I am" is something of a resolution of desire into fixed and sovereign identity, then this project might involve not only learning to speak but to *read* "I am" this way, as in motion, as temporal, as not-I, as deconstructable according to a genealogy of want rather than as fixed interests or experiences.[40] The subject understood as an effect of an (ongoing) genealogy of desire, including the social processes constitutive of, fulfilling or frustrating desire, is in this way revealed as neither sovereign nor conclusive, even as it is affirmed as an "I." In short, if framed in the right political language, this deconstruction could be that which reopens a language and practice of futurity where Nietzsche saw it foreclosed by the logics of rancor and *ressentiment*.

Such a slight shift in the character of the political discourse of identity eschews the kinds of ahistorical or utopian turns against identity politics made by a nostalgic and broken humanist Left, as well as the reactionary and disingenuous assaults on politicized identity tendered by the Right. Rather than opposing or seeking to transcend identity investments, the replacement—even the admixture—of the language of "being" with "wanting" would seek to exploit politically a recovery of the more expansive moments in the genealogy of identity formation, a recovery of the moment prior to its own foreclosure against its want, prior to the point at which its sovereign subjectivity is established through such foreclosure and through eternal repetition of its pain. How might democratic discourse itself be invigorated by such a shift from ontological claims to these kinds of more expressly political ones, claims which, rather than dispensing blame for an unlivable present, inhabited the necessarily agonistic theater of discursively forging an alternative future?

NOTES

1. The Local and the Global," in *Culture, Globalization, and the World System: Contemporary Conditions for the Representation of Identity*, ed. Anthony King (Albany: State University of New York Press, 1991), p. 24.

2. "An identity is established in relation to a series of differences that have become socially recognized. These differences are essential to its being. If they did not coexist as differences, it would not exist in its distinctness and solidarity. . . . Identity requires difference in order to be, and it converts difference into otherness in order to secure its own self-certainty." William Connolly, *Identity/Difference: Democratic Negotiations of Political Paradox* (Ithaca: Cornell University Press, 1991), p. 64.

   I cite from Connolly rather than the more obvious Derrida because Connolly is exemplary of the effort *within* political theory to think about the political problem of identity working heuristically with its linguistic operation. I cite from Connolly, as well, because the present essay is in some ways an extension of a conversation began at a 1991 American Political Science Association roundtable discussion of his book. In that discussion, noting that Connolly identified late modernity as producing certain problems for identity but did not historicize politicized identity itself, I called for such an historicization. To the degree that the present essay is my own partial response to that call, it—as the notes make clear—is indebted to Connolly's book and that public occasion of its discussion.

A short list of others who have struggled to take politicized identity through and past the problem of political exclusion and political closure might include: Stuart Hall, Trinh T. Minh-ha, Homi Bhabha, Paul Gilroy, Aiwah Ong, Judith Butler, Gayatri Spivak, Anne Norton.

3. Locke's (1689) "Letter Concerning Toleration" signals this development in intellectual history. The three hundred-year process of eliminating first the property qualification, and then race and gender qualifications in European and North American constitutional states heralds its formal political achievement.

4. "On the Jewish Question," in *The Marx-Engels Reader* (second edition), ed. R. Tucker (New York: Norton, 1974), p. 34.

5. John Locke, *Letter on Toleration*; John Stuart Mill, "On Liberty"; George Kateb, "Democratic Individuality and the Claims of Politics," *Political Theory*, August 1984.

6. In the "Jewish Question," Marx argues, "far from abolishing these *effective* differences [in civil society, the state] exists only so far as they are presupposed; it is conscious of being a political state and it manifests its universality only in *opposition* to these elements" (p. 33). See also Marx's *Critique of Hegel's Philosophy of Right*, ed. J. O'Malley (Cambridge: Cambridge University Press, 1970), pp. 91 and 116.

7. Ernesto Laclau, "Universalism, Particularism and the Question of Identity," in this volume. Laclau is here concerned not with the state but with the possibility of retaining a "universal" in social movement politics where a critique of bourgeois humanist universalism has become quite central. Interestingly, Laclau's effort to preserve a universalist political ideal from this challenge entails making this ideal even more abstract, pulling it further away from any specific configuration or purpose than the distance ordinarily managed by liberal discourse. Laclau's aim in voiding the universal completely of body and content is only partly to permit it to be more completely embracing of all the particulars; it is also intended to recognize the *strategic* value of the discourse of universality, the extent to which "different groups compete to give

their particular aims a temporary function of universal representation." But how, if universal discourse may always be revealed to have this strategic function, can it also be taken seriously as a substantive value of democracy?

8. Jürgen Habermas's *Legitimation Crisis*, trans. T. McCarthy (Boston: Beacon, 1975) and James O'Connor's *Fiscal Crisis of the State* (New York: St. Martin's Press, 1973) remain two of the most compelling narratives of this development. Also informing this claim are Max Weber's discussion of bureaucracy and rationalization in *Economy and Society*, Sheldon Wolin's discussion of the "mega-state" in *The Presence of the Past*, as well as the researches of Claus Offe, Bob Jessop, and Fred Block.

9. To be fully persuasive, this claim would have to reckon with the ways in which the articulation of African-American, feminist, queer or Native American "values" and cultural styles have figured centrally in many contemporary political projects. It would have to encounter the ways that the critique of cultural assimilation which I alluded to in this essay has been a critical dimension of identity politics. Space prohibits such a reckoning, but I think its terms would be those of capitalism and style, economics and culture, counterhegemonic projects and the politics of resistance.

10. It is, of course, also the abstraction of politicized identity from political economy that produces the failure of politicized identities to encompass and unify their "members." Striated not only in a formal sense by class, but divided as well by the extent to which the suffering entailed, for example, in gender and racial subordination, can be substantially offset by economic privilege, insistent definitions of Black, or Queer, or Woman sustain the same kind of exclusions and policing previously enacted by the tacitly White, male, heterosexual figure of the "working class."

11. See Ernesto Laclau and Chantal Mouffe, *Hegemony and Socialist Strategy* (London: Verso, 1985), p. 161; Scott Lash and John Urry, *The End of Organized Capitalism* (Madison: University of Wisconsin, 1987), chap. 9; David Harvey, *The Condition of Postmodernity* (Oxford: Blackwell, 1989), chap. 26; Bernice Johnson Reagon, "Coalition Politics: Turning the Century," in *Home Girls: A Black Feminist Anthology*, ed. Barbara Smith (New York: Kitchen Table: Woman of Color Press, 1983), p. 362.

12. In "A Manifesto for Cyborgs," *Feminism/Postmodernism*, ed. L. Nicholson (New York: Routledge, 1990), Donna Haraway writes: ". . . cyborgs are the illegitimate offspring of militarism and patriarchal capitalism, not to mention state socialism. But illegitimate offspring are often exceedingly unfaithful to their origins. Their fathers, after all, are inessential" (p. 193).

13. "Two Lectures," in *Power/Knowledge*, ed. Colin Gordon, (New York: Patheon, 1980), p. 86.

14. "Space, Knowledge, and Power," interview with Paul Rabinow in *The Foucault Reader*, ed. Paul Rabinow (New York: Pantheon, 1984), p. 245.

15. John Rajchman insists that Foucault's philosophy *is* "the endless question of freedom," (p. 124) but Rajchman, too, eschews the question of desire in his account of Foucault's freedom as the "motor and principle of his skepticism: the endless questioning of constituted experience" (p. 7). *Michael Foucault: The Freedom of Philosophy* (New York: Columbia University Press, 1985).

16. "This instinct for freedom forcibly made latent—this instinct for freedom pushed back and repressed, incarcerated within and finally able to discharge and vent itself only on itself. . . ." *Genealogy of Morals*, trans. W. Kaufmann and P. J. Hollindale (New York: Vintage, 1969), p. 87.

17. As Connolly argues, politicized identity also reiterates the structure of liberalism in its configuration of a sovereign, unified, accountable individual. Connolly urges, although it is not clear what would motivate identity's transformed orientation, a different configuration of identity—one which understood itself as contingent, relational, contestatory and social. See *Identity/Difference*, esp. pp. 171–184.

18. Michel Foucault, *Discipline and Punish*, trans. A. Sheridan (New York: Vintage, 1979), pp. 209, 212.

19. *Ibid.*, p. 206.

20. From a draft of "An Ordinance of the City of Santa Cruz Adding Chapter 9.83 to the Santa Cruz Municipal Code Pertaining to the Prohibition of Discrimination."

21. A number of political theorists have advanced this argument. For a cogent account, see pp. 21–27 of *Identity/Difference*.

22. *Genealogy of Morals*, p. 127.

23. *Identity/Difference*, pp. 24–26.

24. *Ibid.*, p. 128.

25. A striking example of this is the way that contemporary natural disasters, such as the 1989 earthquake in California or the 1992 hurricanes in Florida and Hawaii, produced popular and media discourses about relevant state and federal agencies (e.g., the Federal Emergency Management Agency (FEMA)), that come close to displacing onto the agencies themselves responsibility for the suffering of the victims.

26. Tracy Strong, *Friedrich Nietzsche and the Politics of Transfiguration*, expanded edition (Berkeley: University of California, 1988), p. 242

27. *Genealogy*, p. 36.

28. *Thus Spoke Zarathustra*, in *The Portable Nietzsche*, ed. W. Kaufmann (New York: Penguin, 1954), p. 252.

29. *Genealogy of Morals*, pp. 123, 124.

30. *Ibid.*, p. 34.

31. *Zarathustra*, p. 252.

32. *Zarathustra*, p. 251.

33. *Ibid.*, pp. 250-251.

34. *Ibid.*, p. 251.

35. *Ibid.*, p. 251.

36. *Ibid.*, p. 252.

37. *Genealogy*, p. 126. In what could easily characterize the rancorous quality of many contemporary institutions and gatherings—academic, political, cultural—in which politicized identity is strongly and permissibly at play, Nietzsche offers an elaborate account of this replacement of pain with a "more violent emotion" which is the stock in trade of "the suffering":

> The suffering are one and all dreadfully eager and inventive in discovering occasions for painful affects; they enjoy being mistrustful and dwelling on nasty deeds and imaginary slights; they scour the entrails of their past and present for obscure and questionable occurrences that offer them the opportunity to revel in tormenting suspicions and to intoxicate themselves with the poison of their own malice: they tear open their oldest wounds, they bleed from long-healed scars, they make evildoers out of their friends, wives, children, and whoever else stands closest to them. "I suffer: someone must be to blame for it"— thus thinks every sickly sheep. (*Genealogy*, p. 127)

38. This point has been made by many, but for a recent, quite powerful phenomenological exploration of the relationship between historical erasure and lived identity, see Patricia Williams, *The Alchemy of Race and Rights* (Cambridge: Harvard University Press, 1991).

39. Jessie Jackson's 1988 "Keep Hope Alive" presidential campaign strikes me as having sought to configure the relationship between injury, identity and desire in just this way and to have succeeded in forging a "rainbow coalition" *because* of the idiom of futurity it employed—want, hope, desires, dreams—among those whose modality during the 1980s had often been rancorous.

40. In Trinh T. Minh-ha's formulation, "to seek is to lose, for seeking presupposes a separation between the seeker and the sought, the continuing me and the changes it undergoes." "Not You/Like You: Post-Colonial Women and the Interlocking Questions of Identity and Difference," *Inscriptions* 3–4, 1988, p. 72.

ELABORATIONS

Judith Butler

Subjection, Resistance, Resignification: Between Freud and Foucault

> My problem is essentially the definition of the implicit systems in
> which we find ourselves prisoners; what I would like to grasp is the
> system of limits and exclusion which we practice without knowing
> it; I would like to make the cultural unconscious apparent.
>
> Foucault, "Rituals of Exclusion"

Consider, in *Discipline and Punish*, the paradoxical character of what Foucault describes as the subjectivation of the prisoner. The term subjectivation carries the paradox in itself; *assujetissement* denotes the becoming of the subject, but also the process of subjection: one inhabits the figure of autonomy only through becoming subjected to a power, a subjection which implies a radical dependency. For Foucault, this process of subjectivation takes place centrally through the body, and in *Discipline and Punish* the prisoner's body not only appears as a *sign* of guilt, of transgression, as the embodiment of prohibition and the sanction for rituals of normalization, but that body is itself framed and formed through the discursive matrix of a juridical subject. To claim that a discourse "forms" the body is no simple claim, and from the start there must be a distinction between how such a "forming" is not the same as a "causing" or a "determining," much less a notion that bodies are somehow made of discourse pure and simple.

Foucault suggests that the regulation of the prisoner takes place not as an *exterior* relation of power, whereby an institution takes a pregiven individual as the target of its subordinating aims; on the contrary, that individual is formed or, rather, formulated through the discursively constituted "identity" of the prisoner. Subjection is, literally, the *making* of a subject, the principle of regulation according to which a subject is formulated or produced. This notion of subjection is a kind of power that not only unilaterally *acts on* a given individual as a form of domination, but also *activates* or forms the subject. Hence, subjection is neither simply the domination of a subject nor its production, but designates a certain kind of restriction *in* production, a restriction without which the production of the subject cannot take place, a restriction through which that production takes place. Although Foucault occasionally tries to argue that, historically, *juridical* power—power as acting on, subordinating, pregiven subjects—*precedes* productive power, the capacity of power to *form* subjects, it is clear in the case of the prisoner that the subject produced and the subject regulated or subordinated are one, and that the compulsory production is its own form of regulation.

Hence, Foucault warns against those within the liberal tradition who would liberate the prisoner from the prison's oppressive confines, for the subjection signified by the exterior institution of the prison does not act apart from the invasion and management of the prisoner's body, what Foucault describes as the full siege and invasion of that body by the signifying practices of the prison, namely, inspection, confession, the regularization and normalization of bodily movement and gesture, those disciplinary regimes of the body which have led feminists to consult Foucault in order to elaborate the disciplinary production of gender.[1]

The prison thus acts on the prisoner's body, but it does so by forcing the prisoner to approximate an ideal, a norm of behavior, a model of obedience. This is the means by which that prisoner's individuality is rendered coherent, totalized, made into the discursive and conceptual possession of the prison; it is, as Foucault insists, the way in which "he becomes the principle of his own subjection" (203). This normative ideal that is inculcated, as it were, into the prisoner is a kind of psychic identity, or what Foucault will call a "soul." And it is with respect to the soul as an imprisoning effect that Foucault will claim that the prisoner is subjected "in a more fundamental way" than by the spatial captivity of the prison. Indeed, in the citation that

Judith Butler

follows, the soul is figured as itself a kind of spatial captivity, indeed, as a kind of prison which provides the exterior form or regulatory principle of the prisoner's body:

> The man described for us, whom we are invited to free, is already in himself the effect of a subjection (*assujettissement*) much more profound than himself. A "soul" inhabits him and brings him to existence, which is itself a factor in the mastery that power exercises over the body. The soul is the effect and instrument of a political anatomy; *the soul is the prison of the body.* (30, my emphasis)[2]

Although Foucault is here specifying the subjectivation of the prisoner, he appears also to be privileging the metaphor of the prison to theorize the subjectivation of the body. What are we to make of imprisonment and invasion as the privileged figures through which Foucault articulates the process of subjectivation itself, the discursive production of identities? If discourse produces identity through supplying and enforcing a regulatory principle which thoroughly invades, totalizes and renders coherent the individual, then it seems that every "identity," insofar as it is totalizing, acts as precisely such a "soul that imprisons the body." In what sense is this "soul" "much more profound" than the prisoner himself? Does this mean that the soul exists before the body that animates it, and how are we to understand such a claim in the context of Foucault's theory of power?

Rather than answer that question straightaway, one might, for the purposes of clarification, counterpose the "soul" which Foucault articulates as an imprisoning frame with the psyche in its psychoanalytic sense.[3] In the latter case, the ideal of the subject might be understood as the ego-ideal which the superego is said, as it were, to consult in order to measure the ego. This ideal is what Lacan redescribes as the "position" of the subject within the symbolic, the norm which installs the subject within language and, hence, within available schemes of cultural intelligibility. This viable and intelligible being, this subject, is always produced at a cost, and what remains unconscious is precisely that which resists that normative demand by which subjects are instituted. Indeed, the psyche, a notion which includes the unconscious, is very different from the subject: the psyche is precisely that which exceeds the imprisoning effects of the discursive demand to inhabit a coherent identity, to become a coherent subject. The psyche is precisely what resists the regularization and normalization that Foucault ascribes to those normalizing discourses. And yet, those very discourses are said to imprison the body *in the soul*, to animate and contain the body within that ideal frame, and in that sense to reduce the notion of the psyche to the operations of an externally framing and normalizing ideal.[4] This Foucauldian move appears to treat the psyche as if it were nothing other than the recipient of the unilateral effect of the Lacanian symbolic. This transposition of the soul into an exterior and imprisoning frame for the body vacates, as it were, the interiority of the body, leaving that interiority as the malleable surface for the unilateral effects of disciplinary power.

It may seem that I am moving toward a psychoanalytic criticism of Foucault, and in part I am, for I think that the account of subjectivation and, in particular, becoming the principle of one's own subjection, cannot take place without recourse to a psychoanalytic account of the formative or generative effects of restriction or prohibition and that the formation of the subject is not fully thinkable—if it ever is—without recourse to a paradoxically enabling set of grounding constraints. On the other hand, as I elaborate this critique, some romanticized notions of the unconscious defined as resistance itself will come under critical scrutiny, and that criticism will entail the reemergence of a Foucauldian perspective *in* psychoanalysis.

The question of a suppressed psychoanalysis in Foucault—raised by Foucault himself in relation to the "cultural unconscious" quoted above—might be raised more precisely in relation to the problem of locating or accounting for resistance. Where does resistance to or in disciplinary subject-formation take place? Does the reduction of the psychoanalytically rich notion of the "psyche" to that of the imprisoning "soul" eliminate the possibility of a resistance to normalization and to subject-formation, a resistance that emerges precisely from the incommensurability between psyche and subject? How would we understand such a resistance, and would such an understanding entail a critical rethinking of psychoanalysis along the way? Indeed, what I want to propose is not simply a psychoanalytic critique of Foucault, nor simply a Foucauldian response to that psychoanalytic critique, but rather a critical rethinking of the problematic of subjection and resistance that entails a reformulation of both Foucault and Freud.

In what follows, I will ask two different kinds of questions, one of Foucault, and another of psychoanalysis (where this latter term applies variously to Freud and to Lacan):[5] if Foucault understands the psyche in the service

Judith Butler

of normalization, indeed, as an imprisoning effect, then how might he account for the notion of a psychic resistance to normalization? If some proponents of psychoanalysis insist that resistance to normalization is a function of the unconscious, we might well ask whether this guarantee of resistance at the level of the psyche is not a sleight of hand. More precisely, is the resistance upon which psychoanalysis insists socially and discursively produced, or is it a kind of resistance to, an undermining of, social and discursive production *as such*? Consider the claim that the unconscious only and always resists normalization, that every ritual of conformity to the injunctions of civilization is at a cost, and that a certain unharnessed and unsocialized remainder is thereby produced, contesting the appearance of the law-abiding subject: this is a psychic remainder which signifies the limits of normalization. That position in no sense implies that such a resistance wields the power to rework, to rearticulate the terms of discursive demand, the disciplinary injunctions by which normalization occurs. To thwart the injunction to produce a docile body is not the same as dismantling the injunction, or changing the terms of subject-constitution. If the unconscious, or the psyche more generally, is defined as resistance, what do we then make of those unconscious attachments to subjection which imply that the unconscious is no more "free" of normalizing discourse than the subject itself? If the unconscious escapes from a given normative injunction, to what other injunction does it form an attachment? What makes us think that the unconscious is any less structured by the power-relations that pervade cultural signifiers than is the language of the subject? Indeed, we may find an attachment to subjection at the level of the unconscious: What kind of resistance is to be wrought from that?

But even if we grant the point that the resistance of the unconscious to a normalizing injunction guarantees the "failure" of that injunction fully to constitute its subject, does it do anything to alter or expand the dominant injunctions or interpellations of subject-formation itself? What do we make of a resistance that can only undermine, but which appears to have no power to rearticulate the terms, the symbolic terms—to use Lacanian parlance—by which subjects are constituted, that is, by which subjection is installed in the very formation of the subject? This is a resistance which can only establish the incomplete character of any effort to produce a subject through disciplinary means, but it remains impotent to rearticulate the dominant terms of productive power.

Before continuing this interrogation of psychoanalysis, however, let us return to the problem of bodies in Foucault, in order to understand how and why resistance is denied to bodies produced through disciplinary regimes. What is this notion of disciplinary production, and does it work as efficaciously as Foucault appears to imply?

In the final chapter of the first volume of *The History of Sexuality* Foucault asks after a "history of bodies" which would inquire into "the manner in which what is most material and vital in them has been invested."[6] In this formulation, he suggests that power acts not only *on* the body, but also *in* the body; that power not only produces the boundaries of a subject, but pervades the interiority of that subject. In the last formulation, it appears that there is an "inside" to the body which exists before power's invasion. But given the radical exteriority of the soul, how are we to understand "interiority" in Foucault?[7] That interiority will not be a soul, and it will not be a psyche, but what will it be? Is this a space of pure malleability, one which is, as it were, ready to conform to the demands of socialization? Or is this interiority to be called, simply, the body? Has it come to that paradoxical point where Foucault wants to claim that the soul is the exterior form, and the body, the interior space?

Although Foucault wants on occasion to refute the possibility of a body which is not produced through power-relations, it is also clear that sometimes his explanations require that a body maintain a materiality that is ontologically distinct from the power- relations that take that body as a site of investments.[8] Indeed, the term "site" in the above phrase appears, it seems, quite without warrant, for what is the relation between the body as *site* and the investments which that site is said to receive or bear? Does the term "site" stabilize the body in relation to those investments, but deflect the question of how we are to understand the way in which investments establish, contour and disrupt what is in the above taken for granted as the body's "site" (this might be understood as precisely the project in Lacan's "mirror stage")? What constitutes an "investment," and what is its constituting power? Does it have a visualizing function, and can we understand the production of the bodily ego in Freud as the projected or spatialized modality of such investments?[9] Indeed, to what extent does the stabilization of the body's site proceed through a certain projective instability which Foucault cannot quite describe, one which would engage him perhaps in the problematic of the ego as an imaginary function?

Judith Butler

Discipline and Punish offers a different configuration of the relation between materiality and investment. There the soul is taken as an instrument of power through which the body is cultivated and formed. In a sense, it acts as a power-laden schema that produces and actualizes the body itself. We can understand Foucault's references to the "soul" as an implicit reworking of the Aristotelian formulation in which the soul is understood to be the form and principle of the body's matter.[10] Foucault argues in *Discipline and Punish* that the "soul" becomes a normative and normalizing ideal, according to which the body is trained, shaped, cultivated and invested; it is a historically specific imaginary ideal (*idéal speculatif*) under which the body is effectively materialized.

This "subjection" or *assujettissement* is not only a subordination, but a securing and maintaining, a putting into place of a subject, a subjectivation. The "soul brings [the prisoner] to existence"; and, not fully unlike Aristotle, the soul, as an instrument of power, forms and frames the body, stamps it, and in stamping it, brings it into being.

In this formulation, there is no body outside of power, for the materiality of the body, indeed, materiality itself, is produced through, and in a direct relation to, the investment of power. The materiality of the prison, he writes, is established to the extent that (*dans la mésure ou*) it is a vector and instrument of power.[11] Hence, the prison is *materialized* to the extent that it is *invested with power*; or, to be grammatically accurate, there is no prison prior to its materialization; its materialization is coextensive with its investiture with power-relations, and materiality is the effect and gauge of this investment. The prison comes to be only within the field of power-relations, but more specifically, only to the extent that it is saturated with such relations, and that such a saturation is itself formative of its very being. Here the body—of the prisoner and the prison—is not an independent materiality, a static surface or site, which a subsequent investment comes to mark, signify upon or pervade; the body is that for which materialization and investiture are coextensive.

Although the soul is understood to enframe the body in *Discipline and Punish*, Foucault suggests that the production of the "subject" takes place, to some degree, through the subordination and even the destruction of the body. In "Nietzsche, Genealogy, History," Foucault remarks that it is only through the destruction of the body that the subject as a "dissociated unity" appears: "the body is the inscribed surface of events (traced by language and dissolved by ideas), the locus of a dissociated self (adopting the illusion of a substantial unity), and a volume in perpetual disintegration."[12] Here it is precisely at the expense of the body that the subject appears, an appearance which is conditioned in an inverse relation to the disappearance of the body, an appearance of a subject which not only effectively takes the place of the body, but acts as the very soul which frames and forms the body in captivity. Here the forming and framing function of that exterior soul works against the body, indeed, might be understood as the sublimation of the body itself, a production which is the consequence of a displacement and a substitution.

In this redescription of the body in Foucault, I have clearly wandered over into the psychoanalytic vocabulary of sublimation. But since we appear, in some sense, to have arrived there, let me pose a question that might revive the question of subjection and resistance. If the body is subordinated and, to some extent, destroyed, as the dissociated self emerges, and if that emergence might be read as the sublimation of the body, the self, as the ghostly form of the body, then is there some part of the body which is not preserved in sublimation, some part of the body which remains unsublimatable?

This bodily remainder, I would suggest, survives for such a subject in the mode of already, if not always, having been destroyed, a kind of constitutive loss. The body is not a site on which a construction takes place; it is a destruction on the occasion of which a subject is formed. And the formation of this subject is at once the framing, the subordination, the regulation of the body; the mode in which that destruction is preserved (in the sense of sustained and embalmed) *in* normalization.

If, then, the body is now to be understood as that which constitutes the subject in its dissociated and sublimated state, but also that which exceeds or resists any effort at sublimation, how are we to understand the body which is, as it were, negated or repressed such that the subject might live? One might expect the return of the body to a nonnormalizable wildness, and there are of course textual moments in Foucault when something like that happens. But more often than not, in Foucault, the possibility of a subversion or a resistance appears (a) in the course of a subjectivation that exceeds the normalizing aims by which it is mobilized, that is, the example of the "reverse-discourse," or (b) through the convergence with other discursive regimes, whereby the inadvertently produced discursive complexity undermines the teleological aims of normalization.[13] Thus resistance appears as the effect of power, as part of power itself, its self-subversion.

The theorization of resistance is where a certain problem arises which concerns psychoanalysis and, by implication, the limits of subjectivation. For Foucault, the subject who is produced through subjection is not produced at an instant in its totality; it is in the process of being produced, it is repeatedly produced (which is not the same as being produced anew again and again). It is precisely the possibility of a repetition which does not consolidate that dissociated unity, the subject, but which proliferates effects which undermine the force of normalization. The term which not only names, but forms and frames the subject—let us use Foucault's example of homosexuality—is the name which mobilizes a reverse discourse against the very regime of normalization by which it is spawned. This is, of course, not a pure opposition, for it will be the same "homosexuality" which will be deployed first in the service of normalizing heterosexuality and second in the service of its own depathologization; this term will carry the risk of the former meaning in the latter, but it would be a mistake to think that by simply speaking the term one either transcends heterosexual normalization or becomes its instrument. The risk of a renormalization is persistently there: consider the one who, in defiant "outness," declares his/her homosexuality, only then to receive the response, "ah yes, so you are that, and only that," whatever you will say will be read back as an overt or subtle manifestation of your essential homosexuality. (One should not underestimate how exhausting it is to be expected to be an "out" homosexual all the time, whether the expectation comes from gay and lesbian allies or their foes.) Here it is the possibility of resignification, of mobilizing politically what Nietzsche called the "sign-chain" which Foucault cites and reworks from *On the Genealogy of Morals*. For there Nietzsche argued that the uses to which a given sign is originally put are "worlds apart" from the uses to which it then becomes available. This temporal gap between usages produces the possibility of a reversal of signification, but also opens the way for an inauguration of signifying possibilities that exceed those to which the term has been previously bound.

In the above, then, the Foucauldian subject is never fully constituted in subjection; it is repeatedly constituted in subjection; and it is in the possibility of a repetition that repeats against its origin that subjection might be understood to draw its inadvertently enabling power.

From a psychoanalytic perspective, however, we might ask whether this possibility of a resistance to a constituting or subjectivating power can be derived from what is "in" or "of" discourse. For what do we make of the way in which discourses not only constitute the domains of the speakable, but are themselves bounded through the production of a constitutive outside, the unspeakable, the unsignifiable.

From a Lacanian perspective, one might well question whether the effects of the psyche can be said to be exhausted in what can be signified, or whether there is not, over and against this signifying body, a domain of the psyche which contests legibility. If, according to psychoanalysis, the subject is not the same as the psyche from which it emerges, and if, for Foucault, the subject is not the same as the body from which it emerges, then perhaps the body has come to substitute for the psyche in Foucault, that is, as that which exceeds and confounds the injunctions of normalization. Is this a body pure and simple, or does "the body" come to stand for a certain operation of the psyche, one which is distinctly different, if not directly opposed to, the soul figured as an imprisoning effect? Perhaps Foucault himself has invested the body with a psychic meaning that he cannot elaborate within the terms that he uses. How does the process of subjectivation, the disciplinary production of the subject, break down, if it does, in both Foucauldian and psychoanalytic theory; from where does that failure emerge, and what are its consequences?

Consider the Althusserian notion of interpellation, whereby a subject is constituted through being hailed, addressed, named.[14] For the most part, it seems, Althusser believed that this social demand, one might call it a symbolic injunction, actually produced the kinds of subjects it named. He gives the example of the policeman on the street, yelling, "hey you there!" and concludes that the one who is addressed and sited by that call is also in some important way constituted by that call. This scene is clearly a disciplinary one, the policeman's call is an effort to bring someone back in line, and yet at the same time, we might understand this call in Lacanian terms as the call of symbolic constitution. And yet, as Althusser himself concedes, this performative effort of naming can only *attempt* to bring its addressee into being, but there is always the risk of a certain *misrecognition*, and if one misrecognizes that effort to produce the subject, the production itself falters: the one who is hailed may well fail to hear, may well misread the call, may well turn the other way, answer to another name, insist on not being

Judith
Butler

addressed in that way. Indeed, the domain of the imaginary is demarcated by Althusser as precisely that domain which makes *misrecognition* possible: the name is called, and I am sure it is my name, but it is not; the name is called, and I am sure that it is a name that is being called, my name, but it is someone's incomprehensible speech, or worse, someone coughing or worse, a radiator which for a moment approximates a human voice. Or I am sure that no one has noticed my transgression, and that it is not my name that is being called, but only a coughing passerby, the high pitch of the heating mechanism, but it is my name, but even then I do not recognize myself in the subject who is at that moment installed through the name.[15]

Consider the force of this dynamic of intepellation and misrecognition when the name is not a proper name, but a social category[16] and, hence, a signifier that is capable of being interpreted in a number of divergent and conflictual ways. To be hailed as a "woman" or "Jew" or "queer" or "Black" or "Chicana" may be heard or interpreted as an affirmation or an insult, depending on the context (where context is the effective historicity and spatiality of the sign) in which the hailing occurs. If that name is called, there is more often than not a hesitation over whether or how to respond, for what is at stake is whether that temporary totalization performed by the name is politically enabling or paralyzing, whether the foreclosure, indeed the violence, of the totalizing reduction of identity performed by that particular hailing is politically strategic or regressive or, if paralyzing and regressive, also enabling in some way.

The Althusserian use of Lacan centers on the function of the imaginary as the permanent possibility of *misrecognition*, that is, the incommensurability between symbolic demand (the name that is interpellated) and the instability and unpredictability of its appropriation. If the interpellated name seeks to accomplish the identity to which it refers, it begins as a performative process which is nevertheless derailed in the imaginary, for the imaginary is surely preoccupied with the law, structured by the law, but does not immediately obey the law. For the Lacanian, then, the imaginary signifies the impossibility of the discursive, that is, symbolic, constitution of identity. Identity can never be fully totalized by the symbolic, for what it fails to order will emerge within the imaginary as a disorder, a site where identity is contested.

Hence, in a Lacanian vein, Jacqueline Rose offers a formulation of the unconscious as that which thwarts any effort of the symbolic to constitute sexed identity coherently and fully, an unconscious indicated by the slips and gaps that characterize the workings of the imaginary in language. And here I quote from a passage which, I think, has benefitted many of us who have sought to find in psychoanalysis a principle of resistance to given forms of social reality:

> The unconscious constantly reveals the "failure" of identity. Because there is no continuity of psychic life, so there is no stability of sexual identity, no position for women (or for men) which is ever simply achieved. Nor does psychoanalysis see such "failure" as a special-case inability or an individual deviancy from the norm. "Failure" is not a moment to be regretted in a process of adaptation, or development into normality . . . "failure" is something endlessly repeated and relived moment by moment throughout our individual histories. It appears not only in the symptom, but also in dreams, in slips of the tongue and in forms of sexual pleasure which are pushed to the sidelines of the norm . . . there is a resistance to identity at the heart of psychic life.[17]

It might be argued that Foucault, in *Discipline and Punish*, presumes the efficacy of the symbolic demand, its performative capacity to constitute the subject whom it names. In *The History of Sexuality, Volume I*, however, there is both a rejection of "a single locus of Revolt"—which would presumably include the psyche, the imaginary or the unconscious within its purview—and an affirmation of multiple possibilities of resistance enabled by power itself. For Foucault, resistance cannot be *outside* the law, in another register (the imaginary), or in that which eludes the constitutive power of the law:

> there is no single locus of great Refusal, no soul of revolt, source of all rebellions, or pure law of the revolutionary. Instead there is a plurality of resistances, each of them a special case: resistances that are possible, necessary, improbable; others that are spontaneous, savage, solitary, concerted, rampant, or violent; still others that are quick to compromise, interested, or sacrificial; by definition, they can only exist in the strategic field of power relations. But this does not mean that they are only a reaction or rebound, forming with respect to the basic domination an underside that is in the end always passive, doomed to perpetual defeat. (95–96)

This last caricature of power, although clearly written with Marcuse in mind, recalls the effect of the Lacanian law which produces its own "failure" at the level of the psyche, but which can never be displaced or reformulated by that psychic resistance. The imaginary thwarts the efficacy of the symbolic law, but it cannot turn back upon the law itself, demanding or effecting a reformulation of that law. In this sense, psychic resistance thwarts the law in its effects, but cannot redirect the law or its effects. Resistance is thus located in a domain that is virtually powerless to alter the law that it opposes. Hence, psychic resistance presumes the continuation of the law in its anterior, symbolic form and, in that sense, contributes to its status quo. Resistance appears, in such a view, to be doomed to perpetual defeat.

In contrast, Foucault formulates resistance as an effect of the very power that it is said to oppose. This insistence on the dual possibility of being both *constituted* by the law and *an effect of resistance* to the law marks a departure from the Lacanian framework, for where Lacan restricts the notions of social power to that of the symbolic domain, and delegates resistance to the imaginary, Foucault will recast the symbolic as relations of power, and understand resistance as an effect of power itself. Foucault's conception initiates a shift from a discourse on law, conceived as juridical (and presupposing a subject subordinated by power), to a discourse on power which is a field of productive, regulatory and contestatory relations. One might say that, for Foucault, the symbolic produces the possibility of its own subversions, and that these subversions are unanticipated effects of symbolic interpellations. But the notion of "the symbolic" does not address the multiplicity of power-vectors upon which Foucault insists, for power in Foucault not only consists of the reiterated elaboration of norms or interpellating demands, but is formative or productive, malleable, multiple, proliferative and conflictual; moreover, in its resignifications, the law itself is transmuted into that which opposes and exceeds its original purposes. In this sense, disciplinary discourse does not unilaterally constitute a subject in Foucault or, rather, if it does, it constitutes *simultaneously* the condition for the subject's de-constitution. What is brought into being through the performative effect of the interpellating demand is much *more* than a "subject," for the "subject" created is not for that reason fixed in place: it becomes the occasion for a further making. Indeed, I would add, that a subject only remains a subject through a reiteration or rearticulation of itself as a subject, and it may be that this dependency of the coherence of the subject on repetition constitutes the incoherence, the incomplete character of that subject. And this repetition or, better, iterability, thus becomes the non-place of subversion, the possibility of a reembodying of the subjectivating norm which is at once a redirecting of the normativity of the norm.

Consider the inversions of "woman" and "woman," depending on the staging and address of their performance, of "queer" and "queer," depending on its pathologizing or contestatory modes. In each of these examples, it is not a question of an opposition between a reactionary and progressive usage; it is rather a function of the progressive usage requiring and repeating the reactionary in order to effect a subversive reterritorialization.

For Foucault, then, the disciplinary apparatus produces subjects, but, as a consequence of that production, it brings into discourse the conditions for the subversion of that apparatus itself. In other words, the law turns against itself and spawns versions of itself which oppose and proliferate its animating purposes. The strategic question for Foucault is, then, how to work the power relations by which we are worked, and in what direction?

In his later interviews, Foucault suggests that identities are formed within contemporary political arrangements in relation to certain requirements of the liberal state, ones which presume that the assertion of rights and claims to entitlement can only be made on the basis of a singular and injured identity. The more specific identity becomes, the more totalized an identity becomes by that very specificity. Indeed, we might understand this contemporary phenomenon as the movement by which a juridical apparatus produces the field of possible political subjects. Because, for Foucault, the disciplinary apparatus of the state operates through the totalizing production of individuals, and because this totalization of the individual extends the jurisdiction of the state (that is, by transforming individuals into subjects of the state), Foucault will call for a re-making of subjectivity beyond the shackles of the juridical law. In this sense, what we call identity politics is produced by a state which can only allocate recognition and rights to subjects totalized by the particularity that constitutes their plaintiff status. In calling for an overthrow, as it were, of such an arrangement, Foucault is not calling for the release of a hidden or repressed subjectivity, but, rather, for a radical making of subjectivity formed in and against the historical hegemony of the juridical subject:

Judith Butler

Maybe the target nowadays is not to discover what we are, but to refuse what we are. We have to imagine and build up what we could be to get rid of this kind of political "double bind," which is the simultaneous individualization and totalization of modern power structures. . . . The conclusion would be that the political, ethical, social, philosophical problem of our days is not to try to liberate us both from the state, and from the state's institutions, but to liberate us from the state and the type of individualization which is linked to the state. We have to promote new forms of subjectivity through the refusal of this kind of individuality which has been imposed on us for several centuries.[18]

Two questions emerge from the above analysis: (1) Why is it that Foucault can formulate resistance in relation to the disciplinary power of sexuality in *The History of Sexuality*, whereas in *Discipline and Punish* disciplinary power appears to determine docile bodies incapable of resistance? Is there something about the relationship of *sexuality* to power that conditions the possibility of resistance in the first text, and a noted absence of a consideration of sexuality from the discussion of power and bodies in the second?

Note that, in the *History of Sexuality*, the repressive function of the law is undermined precisely through becoming itself the object of erotic investment and excitation; the disciplinary apparatus fails to repress sexuality precisely because the apparatus is itself eroticized, thereby becoming the occasion for the *incitement of sexuality* and, therefore, undoing its own repressive aims. (2) With this transferable property of sexual investments in mind, then, we might ask what conditions the possibility of the kind of "refusal" of that type of individuality correlated with the disciplinary apparatus of the modern state that Foucault invites? And how do we account for the *attachment* to precisely that kind of state-linked individuality which reconsolidates the juridical law? To what extent has the disciplinary apparatus that attempts to produce and totalize identity become an abiding object of passionate attachment. Certainly, we cannot simply throw off the identities we have become, and Foucault's call to "refuse" the identities we have become will certainly be met with resistance. If we reject theoretically the source of resistance in a psychic domain that is said to precede or exceed the social,[19] as we must, can we then reformulate psychic resistance *in terms of the social* without that reformulation becoming a domestication or normalization? (Must the social always be equated with the given and the normalizable?) In particular, how are we to understand not merely the disciplinary production of the subject, but the disciplinary cultivation of *an attachment to subjection*?

Such a postulation may raise the question of masochism, indeed, the question of masochism in subject-formation, and yet it does not yet answer the question of the status of "attachment" or "investment." Here the grammatical problem emerges, in which an attachment appears to precede the subject who might be said to "have" it; and yet, it seems crucial to suspend the usual grammatical requirements, and to consider an inversion of terms such that certain attachments precede and condition the formation of subjects (the visualization of libido in the mirror stage, the sustaining of that projected image through time as the discursive function of the name). Is this, then, an ontology of libido or investment that is in some sense prior to and separable from a subject, or is it rather that every such investment is, from the start, bound up with a reflexivity that is stabilized (within the imaginary) as the ego? If the ego is composed of identifications, and identification is the resolution of desire, then the ego is the residue of desire, the effect of incorporations which, Freud argues in *The Ego and the Id*, trace a lineage of attachment and loss.

To what extent does becoming a subject require/presuppose a passionate attachment to subjection? And is this not an attachment to subjection that safeguards against the dissolution into psychosis, the conjured spectre of a dissolution of the subject itself through an abrogation of its founding prohibitions; in other words, when understood as a safeguard against psychosis, is not the attachment to subjection at the heart of subject-formation not a sustaining subjection of some crucial kind?

In a longer version of this paper, I plan to read the portion of *Civilization and its Discontents* on the formation of conscience, in which it is precisely the attachment to prohibition which founds the subject in its reflexivity. Under the pressure of the ethical law, a subject emerges who is capable of reflexivity, that is, who takes him/herself as an object, and so mistakes him/herself, since he/she is, by virtue of that founding prohibition, at an infinite distance from his/her origin. Only on the condition of a separation enforced through prohibition does a subject emerge, which is formed through the attachment to prohibition (an obedience to it, but also an eroticization of it). And this prohibition is all the more savory precisely because it is bound up in that narcissistic circuit that wards off the dissolution of the subject into psychosis.[20]

Judith Butler

We might understand Foucault to have misunderstood the process of subjection, inasmuch as he maintained that a subject is formed and then invested with a sexuality, invested with a sexuality by a regime of power. If the very process of subject-formation requires a preemption of sexuality, a founding prohibition which at once prohibits a certain desire, but also a prohibition which becomes itself the aim of desire, then it appears that a subject is formed through the prohibition of a sexuality, where that sexuality—and the subject who is said to bear it—become formed by that prohibition. This last view disputes the Foucauldian notion that psychoanalysis presumes the exteriority of the law to desire, for it maintains that there is no desire without that law, that law forms and sustains the very desire that it prohibits; indeed, prohibition becomes an odd form of preservation, a way of attaching a desire to the law that prohibits it, a way of eroticizing the law which would abolish eroticism, but which only works through compelling eroticization, making the law and its prohibitions into the final object of desire.[21] In this sense, a "sexual identity" is to a certain extent a productive contradiction in terms, for identity is formed through a prohibition on some dimension of the very sexuality it is said to bear, and sexuality, when it is tied to identity, is always in some sense undercutting itself.

But this is not necessarily a static contradiction, for the signifiers of identity are not structurally determined in advance. If Foucault could argue that a sign could be taken up, used for purposes counter to those for which it was designed, then he understood that even the most noxious terms could be owned, that the most injurious interpellations could also be the site for a radical reoccupation and resignification. But what is it that lets us occupy the discursive site of injury or, rather, how is it that we are animated, mobilized by, that discursive site and its injury, such that our very attachment to it becomes the condition for our resignification of it? Called by an injurious name, I come into social being, but because a certain attachment to my existence is to be assumed, a certain narcissism takes hold of any term that confers existence, I am led to embrace the terms that injure me, precisely because they constitute me socially. One might understand the self-colonizing trajectory of certain forms of identity politics as symptomatic of this paradoxical embrace of the injurious term. As a further paradox, then, it is only by occupying—being occupied by—that injurious term that I become enabled to resist and oppose that term, and the power that constitutes me is recast as the power I oppose. In this way, a certain place for psychoanalysis is secured, in the sense that any mobilization against subjection will take subjection itself as its resource, and that an attachment to an injurious inter-pellation by way of a necessarily alienated narcissism will become the con-dition by which a resignification of that interpellation becomes possible. This will not be an unconscious outside power, but rather something like the unconscious of power itself, in its traumatic and productive iterability.

If, then, we understand certain kinds of interpellations to be identity-conferring, then those injurious interpellations will constitute identity through injury. This is not the same as saying that such an identity will remain always and forever rooted in its injury as long as it remains an iden-tity, but it does imply that the possibilities of resignification will rework and unsettle that passionate attachment to subjection without which sub-ject-formation—and reformation—cannot succeed.

NOTES

My thanks to Wendy Brown for her help with this essay, and for her essay, "Wounded Attachments," included in this volume, with which this essay was written in tandem.

1. See Sandra Bartky, *Femininity and Domination* (New York: Routledge, 1990).
2. "L'homme dont on nous parle et qu'on invité a liberer est déjà en lui-même l'effet d'un assujettissement bien plus profond que lui. Une 'âme' l'habite et le porte a l'existence, qui est elle-même une pièce dans la mâitrise que le pouvoir exerce sur le corps. L'âme, effet et instrument d'une anatomie politique; l'âme, prison du corps." Michel Foucault, *Surveillance et punir: Naissance de la prison* (Paris: Gallimard, 1975), p. 34.
3. It is important to distinguish between the notion of the psyche, which includes the notion of the unconscious, and that of the subject, whose formation is conditioned by the exclusion of the unconscious.
4. For an extended and rich discussion of how norms work to subjectivate and, in particular, how norms are to be understood as transitive actions, see Pierre Macherey, "Towards a Natural History of Norms," in *Michel Foucault/Philosopher*, trans. and ed., Timothy J. Armstrong (New York: Routledge, 1992), pp. 176–191. In that same volume, for a discussion

of Foucault as writing indirectly about Lacan, see Jacques-Alain Miller, "Michel Foucault and Psychoanalysis," pp. 58–63. On the problem of the dynamic relation between ethical demands and the subjectivity to whom they are addressed, see the very useful comparative discussion of Foucault and Lacan in John Rajchman, *Truth and Eros: Foucault, Lacan, and the Question of Ethics* (New York: Routledge, 1991).

5. This is not meant to suggest that psychoanalysis is only to be represented by these two figures, but only that it will be for the purposes of this analysis.

6. Foucault, *The History of Sexuality, Vol. I: An Introduction*, trans. Robert Hurley (New York: Random House), p. 152. The French reads: "non pas donc 'histoire des mentalités' qui ne tiendrait compte des corps que par la manière dont on les aperçues ou dont on leur a donné sens et valeur; mais 'histoire des corps' et de la manière dont on a *investi* ce qu'il y a de plus *material*, de plus vivant en eux," Foucault, *La volonté de savoir* (Paris: Gallimard, 1978) p. 200.

7. This is a question raised in a very different way by Charles Taylor, when he asks whether there is a place for Augustinian "inwardness" in Foucault, in "Foucault on Freedom and Truth" in David Couzens Hoy, ed. *Foucault: A Critical Reader* (New York and Oxford: Blackwell, 1986), p. 99.

8. See my "Foucault and the Paradox of Bodily Inscriptions" in *Journal of Philosophy*, vol. LXXXVI, No. 11, November, 1989.

9. See discussions of the bodily ego in Freud, "The Ego and the Id," *The Standard Edition*, XIX, p. 26; and in Margaret Whitford, *Luce Irigaray: Philosophy in the Feminine* (London: Routledge, 1991), pp. 53–74.

10. See "Bodies that Matter" in my *Bodies that Matter: On the Discursive Limits of "Sex"* (Routledge: New York, 1993), pp. 32–36, for a fuller explanation of Foucault's reworking of Aristotle.

11. "What was at issue was not whether the prison environment was too harsh or too aseptic, too primitive or too efficient, but its very materiality as an instrument and vector of power [c'etait sa materialité dans la mesure ou elle est instrument et vecteur de pouvoir]," *Discipline and Punish*, p. 30; *Surveiller et punir*, p. 35.

12. See Foucault, "Nietzsche, Genealogy, History", in *The Foucault Reader*, ed. Paul Rabinow (New York: Pantheon, 1984).

13. See "Shahbano," Zakia Pathak and Rajeswari Sunder Rajan, in Butler and Scott, eds., *Feminists Theorize the Political* (New York: Routledge, 1992).

14. Louis Althusser, "Ideology and Ideological State Apparatuses (Notes towards an investigation), *Lenin and Philosophy and Other Essays* (New York: Monthly Review Press), pp. 170–77.

15. For an excellent book that appropriates this Althusserian problematic for feminism, see Denise Riley, *Am I that Name? Feminism and the Category of "Women" in History* (New York: MacMillan, 1988).

16. See Slavoj Žižek on the social interpellation of the proper name in *The Sublime Object of Ideology* (London: Verso, 1989), pp. 87–102.

17. Jacqueline Rose, *Sexuality in the Field of Vision* (London: Verso, 1987), pp. 90–91.p

18. Foucault, "The Subject and Power," *Michel Foucault: Beyond Structuralism and Hermeneutics*, eds. Hubert L. Dreyfus and Paul Rabinow (Chicago: University of Chicago Press, 1982), p. 212.

19. See the preface to *Formations of Fantasy*, eds. Victor Burgin, James Donald and Cora Kaplan (London: Methuen, 1986) for a psychoanalytic warning against "collapsing" the psychic and the social.

20. In the above, the terms "attachment" and "investment" might be understood as intentional in the phenomenological sense, that is, as libidinal movements or trajectories which always take an object. There is no free-floating attachment which then takes an object; rather, an attachment is always an attachment *to* an object, where that to which it is attached alters the attachment itself. The transferability of attachment presupposes that the object to which an attachment is made may change, but there will always be that attachment, and there will always be some object, and that this action of binding to (tied always to a certain warding off) is the constitutive action of attachment.

This notion of attachment seems close to certain efforts to account for drives in nonbiologistic terms (to be distinguished from those efforts that take the biological seriously). Here one might seek recourse to Gilles Deleuze's reading of drives in *Présentation de Sacher-Masoch* (1967) (*Coldness and Cruelty*, Zone Books), in which he suggests that drives may be understood as the pulsionality of positing or valuation. See also Jean Laplanche's recent discussions, in which "the drive" becomes indissociable from its cultural articulation: "we think it necessary to conceive of a dual expository stage: on the one hand, the preliminary stage of an organism that is bound to homeostasis and self-preservation, and, on the other hand, the stage of the adult cultural world in which the infant is immediately and completely immersed," in *Jean Laplanche: Seduction, Translation, Drives*, eds. John Fletcher and Martin Stanton (London: Institute of Contemporary Arts, 1992), p. 187.

21. See my "Stubborn Attachments: A Rereading of Hegel's `Unhappy Consciousness'," in Tillotama Rajan, ed. *Intersections: Nineteenth Century Philosophy and Contemporary Theory* (Albany: SUNY Press, forthcoming).

ELABORATIONS

Fredric Jameson

On *Cultural Studies*

The desire called Cultural Studies is perhaps best approached politically and socially, as the project to constitute a "historic bloc," rather than theoretically, as the floor plan for a new discipline. The politics in such a project are, to be sure, "academic" politics, the politics within the university, and, beyond it, in intellectual life in general, or in the space of intellectuals as such. At a time, however, when the Right has begun to develop its own cultural politics, focused on the reconquest of the academic institutions, and in particular of the foundations and the universities themselves, it does not seem wise to go on thinking of academic politics, and the politics of intellectuals, as a particularly "academic" matter. In any case, the Right seems to have understood that the project and the slogan of Cultural Studies (whatever that may be) constitutes a crucial target in its campaign and virtually a synonym for "political correctness" (which may in this context be identified simply as the cultural politics of the various "new social movements": antiracism, antisexism, antihomophobia, and so forth).

But if this is so, and Cultural Studies is to be seen as the expression of a projected alliance between various social groups, then its rigorous formulation as an intellectual or pedagogical enterprise may not be quite so important as some of its adherents feel, when they offer to begin the Left sectarian warfare all over again in the struggle for the correct verbal rendering of the cultural studies party line: not the line is important, but the possibility for social alliances that its general slogan seems to reflect. It is a symptom rather than a theory; as such, what would seem most desirable is a cultural studies analysis of Cultural Studies itself. This also means that what we require (and find) in the recent collection, *Cultural Studies*,[1] edited by Lawrence Grossberg, Cary Nelson and Paula A. Treichler, is merely a certain comprehensiveness and general representativity (something forty contributors would seem to guarantee in advance), and not the absolute impossibility of the thing being done some other way or staged in a radically different fashion. This is not to say that absences from or gaps in this collection, which essentially reprints the papers delivered at a conference on the subject held in Urbana-Champaign in Spring 1990, are not significant features deserving of comment: but the comment would then take the form of a diagnosis of this particular event and the "idea" of Cultural Studies it embodies, rather than of a proposal for some more adequate alternative (conference, "idea," program, or "party line"). Indeed, I should probably lay my cards on the table at once and say that, as important (indeed, as theoretically interesting) as I think it is to discuss and debate the matter of Cultural Studies right now, I don't particularly care what ultimate form the program ends up taking, or even whether an official academic discipline of this kind comes into being in the first place. That is probably because I don't much believe in the reform of academic programs to begin with; but also because I suspect that, once the right kind of discussion or argument has taken place publicly, the purpose of Cultural Studies will have been achieved anyway, regardless of the departmental framework in which the discussion has been carried out. (And I specifically mean this remark to have to do with what I take to be the most crucial practical issue at stake in the whole matter, namely the protection of the younger people writing articles in this new "field," and their possibility of tenure.)

I guess I also have to say, against definitions (Adorno liked to remind us of Nietzsche's dismissal of the attempt to *define* historical phenomena as such), that I think we already know, somehow, what Cultural Studies is; and that "defining" it means removing what it is not, removing the extraneous clay from the emergent statue, drawing a boundary by instinct and visceral feel, trying to identify what it is not, so comprehensively that finally the job is done whether a positive "definition" ever ends up emerging.

Fredric
252 *Jameson*

Whatever it may be, it came into the world as the result of dissatisfaction with other disciplines, not merely their contents but also their very limits as such. It is thus in that sense postdisciplinary; but despite that, or perhaps for that very reason, one of the crucial ways in which Cultural Studies continues to define itself turns on its relationship to the established disciplines. It may therefore be appropriate to begin with the complaints from allies in those disciplines about the neglect by an emergent Cultural Studies of aims they consider fundamental; eight further sections will deal with groups; Marxism, the concept of articulation, culture and libido, the role of intellectuals, populism, geopolitics, and, in conclusion, Utopia.

IT'S NOT MY FIELD!

The historians seem particularly perplexed by the somewhat indeterminable relationship of the cultural people to archival material. Catherine Hall, the author of one of the more substantive pieces in the collection—a study of the ideological mediation of English missionaries in Jamaica—after observing that "if cultural history isn't a part of cultural studies, then I think there's a serious problem" (272), goes on to say that "the encounter between mainstream history and cultural studies in Britain has been extremely limited" (271). That could, of course, be fully as much the problem of mainstream history as of Cultural Studies; but Carolyn Steedman goes on to examine the matter more pointedly, suggesting some basic methodological differences. Collective versus individual research is only one of these: "Group practice is collective; archive research involves the lone historian, taking part in an undemocratic practice. Archive research is expensive, of time and of money, and not something that a group of people can practically do, anyway" (618). But when she tries to formulate the distinctiveness of the Cultural Studies approach in a more positive way, it comes out as "text-based." The cultural people analyze handy texts, the archival historian has to reconstruct, laboriously, on the basis of symptoms and fragments. Not the least interesting part of Steedman's analysis is her suggestion of an institutional, and more specifically educational, determinant in the emergence of the "text-based" method: "Was the 'culture concept' as used by historians . . . actually invented in the schools, between about 1955 and 1975? In Britain, we do not even have a social and cultural history of education that allows us to think that this might be a question"

(619–620). She does not, however, say in which discipline such a research question might properly belong.

Steedman also suggestively names Burckhardt as a precursor of the new field (no one else does); and she briefly engages with the New Historicism, whose absence from these pages is otherwise very significant indeed (save for a moment in which Peter Stallybrass denies having any kinship with the rival movement). For the New Historicism is surely basic competition, and on any historical view a kindred symptom with Cultural Studies in its attempt to grapple analytically with the world's new textuality (as well as in its vocation to fill the succession to Marxism in a discreet and respectable way). It can of course be argued that Cultural Studies is too busy with the present, and that it cannot be expected to do everything or to be concerned with everything; and I suppose there is a residual afterimage here of the more traditional opposition between the contemporary concerns of students of mass or popular culture and the tendentiously backward-gazing perspective of literary critics (even where the canonized works are "modern" and relatively recent in time). But the most substantial pieces in the collection—besides Catherine Hall's essay, include Lata Mani's study of widow-burning, Janice Radway's essay on the Book of the Month Club, Peter Stallybrass's investigation of the emergence of Shakespeare as an *auteur*, and Anna Szemere's account of the rhetoric of the 1956 Hungarian uprising—are all historical in the archival sense, and *do* tend to stand out like sore thumbs. They ought to be welcome guests, so why does everyone feel awkward?

Sociology is another allied discipline, so close that translation between it and Cultural Studies seems at best difficult if not altogether impossible (as Kafka once observed about the analogous kinship of German and Yiddish). But did not Raymond Williams suggest in 1981 that "what is now often called 'cultural studies' [is better understood] as a distinctive mode of entry into general sociological questions than . . . a reserved or specialized area" (quoted, page 223)? Still, this cross-disciplinary relationship seems to present analogies with that to history: "text-based" work over here, professional or professionalized "research" over there. Simon Frith's complaint is emblematic enough to be quoted in full:

> Now what I've been talking about up to now is an approach to popular music which, in British terms, comes not from cultural studies but from social anthropology and sociology (and I could

cite other examples, like Mavis Bayton's [1990] work on how women become rock musicians). One reason I find this work important is because it focuses on an area and issue systematically (and remarkably) neglected by cultural studies: the rationale of cultural production itself, the place and thought of cultural producers. But what interests me here (which is why this paper is now going to be a different narrative altogether) is something else: compared to the flashy, imaginative, impressionistic, unlikely pop writing of a cultural studies academic like, say, Iain Chambers, the dogged ethnographic attention to detail and accuracy is, as Dick Hebdige once remarked of my sociological approach in contrast to Chambers', kind of dull.(178)

Janet Wolff suggests more fundamental reasons for this tension: "The problem is that mainstream sociology, confidently indifferent if not hostile to developments in theory, is unable to acknowledge the constitutive role of culture and representation *in* social relations" (710). Only it turns out that the feeling is mutual: "Poststructuralist theory and discourse theory, in demonstrating the discursive nature of the social, operate as license to *deny* the social" (711). Quite properly, she recommends a coordination of both ("an approach which integrates textual analysis with the sociological investigation of institutions of cultural production and of those social and political processes and relations in which this takes place" [713]); but this does not do away with the discomfort still felt in the presence of the beast, any more than Cornel West's suggestion that the main advantage of Cultural Studies is that familiar old thing called "interdisciplinary" ("cultural studies becomes one of the rubrics used to justify what I think is a highly salutary development, namely interdisciplinary studies in colleges and universities" [698]). This term spans several generations of academic reform programs, whose history needs to be written and then reinscribed in it in some cautionary way (virtually by definition it is always a failure): but one's sense is that the "interdisciplinary" effort keeps taking place because the specific disciplines all repress crucial but in each case different features of the object of study they ought to be sharing. More than most such reform programs, Cultural Studies seemed to promise to name the absent object, and it does not seem right to settle for the tactical vagueness of the older formula.

Perhaps, indeed, it is *communication* that is the name required: only Communications programs are so recent as to overlap in many ways (including personnel) with the new venture, leaving only communications technology as a distinguishing mark or a feature of disciplinary separation (rather like body and soul, or letter and spirit, machine and ghost). It is only when a specific perspective unifies the various items of study of communications as a field that light begins to be shed, on Cultural Studies as well as on its relations with Communications programs. This is the case, for example, when Jody Berland evokes the distinctiveness of Canadian communication theory as such: nor does this merely amount to some homage to McLuhan and his tradition and precursors, but emerges in a more contemporary form, in her paper, as a whole new theory of the ideology of "entertainment" as such. But she also makes it clear why Canadian theory is necessarily distinct from what she euphemistically refers to as "mainstream communications research" (43), by which US communications theory is meant. For it is clearly the situation of Canada, in the shadow of the US media empire, that gives our neighbors their epistemological privilege, and in particular the unique possibility of combining spatial analysis with the more traditional attention to the media as such:

> The concept of "cultural technology" helps us to understand this process. As part of a spatial production which is both determinant and problematic, shaped by both disciplinary and antidisciplinary practices, cultural technologies encompass simultaneously the articulated discourses of professionalization, territoriality, and diversion. These are the necessary three-dimensional facets of analysis of a popular culture produced in the shadow of American imperialism. In locating their "audiences" in an increasingly wider and more diverse range of dispositions, locations, and contexts, contemporary cultural technologies contribute to and seek to legitimate their own spatial and discursive expansion. This is another way of saying that the production of texts cannot be conceived outside of the production of spaces. Whether or not one conceives of the expansion of such spaces as a form of colonialism remains to be seen. The question is central, however, to arriving at an understanding of entertainment that locates its practices in spatial terms. (42)

What Berland makes clear is that attention to the situation of theory (or the theorist or the discipline) now necessarily involves a dialectic: "As the production of meaning is located [by Anglo-American media theory] in the activities and agencies of audiences, *the topography of consumption is increasingly identified as (and thus expanded to stand in for) the map of the social.* This reproduces in theory what is occurring in practice" (42). The dramatic introduction of a geopolitical dimension, the identification of a certain cultural and communicational theory as Canadian, in sharp opposition to a hegemonic Anglo-American perspective (which assumes its own universality, because it originates in the center and need not mark itself nationally), now radically displaces the issues of the conference and their consequences, as we shall see at greater length later on.

On the other hand, it is unclear what kind of relationship to an emergent Cultural Studies is being proposed here. The logic of collective or group fantasy is always allegorical.[2] This one may involve a kind of alliance, as when the labor unions propose working together with this or that Black movement; or it may be closer to an international treaty of some kind, like NATO or the new free trade zone. But presumably "Canadian communication theory" is not intent on submerging its identity altogether in the larger Anglo-American movement; equally clearly, it cannot altogether universalize its own program, and ask for a blanket endorsement by the "center" of what is necessarily a situated and "dependent" or "semiperipheral" perspective. I suppose that what emerges here is, then, the sense that, at a given point, the analysis in question can be transcoded or even translated: that at certain strategic junctures a given analysis can be read, either as an example of the Cultural Studies perspective, or as an exemplification of everything distinctive about Canadian communication theory. Each perspective thus shares a common object (at a specific conjuncture) without losing its own specific difference or originality (how to name or better to describe this overlap would then be a new kind of problem specifically produced by "Cultural Studies theory").

Nothing better dramatizes this overlap of disciplinary perspectives than the various icons brandished throughout these pages: the name of the late Raymond Williams, for example, is taken in vain by virtually everyone and appealed to for moral support in any number of sins (or virtues).[3] But the text that repeatedly resurfaces as a fetish is very much a book whose multiple generic frameworks illustrate the problem we have been discussing here.

I refer to the study of English youth culture by Paul Willis (not present at this conference, incidentally) entitled *Learning to Labor* (1977). This book can be thought of as a classic work in some new sociology of culture; or as a precursor text from the "original" Birmingham School (of which more below); or yet again as a kind of ethnology, something which now lights up as an axis running from the traditional terrain of anthropology to the new territory claimed by Cultural Studies.

Here, however, what enriches the interdisciplinary "problematic" is the inescapable sense (it may also be so for the other disciplines, but can there equally well be overlooked) that if Cultural Studies is an emergent paradigm, anthropology itself, far from being a comparatively "traditional" one, is also in full metamorphosis and convulsive methodological and textual transformation (as the presence of the name of James Clifford on the Cultural Studies roster here suggests). "Anthropology" now means a new kind of ethnology, a new textual or interpretive anthropology, which—offering some distant family likeness with the New Historicism—emerges fully grown in the work of Clifford and also of George Marcus and Michael Fischer (with the appropriate acknowledgment of the precursive examples of Geertz, Turner, et al.). "Thick description" is then evoked by Andrew Ross, in his pioneering work on New Age culture: "the more exhaustive, or deep, 'ethnographic' study of cultural communities that has produced one of the most exciting developments in recent cultural studies" (537); while the very rhetoric of thickness, texture and immanence is justified by a memorable period of John Fiske, which has the additional merit of bringing out some of the practical stakes of the debate (which are far from boiling down to a battle of mere disciplinary claims and counterclaims):

> I would like to start with the concept of "distance" in cultural theory. Elsewhere I have argued that "distance" is a key marker of difference between high and low culture, between the meanings, practices, and pleasures characteristic of empowered and disempowered social formations. Cultural distance is a multidimensional concept. In the culture of the socially advantaged and empowered it may take the form of a distance between the art object and reader/spectator: such distance devalues socially and historically specific reading practices in favor of a transcendent appreciation or aesthetic sensibility with claims to universality. It encourages rev-

erence or respect for the text as an art object endowed with authenticity and requiring preservation. "Distance" may also function to create a difference between the experience of the art work and everyday life. Such "distance" produces ahistorical meanings of art works and allows the members of its social formation the pleasures of allying themselves with a set of humane values that in the extreme versions of aesthetic theory are argued to be universal values which transcend their historical conditions. This distance from the historical is also a distance from the bodily sensations, for it is our bodies that finally bind us to our historical and social specificities. As the mundanities of our social conditions are set aside, or distanced, by this view of art, so too, are the so-called sensuous, cheap, and easy pleasures of the body distanced from the more contemplative, aesthetic pleasures of the mind. And finally this distance takes the form of distance from economic necessity; the separation of the aesthetic from the social is a practice of the elite who can afford to ignore the constraints of material necessity, and who thus construct an aesthetic which not only refuses to assign any value at all to material conditions, but validates only those art forms which transcend them. This critical and aesthetic distance is thus, finally, a marker of distinction between those able to separate their culture from the social and economic conditions of the everyday and those who cannot. (154)

But the contents of the volume under consideration do not particularly bear out Ross's claim, except for his own lucid study of that uniquely ambiguous "interpretive community" which is the new yuppie culture of the New Age people; whereas Fiske's clarion call does not so much lead us down the road to anthropology as an experimental discipline (and mode of writing), as to a whole new politics of intellectuals as such.

Indeed, Clifford's own paper—a description of his exciting new work on the enthnology of travel and tourism—already implicitly redefines the polemic context by offering a displacement of the traditional ethnographic conception of "fieldwork": "ethnography (in the normative practices of twentieth-century anthropology) has privileged relations of dwelling over relations of travel" (99). This squarely redefines the intellectual and the anthropologist-ethnographer-observer as a kind of traveler and a kind of tourist, and it now at once rewrites the terms of this conference, whose attempt to define that thing called Cultural Studies—far from being an academic and a disciplinary issue—in fact turns on the status of the intellectual as such in relationship to the politics of the so-called new social movements or microgroups.

To put it this way is to make clear the discomfort necessarily triggered among many of the other participants by Clifford's "modest proposal": far from being mere "tourists" or even travelers, most of them want to be true "organic intellectuals" at the very least, if not something more. (But what would that "something more" be, exactly?) Even the cognate notion of the exile or neoexile, the diasporic intellectual invoked by Homi Bhabha (whose remarks on the Rushdie affair—"Blasphemy is the migrant's shame at returning home" [62]—struck me as being extraordinarily pertinent and suggestive), proposes an intermittency or alternation of subject and object, of voice and substance, of theorist and "native," which secures an equally intermittent badge of group membership for the intellectual that is not available to the White male Clifford (or to the present reviewer either).

SOCIAL GROUPS: POPULAR FRONT OR UNITED NATIONS?

But the desire called the organic intellectual is omnipresent here, although it is not often expressed as openly as it is by Stuart Hall himself, when, in one of the grandest utopian moments of the conference, he proposes the ideal of "living with the possibility that there *could* be, sometime, a movement which would be larger than the movement of petit-bourgeois intellectuals" (288). Here is what Hall says about Gramsci in this respect:

I have to confess that, though I've read many, more elaborated and sophisticated accounts, Gramsci's account still seems to me to come closest to expressing what it is I think we were trying to do. Admittedly, there's a problem about his phrase "the production of organic intellectuals." But there is no doubt in my mind that we were trying to find an institutional practice in cultural studies that might produce an organic intellectual. We didn't know previously what that would mean, in the context of Britain in the 1970s, and we weren't sure we would recognize him or her if we managed to produce it. The problem about the concept of an organic intellectual is that it appears to align intellectuals with an emerging historic movement and we couldn't tell then, and can hardly tell now, where that emerging historical movement was to be found. We were organic intellectuals without any organic point of reference; organic intellectuals with a nostalgia or will or hope (to use Gramsci's phrase from another context) that at some point we would be prepared in intellectual work for that kind of relationship, if such a conjuncture ever appeared. More truthfully, we were prepared to imagine or model or simulate such a relationship in its absence: "pessimism of the intellect, optimism of the will." (281)

The Gramscian notion, however, whose double focus structurally includes intellectuals on the one hand and social strata on the other, is most often in the present collection and in the present context not interpreted as a reference to alliance politics, to a historic bloc, to the forging of a heterogeneous set of "interest groups" into some larger political and social movement, as it was in Gramsci, and still seems to be in this formulation by Stuart Hall.

Rather, its reference here seems universally to be that of the "identity politics" of the new social movements, or what Deleuze calls microgroups. Certainly, Cultural Studies has widely been felt to be an alliance space of just this kind (if not exactly a movement in the Gramscian sense, unless you understand its academic ambitions—to achieve recognition and institutional sanction, tenure, protection from traditional departments and the New Right—as a politics, indeed the only politics specific to Cultural Studies as such).[4] Thus, it welcomes together feminism and Black politics, the gay movement, Chicano studies, the burgeoning "postcolonial" study groups, along with more traditional aficionados of the various popular and mass cultures (they can also, in traditional academia, be counted as a kind of stigmatized and persecuted minority), and the various (mostly foreign) Marxist hangers-on. Of the 41 (published) participants, there is a relatively even gender distribution (24 women, 21 men); there are 25 Americans, 11 British, 4 Australians, 2 Canadians, and one Hungarian and Italian, respectively; there are 31 White people, 6 Black people, 2 Chicanos, and 2 Indians (from the subcontinent); and there seem to be at least 5 gay people out of the forty-some. As for the disciplines or departments themselves, they seem to fall out as follows: English takes the lion's share with 11, as might have been predicted; Communications, Sociology and Art History are distant runners-up with 4 each; there are 3 representatives of Humanities programs; 2 each from Women's Studies; Cultural Studies proper, History of Consciousness, and Radio, Television, and Film; while Religion and Anthropology have one representative each.

But these (admittedly very impressionistic) breakdowns do not reflect the group, subgroup or subcultural ideological positions very accurately. As opposed to only four "traditional" feminist papers, for example, there are at least two gay statements. Of the five Black statements, one also raises feminist issues (or rather, it would be more accurate to say that Michele Wallace's paper is a statement of a Black feminist position as such), while two more raise national questions. One of the two Chicano papers is also a feminist statement. There are ten recognizably mass-cultural or popular-cultural topics which tend to displace emphasis from "identity" issues to media ones.

I indulge in this exercise as much to show what seems to have been omitted from the Cultural Studies problematic as what is included in it. Only three papers seem to me to discuss the issue of group identity in any kind of central way (while Paul Gilroy's attack on the slogan, which he translates as "ethnic absolutism," is best examined in another context, below); and of those only Elspeth Probyn's intricately referenced essay makes a stab at a theory of collective identity, or at least of collective enunciation, as such: asking us "to go beyond discrete positions of difference and to refuse the crisis mode of representation . . . to make the sound of our identities count as we work to construct communities of caring" (511). Such sounds seem to be rather wild ones, however, as when we are told "how images of the self can work successfully to annoy, to enervate discursive fixities and extra-discursive expectations" (506).

But the papers by Kobena Mercer and by Marcos Sanchez-Tranquilino and John Tagg are already en route toward something rather different from classic identity theory. Mercer, indeed, opens a path-breaking exploration into the way in which the sixties image of Black militancy was able to serve as a suggestive and a liberating model for the politics of other groups; while Sanchez-Tranquilino displaces the more psychological or philosophical problematic of "identity" back onto the social matter of nationalism: "What is at issue in this resurrection of the *pachuco* in the late 1970s is . . . the representation of . . . militancy through the articulation of the *pachuco* into the politics of identity of a *nationalist* movement. The problems here are the problems of all nationalisms. . . ." (562)

Maybe so: but the nationalisms—let's better say the separatisms—are not present here: feminist, lesbian, gay separatisms are not represented as such, and if there are still any Black separatisms left, they are certainly not here either; of the other ethnic groups, only the Chicanos are here, to represent themselves and perhaps stand in for some of those other movements (but not for the more traditional national *ethnies*, whose problems are interestingly different from these, as witness the debates about Greece as a minor culture[5]); while the "postcolonials" tirelessly make the point (as in the Homi Bhabha essay already referred to) that the diasporic fact and experience is the very opposite of one of ethnic separatism.

This is to say, then, that this particular space called Cultural Studies is not terribly receptive to unmixed identities as such, but seems, on the contrary, to welcome the celebration (but also the analysis) of the mixed, *per se*, of new kinds of structural complexity. Already Bakhtinian tones were invoked to dispel the monologic (and is not cultural separatism the longing for a certain monological discourse?): Clifford wishes "not to assert a naive democracy of plural authorship, but to loosen at least somewhat the monological control of the executive writer/anthropologist" (100), while Stalleybrass's remarkable piece on the invention of "Shakespeare" replaces the modern "single author" with a "network of collaborative relations," normally between two or more writers, between writers and acting companies, between acting companies and printers, between compositors and proofreaders, between printers and censors, such that there is also no single moment of the "individual text" (601). The problematic of the *auteur*, then, reminds us to what degree the narrative notion of a single, albeit collective, agency is still operative in many garden-variety notions of "identity" (and indeed returns on the last page of this anthology in Angela McRobbie's stirring invocation of the mission of Cultural Studies in the 1990s to act "as a kind of guide to how people see themselves . . . as active agents whose sense of self is projected onto and expressed in an expansive range of cultural practices" [730]). But that isolationist conception of group identity would at best open up a space for Cultural Studies in which each of the groups said its piece, in a kind of United Nations plenary session, and was given respectful (and "politically correct") hearing by all the others: neither a stimulating nor a very productive exercise, one would think.

The "identities" in question in the present volume are, however, mainly dual ones: for them Black feminism is the paradigm (but also Chicana feminism, as in Angie Chabram-Dernersesian's lively essay). Indeed, I am tempted to suggest that Cultural Studies today (or at least that proposed by this particular collection and conference) is very much a matter of dual citizenship, of having at least a dual passport, if not more of them. The really interesting and productive work and thought does not seem to happen without the productive tension of trying to combine, navigate, coordinate several "identities" at once, and several commitments, several positions: it is like a replay of Sartre's old notion that the writer is better off having to address at least two distinct and unrelated publics at the same time. Once again, it is in Stuart Hall's reflective and wide-ranging remarks (as one of the precursor or founding figures of the older, Birmingham "Cultural Studies") that the necessity for living with these tensions is affirmed as such (284). To be sure, in this particular passage he means the tension between text and society, between superstructure and base, what he calls the necessary "displacement" of culture out of the social real into the imaginary. But he had also before that recalled the tensions involved in multiple ideological influences and commitments, to Marxism but also to feminism, to structuralism or the "linguistic turn," as so many distinct forces of gravity, which it made up the richness of the school to respond to, rather than to achieve the final synthesis, iron out the contradictions, and flatten these multiple operations out into a single program or formula. The tensions between group identities, one would think, offer a more productive field of force than the interdisciplinary ambivalences discussed earlier, but all this then threatens to be flattened out and defused in a rather different way by the competing disciplinary formula of postmodernism and its version of pluralism, a topic which is here on the whole systematically avoided and eluded, for a reason that now becomes obvious.

CULTURAL STUDIES AS A SUBSTITUTE FOR MARXISM

To stage a frontal assault on postmodernism as such, indeed, and to argue for the philosophical necessity of a Cultural Studies that was something other than a postmodern celebration of the effacement of the boundaries of high and low, the pluralism of the microgroups and the replacement of ideological politics with image and media culture, would require a reassessment of the traditional relationship of the general Cultural Studies movement with Marxism that evidently exceeded the ambitions of the conference. Marxism is there, for the most part, evidently understood as yet another kind of group identity (but then of a very tiny group indeed, at least in the US) rather than as the kind of problematic—and problem!— which Stuart Hall evokes ("the questions that Marxism as a theoretical project put on the agenda . . . questions [which] are what one meant by working within shouting distance of Marxism, working on Marxism, working against Marxism, working with it, working to try to develop Marxism" [279]). Yet it would be all the more important to come to grips with these issues, insofar as, in the US, Cultural Studies, as Michael Denning has argued for its precursor and competitor American Studies,[6] can equally well be seen to be a "substitute" for Marxism as a development of it. But not even Raymond Williams's strategic British reformulation of Marxism as "cultural materialism" receives attention here (nor have the Americans shown much anxiety in general about the problem of avoiding "idealism"); nor is the political will implicit in the Birmingham group fully as much as in Williams generally in much evidence in these pages, about which it needs to be stressed again and again (for both) that Cultural Studies or "cultural materialism" was essentially a political project and indeed a Marxist project at that. When foreign theory crosses the Atlantic, it tends to lose much of its contextual political or class overtones (as witness the evaporation of so much of that from French theory). Nowhere is this process more striking, however, as in the current American reinvention of what was in Britain a militant affair and a commitment to radical social change.

The usual American anti-Marxian litanies are, however, in the current volume only occasionally and perfunctorily intoned. A systemic transformation (which they do not, however, want to call "postmodern," for some reason) is evoked with gusto by Sanchez-Tranquilino and Tagg: "As long as the Museum could be conceived as an Ideological State Apparatus . . . it was possible to imagine another place, another consciousness. . . . Now, with the undermining of these categories and logics, both sides seem to have been flung out or sucked into a gravity-less space. . . . Such forms of sociological explanation have themselves been caught in the internal collapse of the discipline they claim to critique" (556–7).

There is fortunately very little of the silliest of the usual claims, that Marxism is antifeminist or excludes women; but "high feminism" also seems enveloped in another familiar reproach, namely that Cultural Studies does not do Grand Theory anymore ("in which massive, world-historical problems are debated on such a level of generality that they cannot possibly be solved" [Morris, 466]): a reproach that is specifically directed against Marxism, but seems also to secure the fairly thoroughgoing evacuation of any number of other grand theories and grand names besides feminism, psychoanalysis, Lacanianism, deconstruction, Baudrillard, Lyotard, Derrida, Virilio, Deleuze, Greimas and so on (with Raymond Williams—but no longer with Gramsci, Brecht or Benjamin—an exception, and one of the still minimally operative icons of the new movement).

Still, it seems possible that as the noisiest detractors of "grand theory" are the Australians, this particular move may owe something to the idiosyncratic and anarchist roots of Australian radicalism. It is, indeed, from Australia that another, even more sinister variant of this otherwise harmless anti-intellectualism comes, in Tony Bennett's specifically political and "activist" critique of Marxism. After hastening to except the "new social movements" from his own reformist structures on political activity, he describes his position as follows:

> What it *is* to argue against are ways of conducting both of these aspects of political processes [alliances and single-issue politics], and of connecting them to one another, in ways which anticipate—and are envisaged as paving the way for—the production of a unified class, gender, people, or race as a social agent likely to take decisive action in a moment of terminal political fulfillment of a process assigned the task of bringing that agent into being. And it is to do so precisely because of the degree to which such political projects and the constructions which fuel them hinder the development of more specific and immediate forms of political calculation and action likely to improve the social circumstances and possibilities of the constituencies in question. (32)

Laclau/Mouffe versus Gramsci? Versus Lenin? Bennett versus Laclau/Mouffe? The frame of reference is impossible to determine, particularly since no one (on the Left) has ever believed in any "unified class, gender, people, or race" in the first place (and certainly not Gramsci, who has been summarily sent packing in the preceding pages as being no longer "of much service politically" [29]). Bennett's is a genuine "thought of the other," busy tracking down and denouncing the ideological errors of all these enemies on the Left in the shrillest traditions of Althusserian hectoring. Nor does he seem to realize how obscene American Left readers are likely to find his proposals on "talking to and working with what used to be called the ISAs rather than writing them off from the outset and then, in a self-fulfilling prophecy, criticizing them again when they seem to affirm one's direst functionalist predictions" (32). The invitation to stop mouthing Marxist slogans (grand theory) and to enter the (presumably vaguely social-democratic) government may have some relevance in a small country with socialist traditions, but it is surely misplaced advice here (and in any case quite impossible to fulfill). The tone of this essay, given pride of place for alphabetical reasons at the very opening of the volume, is remarkably misleading as to the spirit of the collection as a whole; what is more distressing is the ignorance it betrays about the structural differences of the various national situations today, one of the strong themes of the present volume, and paradoxically one which the Australian contributors themselves play a central role in establishing, as we shall see shortly.

But this particular formulation by Bennett leads on to the fundamental anti-Marxian stereotype, for the passage quoted can readily be translated back into the hoariest of all negative buzzwords, "totalization"—namely some kind of totalitarian and organic homogenization to which the "Marxists" are supposed to subject all forms of difference. In Sartre, however, this originally philosophical term simply meant the way in which perceptions, instruments and raw materials were linked up and set in relationship to each other by the unifying perspective of a project (if you do not have a project or do not want one, it obviously no longer applies). I am not sure whether this concept projects a model exactly (or is constructed according to the image of one); but I suspect it would not matter much, since conceptions of *relationship*—however they attempt to keep their terms distinct and separate—tend to slip into images of an undifferentiated mass. Witness the fortunes of the at least pop-philosophical concept of the "organic" which once designated the radical difference in function between the various organs (one of Marx's fundamental figures in the *Grundrisse* was that of "metabolism"), but now seems to mean turning them all into the same thing. The "organic" has thus, along with "linear history" (a construction I believe we owe to McLuhan), become one of the fundamental poststructural indices of error (at least until "totalization" came along). Of course, one can stop using these words for tactical reasons (and to abridge lexical and philological explanations such as this one); but surely on any dispassionate view the collection under consideration is crammed full of various acts of totalization which it would serve no good purpose to track down and eliminate unless your aim is to return to that kind of simon-pure, solid-color theorization which has, in connection with the politics of an unmixed identity, been argued to be incompatible with the essentially mixed nature of Cultural Studies in the first place.

ARTICULATION: A TRUCK DRIVER'S MANUAL

These acts of totalization are, however, camouflaged by a new figure, which—unlike the Sartrean coinage of totalization itself—has a respectable poststructural theoretical correctness about it (and which, like all figures, displaces the terms of the old one just slightly). This is the omnipresent concept of *articulation*, about which we urgently need a lexical entry in some larger ideological dictionary of the objective spirit of the period. Derived, like "organic," from the body as a reference, it rather designates the bony parts and the connections of the skeleton, than the soft organic organs (and perhaps the rigor and mechanical quality plays some part in its current favor); but is then quickly transferred to speech, as in a very allegory of the "linguistic turn" itself. My sense is that we owe its compulsive use to Althusser (whose influence may then have had some effect on Foucault's even more compulsive figures of segmentation and spatial divisibility), with generalization via Ben Brewster's elegant English-language reinvention, and Poulantzas's political extensions, along with Pierre-Philippe Rey's anthropology, thence to Hindess and Hirst, and on into a generalized theoretical lingua franca, shortly to be rejoined by such current favorites as "to erase," "circulation," "constructed" and the like. What is less often remembered is that Althusser actually found this seemingly Althusserian and structuralist-sounding word in Marx himself, and specifically in the great unfinished program essay of August 1857 which was to have served as the introduction to the *Grundrisse*.[7]

Here *Gliederung* designates the articulation of the categories (and realities) of production, distribution and consumption among each other (in this form it is a suggestive model whose application remains to be explored). Meanwhile, it is important to stress the well-nigh independent and extraordinarily rich development of the concept of articulation by the Birmingham School itself, at a crucial moment in its history when the intersections of race, gender and class became an urgent theoretical problem. Catherine Hall's formulation is here canonical:

> I don't think that we have, as yet, a theory as to the articulation of race, class, and gender and the ways in which these articulations might generally operate. The terms are often produced as a litany, to prove political correctness, but that does not necessarily mean that the forms of analysis which follow are really shaped by a grasp of the workings of each axis of power in relation to the others. Indeed, it is extremely difficult to do such work because the level of analysis is necessarily extremely complex with many variables in play at any one time. Case studies, therefore, whether historical or contemporary, which carefully trace the contradictory ways in which these articulations take place both in historically specific moments and over time, seem to me to be very important. (270–271)

Perhaps the suggestion of what theory ought to be ("we do not yet have a theory") gives a little too much aid and comfort to those who are allergic to "grand theorizing," since one would have thought that the concept of articulation as referenced here is already very precisely a theory in its own right. It implies a kind of turning structure, an ion-exchange between various entities, in which the ideological drives associated with one pass over and interfuse the other—but only provisionally, for a "historically specific moment," before entering into new combinations, being systematically worked over into something else, decaying over time in interminable half-life, or being blasted apart by the convulsions of a new social crisis. The articulation is thus a punctual and sometimes even ephemeral totalization, in which the planes of race, gender, class, ethnicity and sexuality intersect to form an operative structure. Here is a fuller statement by Stuart Hall:

> The unity formed by this combination or articulation, is always, necessarily, a "complex structure": a structure in which things are related, as much through their differences as through their similarities. This requires that the mechanisms which connect dissimilar features must be shown—since no "necessary correspondence" or expressive homology can be assumed as given. It also means—

since the combination is a structure (an articulated combination) and not a random association—that there will be structured relations between the parts, i.e., relations of dominance and subordination. (579–580)

In reality, a whole poetic is implicit in such analytic terminology, since the very "representation" of such complexes is always problematic. It is not merely the structure of the complex that is not given in advance (as, for example, whether race or gender happen to come first, which one stands as some provisional ultimately determining instance to the other); it is also the language in which the "elements" and their connections are to be described which must be invented. Descriptions of articulation are thus also necessarily auto-referential, in that they must comment on and validate their own linguistic instruments—only preserving the flimsiest and most tenuous survival of an older figural content (the joints or bones operating together, the mechanical sense of sheer connection as such).

Articulation thus stands as the name of the central theoretical problem or conceptual core of Cultural Studies, exemplified over and over again in the volume of the same name, where it is less often foregrounded as such. It can be sensed at work in Constance Penley's rather more Freudian (and also Marxian) notion of lack, contradiction, substitution and compensation-formation, when, in her essay on women's *Star Trek* porn, she places on the agenda:

> the fact that the women fans can imagine a sexual relation only if it involves a childless couple made up of two men, who never have to cook or scrub the tub, and who live three hundred years in the future. I would also argue that *Star Trek* fandom in general is an attempt to resolve another lack, that of a social relation. *Trek* fan culture is structured around the same void that structures American culture generally, and its desire too is that fundamental antagonisms, like class and race, not exist. (495)

But here the public/private or social/sexual articulation is grasped as a kind of dualism that folds the description back into more familiar Freudo-Marxisms like that of Deleuze and Guattari in the *Anti-Oedipus*. One can also represent articulation in terms of models and suggestive influences, as in Kobena Mercer's piece on the sixties (already mentioned), in which the

Black movement and the very ideological and libidinal structure of Black militancy is articulated as a "signifying chain" that can be reproduced in other constituencies. (That it is also a "reversible connecting factor"—and can be rewired back into original new forms of racism—is another point he makes forcefully, in a timely rebuke to a certain omnipresent Cultural Studies triumphalism.) But articulation also implies and indeed grounds allegory as its fundamental expressive structure: thus Janice Radway reminds us of the way in which mass or popular culture has consistently been fantasized as feminine (513): the rotating allegorical structures of collective fantasy are surely, in fact, the basic text of any approach to articulation as symptom or as political program. But these dynamics of articulation will not be clarified until we more fully grasp the consequences implicit in seeing culture as the expression of the individual group.

CULTURE AND GROUP LIBIDO

For culture—the weaker, more secular version of that thing called religion—is not a "substance" or a phenomenon in its own right; it is an objective mirage that arises out of the relationship between at least two groups. This is to say that no group "has" a culture all by itself: culture is the nimbus perceived by one group when it comes into contact with and observes another one. It is the objectification of everything alien and strange about the contact group: in this context, it is of no little interest to observe that one of the first books on the inter-relationship of groups (the constitutive role of the boundary, the way each group is defined by and defines the other), draws on Erving Goffman's *Stigma* for an account of how defining marks function for other people[8]: in this sense, then, a "culture" is the ensemble of stigmata one group bears in the eyes of the other group (and vice versa). But such marks are more often projected into the "alien mind" in the form of that thought-of-the-other we call belief, and elaborate as religion. But belief, in this sense, is not something we ourselves have, since what we do seems to us natural, and does not need the motivation and rationalization of this strange internalized entity; and indeed the anthropologist Rodney Needham has shown that most "cultures" do not possess the equivalent of our concept, or pseudo-concept, of belief (which is thus unmasked as something the translators illicitly project back into nonimperial, noncosmopolitan languages). I have been greatly influenced by Rodney Needham's suggestive *Belief, Language and Experience* (Chicago: University of Chicago Press, 1972).

Still, it happens that "we" also often speak of "our own" culture, religion, beliefs or whatever. These may now be identified as the recuperation of the Other's view of us; of that objective mirage whereby the Other has formed a picture of us as "having" a culture: depending on the power of the Other, this alienated image demands a response, which may be as inconsequential as the denial whereby Americans brush off the stereotypes of the "ugly American" they encounter abroad, or as thoroughgoing as the various ethnic revivals whereby, as in Hindu nationalism, a people reconstructs those stereotypes and affirms them in a new cultural-nationalist politics: something which is never the "return" to an older authentic reality but always a new construction (out of what merely look like older materials).

Culture must thus always be seen as a vehicle or a medium whereby the relationship between groups is transacted. If it is not always vigilantly unmasked as an idea of the Other (even when I reassume it for myself), it perpetuates the optical illusions and the false objectivism of this complex historical relationship (thus the objections that have been made to pseudo-concepts like "society" are even more valid for this one, whose origin in group struggle can be deciphered). Meanwhile, to insist on this translation-program (the imperative to turn concepts of culture back into forms of the relationship between collective groups) offers a more satisfactory way of fulfilling the objectives of the various forms of a sociological Heisenberg principle than does the current individualistic recommendation to reckon back in the place of the observer. In reality, the anthropologist-other, the individual observer, stands in for a whole social group, and it is in this sense that his knowledge is a form of power, where "knowledge" designates something individual, and "power" tries to characterize that mode of relationship between groups for which our vocabulary is so poor.

For the relationship between groups is, so to speak, unnatural: it is the chance external contact between entities which have only an interior (like a monad) and no exterior or external surface, save in this special circumstance in which it is precisely the outer edge of the group that—all the while remaining unrepresentable—brushes against that of the other. Speaking crudely then, we would have to say that the relationship between groups must always be one of struggle or violence: for the only positive or tolerant way for them to coexist is to part from one another and rediscover their isolation and their solitude. Each group is thus the entire world, the collective is the fundamental form of the monad, windowless and unbounded (at least from within).

But this failure or omission of a plausible, let alone a "natural" set of attitudes whereby group relations might be conducted means that the two fundamental forms of group relationship reduce themselves to the primordial ones of *envy* and *loathing*, respectively. The oscillation back and forth between these poles can at least in part be explained by prestige (to use one of Gramsci's categories): an attempt to appropriate the culture of the other group (which, as we have already seen, in effect means inventing the "culture" of the other group) is a tribute and a form of group recognition, the expression of collective envy, the acknowledgment of the prestige of the other group. It seems likely that this prestige is not to be too quickly reduced to matters of power, since very often larger and more powerful groups pay this tribute to the groups they dominate, whose forms of cultural expression they borrow and imitate. Prestige is thus more plausibly an emanation of group solidarity, something a weaker group often needs to develop more desperately than the larger complacent hegemonic one, which nonetheless dimly senses its own inner lack of the same cohesion and unconsciously regrets its tendential dissolution as a group as such. "Groupie-ism" is another strong expression of this kind of envy, but on an individual basis, as members of the dominant "culture" opt out and mimic the adherence to the dominated (after all that has been said, it is probably not necessary to add that groupies are thus already in this sense potential or proto-intellectuals).

As for group loathing, however, it mobilizes the classic syndromes of purity and danger, and acts out a kind of defense of the boundaries of the primary group against this threat perceived to be inherent in the Other's very existence. Modern racism (as opposed, in other words, to postmodern or "neo" racism) is one of the most elaborated forms of such group loathing—inflected in the direction of a whole political program; it should lead us on to some reflection on the role of the stereotype in all such group or "cultural" relations, which can virtually, by definition, not do without the stereotypical. For the group as such is necessarily an imaginary entity, in the sense in which no individual mind is able to intuit it concretely. The group must be abstracted, or fantasized, on the basis of discrete individual contacts and experiences which can never be generalized in anything but abusive fashion. The relations between groups are always stereotypical insofar as they must always involve collective abstractions of the other group, no matter how sanitized, no matter how liberally censored and imbued with respect. What it is politically correct to do under such circumstances is to allow the other group itself to elaborate its own preferential image, and then to work with that henceforth "official" stereotype. But the inevitability of the stereotypical—and the persistence of the possibility of group loathing, racism, caricature and all the rest it cannot but bring with it—is not thereby laid to rest. Utopia could therefore, under those circumstances, only mean two different kinds of situations, which might in fact turn out to be the same: a world in which only individuals confronted one another, in the absence of groups; or a group isolated from the rest of the world in such a way that the matter of the external stereotype (or "ethnic identity") never arose in the first place. The stereotype is indeed the place of an illicit surplus of meaning, what Barthes called the "nausea" of mythologies: it is the abstraction by virtue of which my individuality is allegorized and turned into an abusive illustration of something else, something nonconcrete and nonindividual. ("I don't join organizations or adopt labels," says a character in a recent Austrian movie. "You don't have to," replies his friend, "You're a Jew!") But the liberal solution to this dilemma—doing away with the stereotypes or pretending they don't exist—is not possible, although fortunately we carry on as though it were for most of the time.

Groups are thus always conflictual; and this is what has led Donald Horowitz, in the definitive study of international ethnic conflict,[9] to suggest that, although what he takes to be Marxism's economic or class account of such conflicts is unsatisfactory, Marx may have unwittingly anticipated a fundamental feature of modern ethnic theory in his notion of the necessarily dichotomous structure of class conflict as such: ethnic conflicts, indeed are, for Horowitz, always tendentially dichotomous, each side ending up incorporating the various, smaller, satellite, ethnic groups in such a way as to symbolically reenact a version of Gramscian hegemony, and Gramscian hegemonic or historic blocs as well. But classes in that sense do not precede capitalism, and there is no single-shot Marxian theory of "economic" causality: the economic is most often the forgotten trigger for all kinds of noneconomic developments, and the emphasis on it is heuristic and has to do with the structure of the various disciplines (and what they structurally occult or repress), rather than with ontology. What Marxism has to offer ethnic theory is probably, on the contrary, the suggestion that ethnic struggles might well be clarified by an accompanying question about class formation as such.

Fredric Jameson

Fully realized classes, indeed, classes in and for themselves, "potential" or structural classes that have finally, by all kinds of complicated historical and social processes, achieved what is often called "class consciousness," are clearly also groups in our sense (although groups in our sense are rarely classes as such). Marxism suggests two kinds of things about these peculiar and relatively rare types of groups. The first is that they have much greater possibilities for development than ethnic groups as such: they can potentially expand to become coterminous with society as a whole (and do so, during those unique and punctual events we call revolutions), whereas the groups are necessarily limited by their own specific self-definition and constitutive characteristics. Ethnic conflict can thus develop and expand into class conflict as such, whereas the degeneration of class conflict into ethnic rivalry is a restrictive and centripetal development.

Indeed, the alternation of envy and loathing constitutes an excellent illustration of the dialectic of class and group in action: whatever group or identity investment may be at work in envy, its libidinal opposite always tends to transcend the dynamics of the group relationship in the direction of that of class proper. Thus, anyone who observed the deployment of group and identity hatred in the 1992 Republican National Convention—the race and gender hostility so clearly marked in the speeches and the faces of characteristic "cultural counterrevolutionaries" like Pat Buchanan—understood at once that it was fundamentally class hostility and class struggle that was the deeper stake in such passions and their symbolisms. By the same token, the observers who felt that symbolism and responded to the Republican Right in kind can also be said to have had their smaller group-and-identity consciousness "raised" in the direction of the ultimate horizon of social class.

The second point follows from this one, namely that it is only after the modulation of the ethnic into the class category that a possible resolution of such struggles is to be found. For, in general, ethnic conflict cannot be solved or resolved; it can only be sublimated into a struggle of a different kind that *can* be resolved. Class struggle, which has as its aim and outcome not the triumph of one class over another but the abolition of the very category of class, offers the prototype of one such sublimation. The market and consumption—that is to say, what is euphemistically called modernization, the transformation of the members of various groups into the universal consumer—is another kind of sublimation, which has come to look equally as universal as the classless one, but which perhaps owes its success predominantly to the specific circumstances of the postfeudal North American commonwealth, and the possibilities of social leveling that arose with the development of the mass media. This is the sense in which "American democracy" has seemed able to preempt class dynamics and to offer a unique solution to the matter of group dynamics discussed above. We therefore need to take into account the possibility that the various politics of difference—the differences inherent in the various politics of "group identity"—have been made possible only by the tendential leveling of social identity generated by consumer society; and to entertain the hypothesis that a cultural politics of difference becomes itself feasible only when the great and forbidding categories of classical Otherness have been substantially weakened by "modernization" (so that current neoethnicities may be distinct from the classical kind as neoracism is from classical racism).[10]

But this does not spell a waning of group antagonisms, but precisely the opposite (as can be judged from the current world scene), and it is also to be expected that Cultural Studies itself—as a space in which the new group dynamics develop—will also entail its quotient of the libidinal. The energy exchanges or ion formations of "articulation" are not, indeed, likely to take place neutrally, but to release violent waves of affect—narcissistic wounds, feelings of envy and inferiority, the intermittent repugnance for the others' groups. And in fact this is precisely what we observe to be at work in some of the most remarkable papers in the present collection.

Thus, in one of its most dramatic moments, Douglas Crimp traces a liberal-tolerant practice of AIDS cultural politics through to the point at which it becomes clear that the photographic and video documentation in question, ostensibly intended to inspire pity and sympathy for what are always called the "victims," in reality constitute "*phobic* images, images of the terror at imagining the person with AIDS as still sexual" (130). This liberalism, then, comes with a price, namely the possibility for the liberal middle-class sympathizer to omit an imagination of the sick person as a sexual being; the implication is that a liberal tolerance for gays and lesbians generally requires this more fundamental imaginative repression of awareness of sexuality as such. Here the sexual or gender plane lends a powerful anticathexis or loathing to the social one, and enables a development of mass reaction and hatred that can be mobilized well beyond this particular target group, and made available for alliance politics of a different and more alarming type.

For loathing and envy are very precisely the affective expressions of the relations of groups to one another, as has been argued above: insofar as the object of Cultural Studies can be defined as the cultural expression of the various relationships groups entertain with each other (sometimes on a global scale, sometimes within a single individual), the semiotics of disgust and of group envy ought to play a larger part here than it does. In that respect, the central exhibit is a remarkable article by Laura Kipnis, whose title "(Male) Desire and (Female) Disgust: Reading *Hustler*," does not make it clear enough that one of its central theses has to do with the way in which—following the spirit of Bourdieu's *Distinction*—class consciousness here borrows the trappings of physical repugnance:

> the transcoding between the body and the social sets up the mechanisms through which the body is a privileged political trope of lower social classes, and through which bodily grossness operates as a critique of dominant ideology. The power of grossness is predicated on its opposition from *and to* high discourses, themselves prophylactic against the debasement of the low. . . . (376)

But Kipnis goes even further than this (and than Bourdieu himself) in the way in which, as is appropriate in dealing with a class consciousness that is by definition a relationship and a form of struggle, she takes on the intricate matter of the "subject positions" involved in this act of cultural aggression (in which, at least for openers, women are allegorized as gentility and high culture and men, by way of what Jeffrey Klein calls "a blue-collar urge" [391], as lower class):

> . . . there is the further discomfort at being addressed as a subject of repression—as a subject with a history—and the rejection of porn can be seen as a defense erected against representations which mean to unsettle her in her subjectivity. In other words, there is a violation of the *idea* of the "naturalness" of female sexuality and subjectivity, which is exacerbated by the social fact that not all women *do* experience male pornography in the same way. (380)

But this analysis of intercollective subjectivities and subject positions leads us virtually to the borderlines of a whole new field, which is no longer either anthropology or sociology in the traditional sense, but which certainly restores to culture its hidden inner meaning as the space of the symbolic moves of groups in agonistic relation to each other. One other essay, bell hooks's "Representing Whiteness in the Black Imagination," occupies this area as its own; its account of the visceral fear of White people in the Black imagination has something of the vividness of a work of art in its own right (not necessarily the highest compliment in the present context, I realize).

Yet such a new field is neither so accessible nor so easy of realization as I may have unwittingly suggested: there are barriers, and they are not automatically overcome even by the least self-indulgent introspection or the most controlled autobiographical exploration. To see what these are we need to return to Marxism again (indeed, the preceding section constituted a description of the forms taken by totalization in Cultural Studies). What has not yet been said is the role played by social class in Cultural Studies as currently constituted, which may not be an altogether obvious one, although it has been hinted at in passing.

FREE-FLOATING INTELLECTUALS

Class here essentially takes two forms, in addition to the shifting and aleatory participation of a class "factor" in the various cultural constellations in question (as when class reappears in Kipnis's analysis of a pornographic cultural object, or is fantasized according to a gender allegory). The first form in which class reappears here, charged with an anxiety that is omnipresent in these pages, is through the inconspicuous back door of the role of the intellectual as such. Simon Frith designates it with some uncharitable bluntness when he says, "from my sociological perspective, popular music is a solution, a ritualized resistance, not to the problems of being young and poor and proletarian but to the problems of being an intellectual" (179). Nor is the professional reference to a "sociological perspective" an idle one, for it conveys a very different conception of the relationship of the intellectual to society than anything Cultural Studies could envisage (when indeed it is willing to conceptualize this embarrassing question), namely, what I am tempted to call "the tragic sense of life" of the great sociologists, from Weber and Veblen to Bourdieu—that glacial disengagement from social phenomena as such which is the very condition of the sociologist's disabused knowledge, and which excludes any activist participation in the social—indeed any political commitment in the usual sense—on pain of losing the very insights, the very power of demystification, paid for by just this epistemological separation from the human.

This is, I believe, a "bourgeois" (or pre-Marxist) view of the matter, but it expresses the conviction of a very real truth, which is none other than the "Heisenberg principle" of the status of the intellectual as observer, the sense that it is precisely that status—itself a social reality and a social fact—that intervenes between the object of knowledge and the act of knowing. Such sociology is in any case constituted by a passion for seeing through the ideologies and the alibis which accompany the class and group struggles of the social and entangle those in ever higher levels of cultural complexity; if now we become aware that such lucidity as to the real mechanisms of social relationship demands the price of a single white lie, a strategic blind spot in the area of the intellectual, the occupation of everything that is social about our own observer's viewpoint itself, the renunciation of social commitment, the attempt to surrender social knowledge from action in the world, indeed the very pessimism about the possibility of action in the world in the first place, will come to seem an act of atonement for this particular (structural) original sin. For the intellectual is necessarily and constitutively at a distance, not merely from her or his own class of origin, but also from the class of chosen affiliation; even more relevant in the present context, she is also necessarily at a distance from the social groups as well; and the ontological security of the militants of the new social movements is deceptive, who were able to feel that because they were women, Blacks, or ethnics, as intellectuals they counted as members of those "peoples," and no longer had to face the dilemmas of the classic intellectual with his Hegelian "unhappy consciousness." But we now know this is impossible, particularly since the question of the intellectual has been rewritten in the new paradigm as the problem of representation as such, about which there is some agreement that it is neither possible nor desirable. On the older paradigm, however, the intellectual was most lucidly conceived of as what Sartre called an "objective traitor," an impersonal and unintentional Stalinist crime for which no solution can be found, but only expiation or bad faith. Where Sartre was always closest to Marxism was in this conviction that when you cannot resolve a contradiction, it is best and most authentic to hold onto it in wrenching self-consciousness; or at least, that is preferable, as anything else always is, to repression and the artificial working up of this or that form of good conscience. This is not inconsistent with a Utopian position, in which, with Stuart Hall, we can try to act as though the group whose "organic intellectual" we try to be already existed; or, remembering that other remark of Gramsci that "everyone is an intellectual," we can also suffer the class and blood guilt of the contemporary intellectual situation, in the hopes of some future abolition of classes altogether, and thus, with them, of everything now conflicted about the smaller groups now buffeted by the force field of class struggle.

In the light of this dilemma, Foucault's *ad hoc* invention of the category he calls "the specific intellectual" seems trivial; while beyond it, the old Maoist solution itself seems a tragic impossibility, in which by going back to the factory or the field the intellectual is promised some reimmersion in the group, which will cleanse him of that particular original sin which is the crime of being an intellectual. But this is also called populism, and it remains very much alive, not least in the pages of the volume under review. The negative symptom of populism is very precisely the hatred and loathing of intellectuals as such (or, today, of the academy that has seemed to become synonymous with them).[11] It is a contradictory symbolic process not unlike Jewish anti-Semitism, since populism is itself very precisely an ideology of intellectuals (the "people" are not "populist"), and represents a desperate attempt on their part to repress their condition, and to deny and negate its facts of life. In the Cultural Studies area, it is, of course, the name of John Fiske that has primarily been associated with a certain populist stance toward culture:

> Politics have never been far below the surface in my attempt to think critically about the relationships between dominant and subordinated habituses in cultural theory. I hope we can narrow the gap and increase the travel between them because by doing so I believe we can help change the relationship between the academy and other social formations, in particular those of the subordinate. Many of those living within such subordinated formations find little pertinence between the conditions of their everyday lives and academic ways of explaining the world. It is in none of our interests to allow this gap to grow any wider, particularly when we consider that many of the most effective recent movements for social change have involved allegiances between universities and members of repressed or subordinated social formations. (164)

Fredric Jameson

Here and throughout a few hardy souls dare to express the opinion that academics are also people; but no one seems particularly enthusiastic about the prospect of undertaking an ethnology of *their* culture, fearing, perhaps rightly, the anxieties and the dreariness of such self-knowledge, which Pierre Bourdieu has unremittingly pursued in France (but, after all, there is a way in which populism and anti-intellectualism are a specifically—one even wants to say an exceptionally—American matter). The primary reproach to Fiske's work lies elsewhere, and seems to turn very precisely on the ambiguity of culture or the superstructure about which Stuart Hall warned, on its tendency, as an object, to displace itself away from the social, to reaffirm its semi-autonomy, "to instantiate a necessary delay . . . something decentered about the medium of culture . . . which always escapes and evades the attempt to link it, directly and immediately, with other structures" (284). Fiske's work builds on this very gap, affirming the presence of economic oppression and social exploitation, at the same time that it reads culture as a set of "resources to fight against those constraints" (157). The fear is not only that, as with Marx's supposedly infamous view of religion,[12] that fight may be only an imaginary one; it is even more the suspicion that it is the intellectual himself who may here be using the celebration of mass culture as a ritual to conjure his particular structural "distance" and to participate, like Edward Curtis, in the dances and solidarity of the ethnic tribe itself. (Interestingly, one of the really interesting "textual" studies in this collection, William Warner's paper on *Rambo*, affirms the operativity of pain in this mass-cultural text, as a way in which the American public assuages its guilt at the loss of the war by way of images of the physical suffering of its hero; in general, a little more attention to the "negative emotions," in popular culture as well as in its analysis, would have enhanced the credibility of the volume.)

But it is Michele Wallace who raises these issues most sharply in her exploration of the ironies of representation in the micropolitics of Cultural Studies: after repudiating the claims of others to "represent" Black feminism, and after describing the tensions within it between subversion and institutionalization (or commercial stardom, as in the actors of *The Color Purple*), she goes on to problematize the thing itself, following Gayatri Spivak's famous query, "Can the subaltern speak?":

> What I am calling into question is the idea that black feminism
> (or any program) should assume, uncritically, its ability to speak

for black women, most of whom are poor and "silenced" by inadequate education, health care, housing, and lack of public access. Not because I think that black feminism should have nothing to do with representing the black woman who cannot speak for herself but because the problem of silence, and the shortcomings inherent in any representation of the silenced, need to be acknowledged as a central problematic in an oppositional black feminist process. (663)

This modesty, along with Cornel West's forthright call to the participants to recognize and acknowledge themselves as *American* intellectuals (and to take up the burden of American cultural history, which, along with "American Studies," is also strangely absent here), may offer the most satisfactory way of working through or working out the dilemma of the cultural intellectual.

It is, however, not the only one, and surely the most innovative treatment of the intellectual in this conference lies in the new model of the intellectual as "fan": "Some of the most exciting work being done in Cultural Studies, as you know, is ethnographic, and positions the critic in some respects as a 'fan' " (Ross 553). It is at least a somewhat more attractive image and role than that of the "groupie" of sixties vintage, and implies the transformation of group or ethnic identity (to which the "groupie" was attracted as a moth to the flame) into practices and performances which one could appreciate like a not-unparticipatory spectator. This surely reflects the properly postmodern transformation of ethnicity into neoethnicity, as the isolation and oppression of groups is lifted up (in a properly Hegelian *Aufhebung*, which preserves and cancels that at one and the same time) into media acknowledgment and the new reunification by the image. But it is not an unproblematical solution either: for the new fan is something like a fan of fans, and both Constance Penley, in her account of *Star Trek* culture, and Janice Radway, in her classic book on the romance, are careful to document the distance that has to be overcome between the "real" fans and their academic ethnographer. Simon Frith goes even further than this: "if, as is variously suggested in this book, fans are 'popular' (or organic) intellectuals, then they may well have the same anxieties about being fans (and take comfort from the same myths) as the rest of us" (182). This is to underscore a peculiarly Derridean turn in the transformation of the "people" into "fans":

Fredric Jameson

where the first of these was a primary substance, calmly persisting in its essence, and exercising a powerful gravitational effect on the insubstantial intellectuals who fluttered near it, the new version opens up a hall of mirrors in which the "people" itself longs to be a "people" and be "popular," feels its own ontological lack, longs for its own impossible stability, and narcissistically attempts, in a variety of rituals, to recuperate a being that never existed in the first place. That would, to be sure, lead us on to a more psychoanalytic view of groups and ethnic conflict (perhaps along the lines proposed by Slavoj Žižek); but it would also considerably dampen the enthusiasm of populist intellectuals for a collective condition not much better than their own.

All of which supposes that the "people" in question still somehow refers to that television-watching, beer-drinking population of middle-to-lower-class jobholders (or unemployed) who, Black or White, male or female, are generally fantasized to constitute some larger fundamentally ethnic social reality. But what if it were otherwise? Indeed, Meaghan Morris remarks ominously, "this process does not extend to involvement with the one figure who in fact remains . . . quite unredeemably 'other'—the bureaucrat" (465). Andrew Ross, meanwhile, seems at various moments in his contribution to realize that what is more ambiguous, for a Cultural Studies public, about his own object of study ("New Age technoculture") is that the New Age people may not really any longer be "popular" in this populist sense, but rather, far more fatefully, *middlebrow*. (Indeed, the originality and importance of Janice Radway's work-in-progress, on the Book of the Month Club, lies in its promise to show the very construction of the middlebrow as such, and the social and political function of that construction as a kind of repression or displacement of the popular). Finally, in one of the truly chilling and comical moments in this conference, Ian Hunter describes just this ultimate First Contact with the bureaucratic Other:

> The problem with aesthetic critique—and with cultural studies to the degree that it is still caught in its slipstream—is that it presumes to comprehend and judge these other cultural regions from a single metropolitan point, typically the university arts faculty. To travel to these other regions though—to law offices, media institutions, government bureaus, corporations, advertising agencies—is to make a sobering discovery: They are already replete

with their own intellectuals. And they just look up and say, "Well, what exactly is it that you can do for us?" (372)

POPULISM AS DOXA

One cannot, however, leave the matter of populism without a final, more general complaint, which touches on a few of the theoretical and verbal rituals of this ideology. Raymond Williams's *Keywords* being so crucial a reference throughout, it might be desirable to think of a companion volume, to be called *Buzzwords* (and which one imagines looking, for our era, something like Flaubert's twin *Dictionary of Received Ideas* and *sottisier* of commonplaces). Failing that, one might propose, as a form of philosophical hygiene, that for ten years or so we simply stop using the two words, *power* and the *body*. Nothing is more disembodied than such references to the body, except where, as in Laura Kipnis's article on *Hustler* already referred to, or in Douglas Crimp's, it generates some real visceral effects; materialism is scarcely achieved by the corporeal litany, which seems if anything to be a sop thrown to the (admittedly) materialist culture of the masses under Bourdieu's watchful eye. The materialism of the body is the eighteenth-century mechanical materialism, and is fashioned on the medical model (whence the role of Foucault in both these obsessional conducts); it should not be confused with a historical materialism that turns on *praxis* and on the mode of production.

But in a more general way, we must be very suspicious of the reference to the body as an appeal to immediacy (the warning goes back to the very first chapter of Hegel's *Phenomenology*); even Foucault's medical and penal work can be read as an account of the construction of the body which rebukes premature immediacy. In any case, structuralism and psychoanalysis both work energetically at the demystification of the illusions of bodily intimacy most strongly suggested by "desire"; the theme of torture does not refute this but rather confirms it by making the wordless individual bodily experience the most isolated of all and the most difficult of access. But the fascination today with pornography, torture and violence is the sign of the loss of that immediacy and the longing for the impossible physically concrete, rather than the proof by the *Zeitgeist* that it lies all around us ready to hand: in fact what lies all around us are, rather, images and information stereotypes of the body, which are themselves the most powerful source of interference when it comes to a full phenomenological approach to the body itself. This last is, therefore, a theme that is always to be historically problematized, and never taken as an interpretive code in its own right, at least not for us, here and now.

As for *power*, about which it is frequently suggested in the pages of the volume under consideration that it is what Cultural Studies is all about ("share a commitment to examining cultural practices from the point of view of their intrication with, and within, relations of power" [Bennett 23]), it is an even more dangerous and intoxicating slogan for intellectuals, who thereby feel themselves closer to its "reality" than they may actually be. My sense is that interpretations in terms of power must come as punctual demystifications, de-idealizations, and involve thereby a certain shock, a painful rebuke to our own habits of idealization in the first place. Certainly, the realm of culture is a privileged space for such shock effects, for given the amphibiousness of the superstructures (and that tendency to be displaced away from their context of which Stuart Hall spoke), the revelation, at this or that historical point, that culture is socially functional, that it stands in thrall and service to the institutions, and that its veneer of the aesthetic or of leisure time, the restorative or even the utopian, is false and a lure—this kind of timely reminder can only be a healthy one, particularly for cultural intellectuals. But if everything is power, then we neither require that reminder, nor can it retain any of its demystificatory force (which also had the benefit of calling us into question as intellectuals in the process). In that case "power" is as satisfactory an explanation as the "*vertu dormitive*" of opium; if it is everywhere, then there is not much point talking about it (Foucault could do so only because as a historian he sought to trace out the *emergence* of a new scheme of modern power). What is indeed the advantage in stigmatizing the power of that corporate bureaucrat who made his unexpected appearance in these pages a moment ago? Would it not be more useful to look at the structure of the multinational corporations themselves, with a view toward determining the mode of influence and production of a properly corporate culture? But there is a confusion when the individual experience of domination, in acts of racism or *machismo*, authoritarianism, sadism, conscious or unconscious personal brutality, is transferred to social phenomena which are a good deal more advanced and complicated than that: Konrad and Szelenyi indeed pointed out some time ago that the realm of experience of capitalist cultural production is a relatively old-fashioned or underdeveloped, retrogressive enclave within late capitalism.[13] It hearkens back to the entrepreneurial moment, elsewhere in corporate society long since vanished and present only as nostalgia (the yuppie rhetoric of the market is thus a cultural symptom which demands textual analysis in its own right). It is therefore not surprising that a kind of feudal picture of personal domination and subordination is sometimes carried over into the faceless corporate universe; but in that case it is a text to be analyzed, rather than an interpretive code still useful in the deciphering of other contemporary social texts (forms of personal or symbolic brutality, however, probably tending to reflect an absence of power in the social sense, rather than its acting out).

But by way of this anachronism, a whole liberal political theory and ideology then pours into Cultural Studies (and other disciplines); for the rhetoric of "power" carries a good deal more in its baggage—a repudiation of economic analysis, for example, a kind of forthright anarchistic stance on the thing itself, the unholy marriage between the heroism of dissidence and the "realism" of "talking to the institutions." The problematic of power, as systematically reintroduced by Weber and then much later by Foucault, is an anti-Marxist move, designed to replace analysis in terms of the mode of production. That opens up new fields and generates rich and fascinating new material; but users should be aware of its secondary ideological consequences; and intellectuals should above all be wary of the narcissistic intoxications of its knee-jerk invocation.

THE GEOPOLITICAL IMPERATIVE

This is, then, the moment, not merely to say what ought to be done in the void left by these two buzzwords, and in the ideological loose ends at which the critique of populism may well leave us, but also to show how, in fact, many of the papers in the collection are already moving in just that direction.

This is the fundamentally spatial dimension of Cultural Studies (already underscored by Jody Berland), which can at first be sensed in the discomfort with American parochialism and exceptionalism tactfully voiced by some of the foreigners. Thus Stuart Hall, who pronounces himself "dumbfounded":

> the enormous explosion of cultural studies in the U.S., its rapid
> professionalization and institutionalization, is not a moment which

any of us who tried to set up a marginalized Centre in a university like Birmingham could, in any simple way, regret. And yet I have to say, in the strongest sense, that it reminds me of the ways in which, in Britain, we are always aware of institutionalization as a moment of profound danger. (285)

And we have already seen some of the Australians reflecting on the different meaning and significance of cultural institutions in the US (which, unlike their own, are mostly private), without necessarily drawing differential consequences (but see also Graeme Turner on Australian and Canadian differences [644–645]). To talk about it this way seems to introduce the theme of the nation as such (which indeed becomes a significant preoccupation here); but that may be too restricted and misleading.

It is rather a specific global constriction that Meaghan Morris has in mind in a splendid and illuminating outburst:

This exchange makes me realize that I haven't been explicit enough about why "Eurocentrism" should worry me at a rudimentary level at a conference like this. It's a restlessness I have, rather than a position I can expound, and maybe it came through in my speech rather than in the text of my paper. I'm restless about the map of cultural studies being constructed at this conference, about what's not *on* that map, rather than what is. We've talked about local and global relations in a world where Japan, South Korea, Hong Kong, Taiwan, Singapore, or Indonesia simply don't exist, certainly not as *forces* in emergent structures of world power. The one time I heard somebody mention the Pacific Rim, it turned out to be a way of talking about relations between North and Central and South America—another way of staying on the American land mass, not a way of crossing the ocean. I'm not making a plea for inclusiveness, it's just that certain globalizing structures have potential, if "only" on the economic level, to affect people's lives everywhere in the future, and they aren't "centered" now in quite the same old *doubled* way (UK/USA, or USA/USSR), that traditional critiques of Eurocentrism sometimes Eurocentrically assume. To ignore this seems to me to be a political error. (476)

There is much to be said about this moment, in some ways one of the climaxes of the conference. One might remark that "Eurocentrism" does not quite seem the word anymore, for what is surely an American parochialism: even if informed by European canonical perspectives (and very much imbued with the return of the repressed, scarcely unconscious Anglophilia—after the Francophilia of the preceding moment of high theory), these are now the perspectives of an American NATO view of the world for which the old Europe is not much more significant for us than Birmingham for the new US Cultural Studies. Europe and Britain are surely live-wire issues for the Australians, and even the Canadians here, more than they are for the Americans; and perhaps this is a deeper undertone and implication of Meaghan Morris's reproach, that we are not sufficiently worried about our European and Oedipal link, we are too complacent about it. But in the same sense, the new Pacific Rim culture she celebrates here may be a different kind of liberation for Australia than for Americans intent on at least sharing it with the Japanese. And she dismisses Latin America, an oversight remedied by Donna Haraway, whose picture of an analogous Pacific culture it is instructive to juxtapose at this point:

> I grew up in a town in Colorado where I thought the Atlantic
> Ocean began somewhere in Kansas and that anything that happened East of Kansas City counted as the East Coast. And I know
> Cornel grew up in California, but I think maybe you've been in the
> East too long. Paul's Atlanticist reformulation of African heritage,
> African culture, and African-Americans reformulated a lot of issues
> for me. But it's a California statement I want to make. It has to do
> with seeing the world in relationship to Latin America, Central
> America, Mexico, living in conquest territory so that it almost
> seems like Quebec is part of California rather than part of the
> world you're talking about. It's the sense of the Pacific. I think of
> Bernice Johnson Reagon's speech on coalition politics which took
> place at a West Coast women's music festival and is an absolutely
> canonical text in U.S. feminism and in the constructions of the category, "women of color," but also of a feminist cultural politics and
> a vision of a new world cultural politics. None of this is caught by
> the tendency to build the world as black/white and America/
> Britain, with a little bit of Australia and Canada thrown in. This

particular global mapping leaves out these really crucial questions. (703)

All of which may seem to confirm the Clifford view of Cultural Studies as a model based on travel and tourism: but this would be to neglect deeper and more interesting tensions, those for example expressed in a sharp exchange between Morris and Paul Gilroy, whose remarkable proposal to acknowledge and reconstruct a properly Black Atlantic culture seems on first glance to present some symmetrical analogies to the Pacific Rim vision. But Gilroy has a somewhat different agenda: "The specificity of the black Atlantic can be defined on one level through this desire to transcend both the structures of the nation-state and the constraints of ethnicity and national particularity" (194–5; we have already seen that Gilroy's is an explicit repudiation of the "politics of identity" or of cultural separatism). But Gilroy can (and must) resist the divisive pull of a celebration of British or US cultural exceptionalism (even when that is staged in terms of the exceptionalism of Black-British or African-American culture): the great floating decentered archipelago of the Caribbean is there to authorize such resistance. Perhaps, however, the Australians and the Canadians cannot so easily jettison the determinant problem and category of the nation, as Jody Berland thinks:

> The reason I refused the idea of identity in terms of a historical tradition in the struggle around communications was that, in Canada, it's both impossible and compulsory to talk about the problem of identity. It's a complete double-bind: one has to talk about it constantly because it's a problem, but you can't talk about it because as soon as you start you're in danger of imposing a singular definition on something which isn't singular at all. (52)

The discomfort seems to have to do in part with the words "nation" and "national," which evidently still vehiculate the baggage of the older autonomous nation-state, and give rise to the apprehension that one is still talking about the national culture, the national *topoi* (as Morris calls them in her interesting sketch of the Australian version of these), the national allegories, in a kind of separatist or cultural-nationalist way. For that structural allegory of Cultural Studies to the "unmixed" which I mentioned above, this is clearly decisive, and it plays a greater role in Gilroy's reaction than in Morris's remarks. But it should be added that autonomy is the great political question of the postmodern age: Communism itself foundered on the impossibility of autarchy (even of socialism in several countries) in the multinational era. We should thus see nationalism, not as the vice and the toxic symptom of the immediate post-World War II era, but, rather, as itself a kind of nostalgia for a social autonomy no longer available for anyone; while "nation" today ought to be used as the word for a term within a system, a term which ought now always to imply relationality (of a more than binary type). Indeed, it is the need for some new relational discourse on these global and spatial matters which makes itself felt through such uneasy debates.[14] The new requirement is not—as with the multiple subject-positions and, as it were, the internal structural problems of cultural identity—a matter of articulation, so much as it is one of the superposition of incommensurable dimensions: Morris quite rightly asks us "to think of cultural studies as a discipline capable of thinking the relations between local, regional, national, and international frames of action and experience" (470): but the word "representation" might be even more suggestively substituted for the notion of merely "thinking" those relations. It is then curious that she should so insistently refuse the model offered by David Harvey in his splendid *Condition of Postmodernity*: it need not be the final word on anything, to be sure, but it is one way of mapping the new global system from which we can begin (indeed, she says herself that her alternate models "use similar economic arguments to Harvey's" [474]), but maybe the Marxism is just a bit too much; and perhaps it is Eurocentric as well? (Indeed, in one remarkable moment [455] she seems to be attributing the seemingly feudal battle cry "For England and Marxism!" to Terry Eagleton, something the Irish comrades need never hear about.) Still, hers is far and away the richest and most stimulating discussion both of a national cultural self-representation and of the urgent international dimensions still missing from Cultural Studies: it is embarrassing that none of the Americans think any of these thoughts (which Clifford, to be sure, echoes in a more reflective/contemplative way).

CONCLUSIONS AND UTOPIA

It is time to sum up the lessons of the book (the lessons I have learned from the book): something best done in the form of future tasks, of an agenda, although not necessarily an agenda for "Cultural Studies" in the narrower

Fredric Jameson

institutionalized or would-be disciplinary sense we have also seen emerging from the collection. That agenda would include groups, articulation and space; and it would also open a new entry (so far mostly blank) for commodification and consumption. The phenomenon of group struggle—in bell hooks and in Mercer, for example—reminds us that, no less than for class, cultural texts, when properly decoded, can always be expected to constitute so many messages in this symbolic process, and to stand as so many distinct strategic or tactical moves in what is an enormous *agon*. It is therefore clear that the hermeneutic appropriate to social class also demands to be applied here, in a situation in which stable cultural objects, works or texts, are to be rewritten as dialogically antagonistic moves in struggle between groups (which very specifically includes the achievement of group consciousness as one of its aims), moves which tend to express themselves affectively in the form of loathing or envy.

This methodology no longer seems quite so useful when, as in so many of the contributions here, the phenomenon of group relationship is interiorized, and becomes a matter for mixed feelings, multiple subject positions, productive schizophrenia or unhappy co-consciousness: it being understood that all these things can characterize the collective condition of a group as well. Here, then, the model of articulation seems again to reimpose itself, and we pass from the dialectical (in the case of intergroup struggle) to the structural, in this particular field which is that of group interrelationship, intragroup phenomena, or the construction of larger molar group units. The poetics of this moment also seems relatively distinct from that of the first one, where a text could be translated into a symbolic and strategic value which it possessed simultaneously with its surface value or organization. Here translation takes the form of transcoding, or synonymity within a given term: for it is the possibility of any given term to bear several distinct meanings at the same time that allows the sharing of a text between several distinct codes (and the groups whose language they constitute). Here group connection is enabled by the transfer of a crucial seme or atom, which binds the codes together momentarily by way of its own polysemousness.

But these first two zones of meaning and analysis are still safely contained within "Cultural Studies," now understood as some vast Popular Front or populist carnival. The third dimension emerges only when we reach the edge of that and look out upon the true Other, the bureaucrat or corporate figure who stands in for late capitalism itself and its now-global institutions. It is because this Other can no longer be assimilated into the structures previously described that relations with it must be modeled on an external or spatial mode, and demand a kind of geographical analysis for which we have as yet no particularly adequate language (my implication that it will turn out to be neither dialectical nor structural is little more than an impression and a possible starting point). This is then the moment when our own social role and status as intellectuals return with a vengeance, since it is a role which is mediated by geopolitics, its value conferred by the world system itself and by our positioning within it. It then returns upon our individual readings and analyses to enforce a new requirement of geographic reflexivity or geopolitical self-consciousness, and to demand the validation of some account of the "national" situation from within whose standpoint the analysis has been made: it being understood that "national" is now merely a relational term for the component parts of the world system, which might also be seen as the superposition of various kinds of space (local and regional as well as national, the geographical bloc as well as the world system itself). In that case, US Cultural Studies, as here, would have to sign its address a little more self-consciously to its contributions.

But who says the US says global capitalism itself: and the move on into the culture of that, and the dynamics of that truer Other than any of the microgroups at play here, demands the return to some form of commodity analysis, of which—save for Jody Berland's suggestive pages on the ideology of "entertainment"—there is little enough trace in the volume. Perhaps, in a kind of populist way, it is felt that to treat these cultural products as commodities about to be swept off in the purely formal process of consumption is somehow to demean them and to diminish their dignity, to overlook their other social and group functions (outlined above). But that need not be the case for an analysis of the right complexity, although it is certain that for consumption, as a culture and a collective form of addiction, the act of consumption is an empty one, indifferent to the specific contents of a given object and thus relatively unpropitious for an analysis that would want to do it justice in substantive detail. Still, conflict, alienation, reunification, what used to be called the inauthentic, have to be given their due; nothing truly interesting is possible without negativity; error or ideology, false appearance, are also objective facts that have to be reckoned back into truth; the standardization of consumption is like a sound barrier which con-

Fredric Jameson

fronts the euphorias of populism as a fact of life and a physical law at the upper reaches of the spectrum.

Beyond that lies Utopia, also secretly at work everywhere in these pages, wherever the most obscure forms of enjoyment and group celebration or narcissism are to be found. But it must also be named, without which its half-life decays with unbelievable speed on exposure to the smog-filled light and polluted air of current reality. Donna Haraway names it here, in an essay of such range and complexity that I cannot do it justice, let alone in these concluding pages: suffice it to say that in an immense wheeling and slowly rotating movement, she designates a succession of radically Other or alternative spaces to aspects of our own—the rain forest to our social space; the extraterrestrial to our physical one; the biomedical microcosm to our still conventional bodies; and the science fictional macrocosms to our still conventional minds. Let these Utopias then move as a kind of starry firmament over this collection, as indeed over Cultural Studies in general.

NOTES

1. Lawrence Grossberg, Cary Nelson and Paula A. Treichler, eds., *Cultural Studies* (New York: Routledge, 1992), internal page references to this text.

2. As in "the unhappy *marriage* of Marxism and feminism": see Jane Gallop's recent *Around 1981: Academic Feminist Literary Theory* (New York: Routledge, 1992) for a more elaborate exploration of the allegorical models by way of which an emergent feminism has sought to tell itself the story of that emergence.

3. One must also mention Dick Hebdige's *Subculture* (London: Methuen, 1981), which, more than any other single work, invented the style and stance repeatedly adopted in the present conference.

4. See, in particular, the rather triumphalistic program article by one of the organizers of the conference: Cary Nelson, "Always Already Cultural Studies," *Journal of the Midwest Modern Language Association* 24, No. 1 (1991), pp. 24–38.

5. Fredric Jameson, "Commentary," *Journal of Modern Greek Studies* 8 (1990), pp. 135–39.

6. Michael Denning, " 'The Special American Conditions': Marxism and American Studies," *American Quarterly* 38, No. 3 (1986), pp. 356–80.

7. See the 1857 Preface to the *Grundrisse*; as well as Louis Althusser and Etienne Balibar, *Reading Capital* (London: Verso, 1970), pp. 174ff, 207. I am indebted to Perry Anderson and Ken Surin for their assistance in this hit-and-run genealogy; Jose Ripalda Crespo assures me that the history of the concept beyond Marx is banal and lost in the night of medieval scholasticism. Meanwhile, the latest and most familiar use of this term, in Ernesto Laclau and Chantal Mouffe's remarkable anatomy of alliance politics, *Hegemony and Socialist Strategy* (London: Verso, 1985), pp. 105ff, does not attribute the concept historically (it is, however, not to be found in Gramsci). Finally, I am told by both Michael Denning and Andrew Ross that the fundamental image whereby this was always conveyed in Birmingham—shades of the locomotive of history!—was what in Britain is called the "articulated lorry."

8. Harald Eidheim, "When Ethnic Identity Is a Social Stigma," in *Ethnic Groups and Boundaries*, ed. Fredrik Barth (Boston: Little, Brown, 1969), pp. 39–57. And see Erving Goffman, *Stigma* (New York: Prentice-Hall, 1963). See, also, Bernard McGrane, *Beyond Anthropology* (New York: Columbia University Press, 1989), which breaks new ground in analyzing the succeeding figures of the Other in the Renaissance (in which the Other is an infernal being, on the level with gold and spices), the Enlightenment (in which the Other is pagan and "unenlightened," in the specific sense of being ignorant of "unknown causes"), and in the nineteenth century (where the Other is positioned backward at an earlier point in historical time).

9. Donald Horowitz, *Ethnic Groups in Conflict* (Berkeley: University of California Press, 1985), pp. 90–92. And see, also, Perry Anderson's interesting survey of the concept of "national character" in "Nation-States and National Identity," *London Review of Books* 9 (May 1991), pp. 3–8.

10. Etienne Balibar, "Is There a 'Neo-Racism'?" in Etienne Balibar and Immanuel Wallerstein, *Race, Nation, Class* (London: Verso, 1991), pp. 17–28.

11. See, for example, Constance Penley's telling remarks on the popular feeling that intellectuals—in this case, feminists—are somehow upper class: "The slashers do not feel they can express their desires for a better, sexually liberated, and more egalitarian world through feminism; they do not feel they can speak as feminists, they do not feel that feminism speaks for them" (492).

12. But it is important to stress, as Cornel West does, that religion (and in particular fundamentalism) is a very large and basic component of American mass culture, and in addition, that it is here decidedly underanalyzed and underrepresented.

13. Gyorgy Konrad and Ivan Szelenyi, *Intellectuals on the Road to Class Power* (New York: Harcourt Brace Jovanovich, 1979).

14. That this also holds for cultural production as such is suggested by Simon Frith's work on music culture; for example, "the tension in this world is less than between amateurs and professionals . . . than between local and national reference groups" (176).